BY CHAD ADAMS

Published by

Gun Digest® Books, an imprint of F+W Media, Inc.
Krause Publications • 700 East State Street • Iola, WI 54990-0001
715-445-2214 • 888-457-2873
www.krausebooks.com

To order books or other products call toll-free 1-800-258-0929
or visit us online at www.gundigeststore.com

Cover photography by
Yamil R. Sued/Photoworks, www.hotgunshots.com

All photos by 3-Gun Nation, except where indicated by Yamil R. Sued.

ISBN-13: 978-1-4402-2867-4
ISBN-10: 1-4402-2867-1

Cover Design by Dave Hauser
Designed by Dave Hauser
Edited by Jennifer L.S. Pearsall

Printed in United States of America

Acknowledgements

There are a tremendous number of folks to thank who have made this work possible. 3-gunners Patrick Kelley, Bryan Ray, Bruce Piatt, Rob Romero, Jansen Jones, Mike Voigt, Tommy Thacker, Taran Butler, Tony Holmes, and many more have patiently fielded my calls, returned my e-mails, and more. Match directors Dan Furbee, Andy Horner, JJ and Denise Johnson, Ken Flood, Mike, Rhonda and Travis Gibson and Tenille (Gibson) Chidester at MGM Ironman, Larry Houck, Sheldon Carruth, Kirk Broyles, Gary Welborn, and more have given me and my company access, explained their match design philosophy, and been instrumental in the success of 3GN thus far. A special thanks to NRA Board Member Joe DeBergalis, our patron saint of 3-Gun.

FNH USA's Ken Pfau and Tommy Thacker have been more than influential, and I am one among many who thanks them for providing sponsorship, support staff, knowledge, and even gear for our Tour. Federal Premium, Stag Arms, Cheaper Than Dirt, NSSF, Brownells, DoubleStar, Samson Manufacturing, Timney Triggers, Ruger, MGM Targets, SureFire, Leupold Tactical Opticsand many others also deserve much credit for their contributions. I, we, thank you one and all.

TABLE OF Contents

Intro

3-Gun Nation means a lot of things to a lot of different people in the sport of 3-gun. For some, it's on the periphery of what they do, while others plan their entire shooting careers around the programs and competitive platforms developed by 3-Gun Nation (3GN). Regardless the level of one's involvement, since the debut of 3GN, in 2010, it's hard to argue the dynamic explosion in the popularity of what we like to call the "X-Games of the Shooting Sports."

I discovered 3-gun through my profession, which makes me unique. Most folks' jobs simply don't enable them to go out and try new shooting sports with little financial investment or effort. So, I was lucky, because mine did. However, had I not had such amazing access to the firearms industry, I'm not sure if I ever would have found what has become my passion.

On a fundamental level, I think there's something wrong with that.

I happened to grow up in small-town America, where there wasn't any particular interest, at least to my knowledge, in action shooting. Guns were for hunting, or for defense, or even simply for setting up tin cans and having fun. Football and basketball were sports—real competition. My view of shooting while I was growing up really didn't equate the cool black and tactical guns I liked with any type of "sport" I knew anything about.

So that's the real purpose of this book—an attempt to educate folks, potentially like me, who are not acutely aware of what 3-gun is and how they can get involved. My job has enabled me to get to know the top shooters in the sport, and many of them have helped me along the way, teaching me what I, as a journalist, should be writing about, and how to relay that knowledge to newer shooters. This book is an attempt to take what I've learned from the sport of 3-gun and package it into something useful for anyone interested in playing the game.

This book is for anyone interested in 3-gun, for the top shooters who have driven the sport, for the companies that support it, and for the next great stars of the game, the guys like Rustin Bernskoetter who are out there competing with a philosophy of "shoot until my fingers bleed," as he says. I hope you'll enjoy what's in the pages of this book and come join us in this exploding sport. We're truly looking forward to seeing you on the range.

— *Chad Adams*

CHAPTER 1

3-GUN 101:

An Introduction to America's Fastest Growing Shooting Sport

The sport of 3-gun falls within the discipline known as "action shooting," which really is a politically correct term for *practical* shooting, the sport based on the quest for a higher level of *combat* shooting. While action shooting has been formally presented in America now for several decades, it has taken various shapes.

Today, action shooting has many forms, most of which traces itself back to the formation of the International Practical Shooting Confederation, or IPSC. Later, the United States Practical Shooting Association was formed as the U.S. domain of IPSC, as IPSC is truly international and branches into many countries around the world. The USPSA remains the strongest region, boasting more than 20,000 members nationwide.

(above and opposite page) Match directors sometimes designate specific shooting boxes or shooting area, with fault lines, where shots must be fired to avoid penalty.

The International Defensive Pistol Association (IDPA) is an offshoot of IPSC-style shooting, formed by shooters unsatisfied with the "gamesmanship" perceived to be prevalent within USPSA matches and rules. IDPA currently claims more than 19,000 members, and its competitions differ from IPSC's primarily in their rules structure, which establish competitions leaning more towards self-defense or tactical-style shooting, rather than a test of pure shooting skills, as some view the matches of IPSC. Both USPSA/IPSC and IDPA have been extremely successful in the U.S., but primarily as organizations that promote and sanction pistol competition. 3-gun, while influenced by USPSA rules already in place, has developed outside the vacuum of any one governing body, although 3-Gun Nation is quickly becoming the entity that bridges many matches and clubs together.

A 3-Gun event, or match, is a collection of individual courses of fire, commonly called "stages." During each stage of multiple targets, a competitor, under the direction of a range officer, negotiates that stage— keep in mind that this is an action sport, so there's lots of moving around from place to place, from one bank of targets to another, and so on—engaging each target as described during the stage briefing given by the range officer before the timer buzzer goes off. That briefing varies in its instructions, ranging from strictly regimented courses that must be shot in a specific sequence, to free-form design, where the competitor is free to map their own strat-

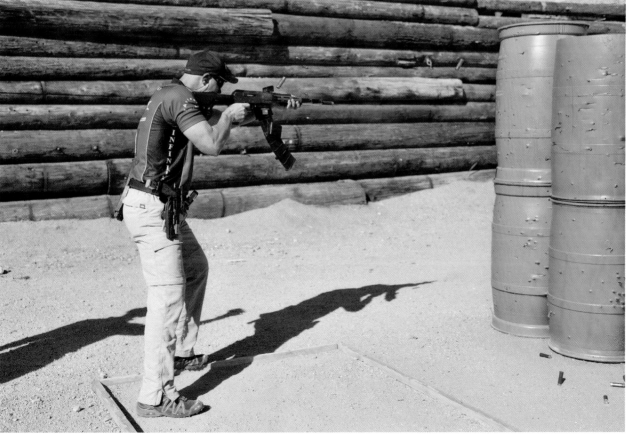

After a stage description read by the range officer, competitors are often given a quick five-minute walk through period to look at the stage.

egy. A stage can have a specific starting area as limited as a small "starting box," outlined by wood or metal staked into the ground. Stages can also have specific shooting areas, where certain targets must be engaged using particular firearms. Fault lines are sometimes present, and they mark the end of an area of movement for a competitor—no shots may be fired outside of a shooting area or forward of a fault line without receiving penalty, which is applied to a shooter's score in extra time.

After the stage briefing, the squad—a designated number of competitors that rotate through the match shooting each of the stages as a unit—is allowed a walk-through period. Often limited to five minutes, competitors get a chance to see

(above) Jerry Miculek prepares for a stage during the 2011 Rocky Mountain 3-Gun.

(left) Junior phenom Katie Harris prepares for a stage during the 2011 Rocky Mountain 3-Gun.

(opposite) Keith Garcia goes over the stage during his walk-through in the 2011 Superstition Mountain Mystery 3-Gun match.

each target, walk the stage as they anticipate they'll run it when it's their time to shoot—this might include planning out where best to reload, how to approach and shoot over, under, or around a barricade, etc.—and ask any questions of the range officer.

It's here that a 3-gun stage can get a bit complicated, and even confusing. At a given match, there are numerous types of targets one might encounter. There are multiple sizes and types of paper targets, with the IPSC-style cardboard torso/head target being the most common. (3-Gun Nation recently developed a new bull's-eye-type paper target that will likely become more common in local club matches.) Steel targets also show up in various forms, ranging from simple knock-over pieces of circular or rectangular steel sitting on top of a target stand, to advanced steel target systems manufactured by MGM Targets and others. Hinged steel "poppers," "plate racks" (six or more pieces of circular steel affixed to a target stand), static steel plates affixed to target stands, and reactive steel targets that move when struck are all used. Auto poppers are popular for rifle stages—here, the popper goes down when hit, then mechanically resets itself without anyone having to go downrange. Most reactive steel targets require a range officer to call "hits" when used in competition. Clay birds are another common target on some stages, and they're usually found in the form of a static target placed on a target stand. Clays are also thrown, just as they might be in

Match directors often use various forms of props and constructions to provide interesting target presentations.

traditional sporting clays, trap, or skeet clay bird games, adding a further degree of difficulty to 3-gun.

Moving targets offer yet another challenge. Often activated when a popper is knocked down, these limited-exposure targets come in many forms. Usually a paper target, the presentation can be moving from side-to-side, often only partially exposed. It can also turn towards the competitor, and then away again after a moment. There is also an "attack target" which accel-

erates toward the competitor before disappearing out of view. Limited-exposure targets can be *extremely* challenging!

Finally, there are the specialty targets—Texas Stars, Spinners, the Propeller Rack—that use gravity and balance to move in various directions. There are many specialty targets, especially the popular ones from MGM Targets, that provide fun and challenging shooting in 3-gun.

Ultimately, depending upon the stage description given by the range officer, all these different types of targets and presentations can be presented for specific or multiple firearms within a given stage—that means 3-gun is a thinking man's game, as much as it is one of pure shooting fundamentals and skill.

As with most action shooting sports, 3-gun is one that is measured in time. When shooting a stage, the competitor, under the direction of the range officer, will "stage" any firearms (i.e., put them in various places throughout the stage for pickup and use when they get to that portion), and, finally, receive the command to "make ready," with a specific firearm. Then, holding a timer that tracks each audible shot, the range officer pushes the timer's button, a loud "beep" goes off, and competitors rip through stages as fast as their skills allow. At the end of the stage, the raw time it took the shooter to complete the stage is recorded, then any penalties for procedurals or targets missed

are applied to form a final stage time, or score. Each stage time is added up, and, as it is with golf, where the fewest strokes win a match, the 3-gun competitor who finishes an event the quickest, penalties included, is the match winner.

Matches vary in size (both competitor number and venue), and form. Major Matches, such as Superstition Mountain Mystery 3-Gun, in Arizona, which I'll cover later in this book, feature 250 or more shooters,

Like most action-shooting disciplines, 3-gun is one in which stages are measured in time—fastest to neutralize all targets is the winner.

(left) Static clay targets are sometimes placed behind falling steel poppers, forcing competitors to slow down during an otherwise extremely fast target array.

(above) Moving paper targets are common in 3-gun, including groups of them activated by a falling popper such as this bank of evil movers put out at the Tarheel 3-Gun match in North Carolina.

(right) It takes only one BB punching through to consider a clay target "broken."

(below) Most 3-gun stages are combinations of various types of paper and steel targets.

utilize a wide array of props and targets, and boast some of the fastest, wide-open types of stages in 3-gun. They often consist of short stages confined to three-wall bermed shooting bays, and the targets and scoring system combine to promote extremely fast shooting. The competition at Blue Ridge Mountain 3-gun, conversely, is a Major Match situated in the rolling hills of Kentucky, which provides a tremendously physically challenging natural terrain course of fire. The scoring and target placement penalize inaccuracy, especially with a rifle, so Blue Ridge becomes a very physical, accuracy-oriented test of skills.

At the local level, match stages are most often contained in shooting bays and limited to 100 yards, although some clubs certainly have the ability to hold long-range rifle stages. Fields of competitors can be anywhere between 20 and 100 in a one-day local club match, offering a wide range of shooting experiences.

No matter what the size or location of the shoot, scoring formulas, rule structures, target presentations, and match styles can vary wildly in the sport—there is, quite literally, a different face to 3-gun nearly everywhere you go. But, this is part of its core, and just one of the many reasons 3-gun is the most exciting discipline in all of shooting.

It takes a tremendous amount of guns and gear to shoot a major 3-gun match.

(left) Gravity moving targets such as a "Texas Star" or "Whirly Gig" will be seen at many matches.

(above) In 2012, 3-Gun Nation, in partnership with Birchwood Casey, developed a new 3GN Pro Series Target for 3-gun.

(below) White, IPSC-style targets are often designated "No Shoot," and competitors receive a penalty each time one is struck.

Tamill R. Sued photo

CHAPTER 2

WHY WE PLAY

The moment comes all at once. Desperately, you run it all through your head one final time—*Shoot four steel on the left, pivot right, load four shotshells moving to the barricade, take three in the first port, six in the left port. Dump shotgun, pick up rifle off table, remember to charge it, go to work … .*

From your periphery you see the last shooters return from setting steel, no more time to plan. You set your guns under direction from the range master, taking sight pictures, checking scopes, turning on red dots. You dry fire your pistol. Finally, there is only the inevitable. Nothing left but to step into the box, close your eyes, take a deep breath, and … .

The beep of the timer shatters the Zen-like world you have created, quiet reflection hammered away by the bass drum that is your pulse, the electric hum of adrenaline synthesizing through your head, racing past thought and carrying you into the moment. *Pop, pop, pop, pop … .*

Not too long ago, most new 3-gunners were, in fact, veteran USPSA pistol shooters who had a fair amount of competition experience. That pistol experience translated into a working knowledge of the competitions themselves and provided a baseline of shooting skills that had been measured under the stress of the clock. Perhaps more importantly, at least for anyone wishing to excel, those shooters came to the sport of 3-gun with a fundamental experience in stage breakdown. In short, these pistol shooters needed only to add a shotgun and rifle to their shooting repertoires (which is plenty, to be sure), and they were off runnin' and gunnin' in 3-gun.

You are now only vaguely aware of the physical, your movements carried out by regimen, and you force yourself to focus on the bare minimum of self-instruction—*get your head down on the stock … front sight, front sight … breathe!*

Shotgun-rifle-pistol it goes, targets crashing in and out of view, sight pictures riding the wave of your heaving chest. "Hit!" bellows the range officer, nearly drowning out the perfect sound of a 55-grain bullet pounding a piece of steel more than four football fields away. It's orchestrated chaos, a crashing wave of excitement, panic, fear, and elation, all at once, all in that moment that belongs to you and you alone.

Welcome to 3-gun.

(above) The face of 3-gun is different at every match and venue, making 3-gun challenging—and never boring.

(right) The margins of error, and the difference between loss and victory, can be extremely small in 3-gun—which make it all the more rewarding.

I am not a champion 3-gunner, nor even an especially good one, in all honesty. I am a journalist by trade, one with unique access to the best shooters on the planet. But that access has had a profound effect on me over the last few years—as soon as I picked up a rifle and sent brass flying, I was immediately hooked on the sport. As 3-gun continues to grow, I am a typical example of the new shooters coming fresh into the game.

I, like a lot of new 3-gunners today, came into this game with very little competition experience and the critical knowledge base that comes with it. To us, 3-gun just flat out looked badass, and we had to give it a try.

You know what? That's all it takes. This game, if you give it any kind of a fair chance, has the ability to quickly morph into an obsession. In that basic way, it's like what golf becomes for the kids who outgrew their fascination with blowing up stuff. But golf is bland by comparison. Three-gun offers *so* much more. It's physical and grinding, and it has a hard edge to it, a 30-second all-out adrenaline dump that demands precision and

timing, while simultaneously requiring you give maximum physical and mental effort. To steal a phrase we use at 3 Gun Nation, "It's the X-Games of the shooting sports."

Unlike most sports, 3-gun is inclusive of the masses. You're not too old or too young, too rich or poor, and men, women, and junior shooters can all play. Even if you don't have any of the gear, chances are someone at the local club will loan you a gun, belt, holster, or shell caddy to get you through your first match. If you let them, many fellow competitors will help coach you, as well, pointing out a weak grip, how to load a shotgun faster, or something so specific such as

why one should move left three steps past the first barricade to most effectively engage an array of steel poppers.

So, 3-gun is an everyman's sport, but it also has an exclusive component to it. Point of fact, anyone can play. Too, at any size match, ranging from your local club to one of the biggest major 3-gun matches in the country, you may be squadded right alongside any number of the top 3-gun competitors in the game—and watching them burn down stages with remarkable speed, skill, and precision is likely to cause *your* engine to run in the red, which translates into a competitor pushing the speed beyond their skill set, resulting in an epic crash-and-burn stage performance. We all go through that—trust me—and, so, again, it's an inclusive sport. But 3-gun, at its highest levels, maintains an air of exclusivity, because the skills demonstrated in this arena—whether it be on sun-baked range bays or a pulse-thumping hillside over a natural terrain course of fire—must be *earned*. While there is almost certainly an elite few who exhibit a natural ability for picking up the game, the rest of us are left with one painful truth: competing with the best 3-gunners in the world takes a dedication unequaled in any other sport.

Still, anyone can have success in 3-gun. That success is, and should be, an ever fluid definition specific to the individual shooter. For me, success at my first match was defined by being safe, not breaking a rule that would get me disqualified, and, despite the inherent frustration from my demonstrated lack of skill and ability compared to others on my squad, having fun. For

While 3-gun is certainly physical, the game is arguably best classified as a mental one, where focus is paramount.

most new 3-gunners, a safe, fun day on the range is the epitome of first-match success.

But, the more you play, the higher the performance ceiling that measures whether you're successful rises. Desired split times on target transitions decrease. Shotgun reloads must be conducted while moving instead of standing still. Or success can mean simply not to time-out on any stage in the match.

As with any sport, as performance improves and expectations begin to rise, so, too, at times, does the level of frustration. Like the golfer who hacks up the course for three hours, furious to the point he's ready to throw his bag of clubs in the lake, the 3-gun shooter will go to war on targets, miss reloads, and not have a clue where their rifle is hitting for nearly an entire match. Then, "it" happens. The shooter takes on that one bank of targets with a shotgun, or possibly even an entire stage,

and everything hits just perfect. Chest heaving, heart thumping, and out of breath, the command to "Unload and show clear" is given, the pistol re-holstered or shotgun returned to the rack and, with nothing more than a knowing look from the other members of the squad, the shooter knows he nailed it to the best of his ability. Better yet, he knows that everyone watching knows it, too. And, once you have that "it" moment, no matter how bad you had been that day or in other matches, you're completely hooked by 3-gun all over again.

"I think I'm addicted to 3-gun because of the challenge and the atmosphere of the matches," Team FNH USA's Dianna Liedorff told me. "There are so many components to the game that it seems like there is always room for improvement—unless you're Daniel (Horner) or Taran (Butler)! There is a great camaraderie with 3-gun shooters, and the natural terrain matches are so unique and beautiful!

"It's also pretty tough!" Liedorff continued. "The days are long and physically challeng-

ing. The weather doesn't always cooperate. With the added bonus from 3-Gun Nation of having money on the line, everyone is stepping up their game, and more shooters are coming to the sport to compete for titles and money!"

As the most challenging of any discipline within the genre of practical shooting, the face of 3-gun changes with every single match. Where one match is wide-open and extremely fast, the next is accuracy driven and painfully technical. Where prop-strewn stages are compacted into square bays at one venue, the next challenge forces competitors to run, jump, and climb over formidable, brutally taxing, natural terrain courses.

"The challenge of being proficient with three guns instead of one is what drew me in," said Colt's Clint Upchurch. "For me, it's kind of like starting over and getting to learn how to shoot all over again. Being presented with the many challenges that 3-gun presents and the great people associated with the sport are what makes it so appealing."

"I enjoy the additional challenge of three different platforms," said Samson Manufacturing's Bryan Ray. "There are many similar skills across rifle, shotgun, and pistol, but the types of targets we engage are obviously very different between the three. A shooter who is lightning quick with a handgun may not be able to shoot a long-range rifle stage very well—and shotgun is its own monster. The competitions are another draw to 3-gun. I don't think a more friendly or helpful group of people can be found within the shooting sports."

While you compete as an individual, teams do exist in the sport, and camaraderie is everywhere and at every level of 3-gun.

HIS

Yamil R. Sued photo

CHAPTER 3

THE TORY BEHIND THE SPORT

I t's unfathomable to imagine where we might be today, in terms of the practical shooting sports, if it weren't for Jeff Cooper and the famous "Leather Slaps," at Big Bear, California. It was there that Cooper was joined by a group of like-minded individuals who'd come together and forever changed pistol craft as we know it.

Cooper, Weaver, Chapman—names that loom in lore over the entire firearms industry—are revered for the sum of their parts. Theirs is a doctrine for combat pistol shooting—the Weaver Grip and Stance, the Southwest Pistol League, Gunsite, the Modern Technique, modern competitive action shooting—all of it traces its roots or influence to Big Bear. Then, in 1976, Cooper and others formed the International Practical Shooters Confederation—IPSC—and the world finally had an organized body dedicated to the promotion of action pistol competition. But, as IPSC, and later USPSA (United States Practical Shooters Association), grew here in America, it wasn't long before a movement within the realm of action shooting began to take shape.

Soldier of Fortune—The Original 3-Gun Match

As action pistol matches gained in popularity, generally informal side matches for shotguns, and even the occasional rifle, began to pop up at local clubs. But it wasn't until a renegade magazine decided to sponsor a tactical-style shooting match that modern 3-gun was born. As such, the *Soldier of Fortune* World Championship 3-Gun Tactical Match is considered the father of all 3-gun competition.

"A milestone event took place in central Missouri, on 26, 27 and 28 September at the Ray Chapman Range in Columbia: The first annual Soldier of Fortune shooting match tested the skill of nearly 100 top-ranked competitors in combat pistol, fighting shotgun and battle rifle events,*"* wrote combat shooting luminary Ken Hackathorn, in the February 1981 issue of *Soldier of Fortune* magazine. *"The match was held in conjunction with the magazine's first annual convention."*

The association with *Soldier of Fortune* magazine set this match apart from the onset. As such, a highly skilled group of law enforcement and military professionals, as well as top-flight civilian competitors, converged on Missouri, for what would be a ground-breaking event in the history of practical shooting.

"The first SOF match was held in September 1980, in Columbia, Missouri," said veteran 3-gunner Mark Passamaneck. "One hundred shooters tested their mettle in an invitation-only match that had a match fee of $25. The terms 'soldier,' 'mercenary,' and 'adventurer' were associated with the competitors, both from a perspective of profession and personality."

"The crew of that first SOF event viewed it first and foremost as an law enforcement training event, and participating officers received a certificate of completion towards training credits if their departments accepted this type of training," explained John Gangl, another veteran 3-gun competitor and owner of JP Rifles. "However, civilians were more than welcome to compete, provided that they could furnish some credentials as to their previous experience in practical shooting, to serve as an indication that they could be expected to understand the basic safety requirements of such an event."

"Casual observers might suggest that such shooting events should be normal for U.S. military and police organizations," Hackathorn continued in his 1981 SOF article. *"Sadly, most training systems have less variety in their practical tests of skill than did this match, but Robert K. Brown and the SOF staff provided a proving ground for practical weapon-craft. Competitors in the invitation-only match were selected for their background and shooting ability. A very high percentage of them came from police or military organizations. The three match weapons were chosen on the basis of their importance in a combat role."*

The inaugural SOF match ran much differently than a major 3-gun match does today. Instead of stages of fire integrated with the use of multiple firearms on each stage (or even all three), the first SOF match really ran each firearm platform as a distinct, separate match, and each with its own champion. The scores were then tallied to formulate an aggregate champion and overall SOF winner.

"There was just one division at the start, and the gear of the top shooters included a .308 rifle, either an H&K 91 or an M1A, a single-stack semi-auto .45 pistol from various makers, and, interestingly enough, the Model 1100 Remington 12-gauge shotgun, which the entire top 10 of the inaugural match all shot," Passamaneck said. "Rifle scores were really what separated the top competitors from the pack."

The first match actually banned the use of rifles chambered in .223 Remington, a far cry from today's events, where AR-15-sytle rifles rule the day. In 1980, H&K 91 and M1A rifles dominated the field and comprised the gun of choice for the entire top 10. FN FALs and M1 Garands were in abundance, as well.

"First, and most critical, was the battle rifle match," Hackathorn wrote. *"Rifle-course ranges extended from 70 to 245 yards. The course consisted of 15 silhouette targets and six steel, falling plates. Time limit was a par time of three minutes. A competitor's score was upped by one point for each second he completed the course under the three-minute par time limit, and one point was deducted for each second over the three-minute-par time. Speed became an important factor. The rifle course had a score value of 360 points at par time. Thus, a rifleman capable of accuracy, fast shooting and quick movement, could increase his score well above the 360-point level.*

"Nine of the competitors managed to score above the 360-par level," Hackathorn continued. *"On the other hand, many shooters were humbled by this course. Most, however, felt—before the event—that target distances were not overly difficult and the shooting would be easy. Faced with the time-limit stress, two 40-yard sprints and having to reload, many shooters discovered that targets became elusive."*

Like much of the early IPSC shooting, Colt 1911s dominated the pistol class at the inaugural SOF. With a high number of law enforcement professional competing, service revolvers chambered in .38 Special were also in use. The course of

fire was one familiar to IPSC shooters of the day.

"They designed a simple course that required a total of 36 rounds," wrote Hackathorn. *"First, a total of 12 rounds were fired from the 25-yard line in two stages, a distance that duplicates the extreme long range normally encountered in combat.*

"Next, a series of drills were fired at the 10 yard line," Hackathorn continued. *"After a total of 18 rounds from this distance, six more rounds were fired from the seven-yard line."*

In the shotgun match, the Remington 1100 was the dominant choice by the top competitors, but, with many military and law enforcement professionals in the mix, there were various pump shotguns on the firing line, as well.

The shotgun match course of fire provided what was certainly one of the earliest practical shooting uses of steel targets for a shotgun stage in the U.S. In it, frangible clay birds were affixed to the center of 18x24-inch steel plates. In the first phase, competitors were armed with shotguns loaded with five rounds of buckshot and were required to break each clay bird from a distance of 25 yards. The drill was repeated at the 15-yard line, with a par time of 4.5 seconds.

In the second phase, competitors fired rifled slugs at silhouette targets, five shots from 25 yards, then a reload and a run forward to a place of "cover," where they fired at three additional targets. While the round count is low by today's major match standards, the use of movement, multiple firing positions and, most importantly,

mixed loads within a single stage (in this case, buckshot and slugs), are hallmarks at many major matches today.

"In both phases, match accuracy was important, and shooting technique really counted," wrote Hackathorn. *"Few people in the U.S. understand the technique of the fighting shotgun. Although the riot gun has a macho image, few users can achieve maximum performance with it. We all have heard gunshop-commando comments about just pointing the riot gun in the general direction, pulling the trigger—and everything will go down. In the SOF practical shotgun match, the big boys knew better. They shot from the shoulder, used a flash-sight picture and achieved well centered hits. All top 10 finishers used Remington 1100 shotguns."*

The inaugural SOF match was won by Raul Walters, a top IPSC pistol competitor and local businessman who went on to found one of the most successful real estate companies in the country (Walters' business success was largely due to the company's financing and real estate deals for a then-fledgling merchant—Wal-Mart). Walters won both the rifle and pistol competitions en route to a four-point overall victory. John Shaw, William Rogers, Charles Byers, and Bill Wilson—top shelf IPSC shooters all—rounded out the top five.

"Looking over the competitor list, one will see names such as Shaw, Enos, Leatham, Hackathorn, Heinie, Wilson, Plaxco, Cirillo, Fowler, and many others associated with firearms 'royalty,'" Passamaneck said. "Many of the founders of IPSC were also some of the pioneers of 3-gun. A large number of the now-famous names in pistol shooting tried their hands at the SOF matches in the early years.

Ironically, it's commonly held today that much of what led to the advent of 3-gun was the result of some within the practical shooting community attempting to make a break away from IPSC. While not completely *untrue*, the match clearly set out to establish an arena that would prepare professional and civilians to better handle firearms in practical application. What few realize, and what I didn't fully understand until being pointed to the *SOF* article, is that IPSC was there in the beginning. From the names of top competitors to the IPSC-style pistol match to Ray Chapman himself running and officiating the event, the founding fathers of practical shooting, of IPSC, has their stamps all over the birth of 3-gun. In fact, an advertisement within the 1981 issue of *SOF* claimed all three matches to be "IPSC-sanctioned," and that the assault rifle match would crown the "First IPSC National Practical Rifle" champion.

Yet, somewhere along the way, a divide emerged between the renegade match and the sanctioning body of practical shooting. For *SOF*'s part, there was advertisement rumored to be featuring porn stars, stories regarding alcohol, and a series of very public trials over contract killings by mercenaries reportedly hired from the classified pages of *Soldier of Fortune*. Around that same time, USPSA was formed as the American region of IPSC, which possibly severed some

connections between the people involved. Whatever the reason, the SOF match, while maintaining the top competitors, lost its association with IPSC/USPSA—and, in turn, and in a very real way, IPSC/USPSA lost much of the sport of 3-gun. While I don't know and can't report the full story of the disconnection, the fact is best illustrated by the reality that USPSA didn't hold its first Multi-Gun Nationals until well over a decade had passed after SOF had ushered in a new era in practical shooting.

"Overall, the SOF three-gun shooting event proved a great success," concluded Hackathorn. *"Thanks must go to Ray Chap-*

man and his staff, who provided a superbly run event and top-quality judges and range officers. Such skill is rarely seen in major events. Chapman and his staff have plenty of expertise, thanks to their participation in other shooting events such as the Bianchi Cup."

With the birth of the SOF event, the sport of 3-gun was off and running—a wild and woolly affair to some, for others, a liberating break from the oppressive structure IPSC-style pistol matches were perceived to have. But, for all, the SOF match represented a new and exciting brand of shooting sports unlike anything any of them had ever seen before.

"The matches, fees, stage complexity, and equipment multiplied considerably after those first few years," Passamaneck said. "As the SOF matches continued on for just over two decades, other groups decided they could depart from SOF and offer a different style of match. The main differences were in divisions and stage design. Courses started to become faster, favoring higher capacity rifles such as the AR-15."

"Three-Gun as been around since the early '80s," said veteran competitor Bruce Piatt. "At the time, the Soldier of Fortune World 3-Gun Tactical Championship was the richest event of the year. Remember,

Veteran competitor Tony Holmes has shot 3-gun for many years and was a winner of the famed Soldier of Fortune Match.

in the early '80s, there were only four major matches to shoot—four, that's it. Steel Challenge, Bianchi Cup, IPSC (pre-USPSA) Nationals, and the Soldier of Fortune 3-Gun. The SOF match was an 'all-surprise stage,' buckshot and slug, long-range rifle, full-power, iron sighted pistol—a true combat match. The match had the highest prize structure of the time: $10,000 to the winner of the top 16 man-on-man shoot-off, not to mention the prizes for the match itself. For many years, the number of 3-gun matches were limited to SOF, USPSA 3-Gun Nationals, and the Miller Invitational 3-Gun Match—yes, Miller Beer sponsored this match in Fulton, New York, every year."

For many top shooters, SOF was an eye-opening experience. Sure, they were accustomed to high-level matches, but mostly ones that relied on known courses of fire, strict range rules, wide-open race equipment, and square shooting bay design. For even the top practical shooters in the country, their first experience in 3-gun proved to be something radically different.

"Nineteen ninety-seven was my first year there," said Tony Holmes. "The first year there was a big learning curve for me. It was basically an all-Tactical match. Scored major/minor with pistol and rifle, all buckshot and 12-gauge only, with a couple of slugs thrown in. Rifles could be shot with only certain battle-approved optics per SOF's guidelines.

"All scoring with rifles was done by optic or iron sights. Each was given 100 points for the highest score posted per stage, and each stage was scored differently. You actually had to read the stage description for each stage and decide how you would attack it—with either speed or points—and points almost always won out. This type of match was different than others, because most of the other 3-gun matches I had been to and seen were being shot with Open guns. Everyone at SOF shot basically Tactical, and rifle was 50/50 as to sights, when I started. In the early years, all guns were iron sights. They started allowing bipods on rifles around 1999."

The SOF match had its own distinct flavor, a characteristic that remains prevalent in the sport of 3-gun today, as each match director and crew put their unique stamp on the game at any given match. But, while that individualism in match design and philosophy flourishes today, it all started with SOF.

"Some felt that the World Championship 3-Gun (WC3G) venue was rather harsh and unaccommodating and may have had somewhat of a boot camp culture to it," said JP Gangl, founder of JP Rifles. "Granted, some of the staff members were a bit over the edge, but all that added to the ambiance. Actually, there is much to be said about a competition in which gamesmanship was frowned upon and complaining or protesting was highly discouraged. Did that make it less fair for shooters? I would submit that, over the long run, it was more than fair, and certainly more expeditious, with the nearly complete lack of whining, nit-picking, re-shoots and protesting that's tolerated in other venues.

"The expectation that a shooter will not be allowed to subvert the stage intent due to some weakness in targets, props, or stage layout allows for more creativity in stage design," Gangl continued. "As it so happens, multi-gun culture, as it exists today, has benefited greatly from the World Championship 3-Gun mind-set. Multi-gun shooters (for the most part) are willing to shoot under a broad range of circumstances—weather, rule sets, and shooting requirements— asking only that equipment classifications are known in advance and somewhat consistent from event to event."

This singular approach to match presentation, not to mention the fact that competi-

tors finally had a venue where they could shoot all three guns in a "practical" competition, immediately elevated the Soldier of Fortune match to among the most revered shooting competitions of its day. While certainly still held on the periphery of the shooting sports, 3-gun had a signature event in the SOF match.

"The WC3G was really analogous to the NRA Bianchi Cup, regarding its stature as an event, complete with semi-formal banquet, a real awards ceremony, and a cash purse," Gangl said. "If it had a problem, that may have been its association with the *Soldier of Fortune* magazine, the perception of which was not accepted in much of the law enforcement community. When the event and the magazine parted company, and the match's name changed to

the World Championship 3-Gun Tactical Match, many more law enforcement agencies accepted the match as an accredited training event for their officers."

Beyond the sometimes over-the-top range staff, the association with a renegade magazine that catered to the world of mercenaries, the awards, and even the cash purse, the attraction for most shooters in the early days of the SOF match was the shooting itself.

"Other concepts that worked very well for the event were the five-man squad format and semi-surprise or full-surprise stage system," Gangl said. "The five-man squad allowed for the four-man team event (with

Bruce Piatt, a five-time winner of the Soldier of Fortune 3-Gun, readies for a stage.

SOF Patch – Though it has been gone for many years, the SOF match lives on today in several major Outlaw 3-gun majors across the country.

a fifth-man spare) and made possible stages on which all five shooters were on the line shooting at once. Again, this resulted in some truly creative stages."

Surprise stages and manageable squad sizes set the stage at SOF for many competitors, and innovative events such as team-on-team shoot-offs set the match apart from most other shooting competitions.

"Although you did not have to participate in the team event and could register as a solo shooter, many teams did compete, and the five-man squad allowed them to stay together during the entire match and be slotted together for the team shoot-off elimination stage, a great concept in itself. There is no doubt that the team stage and team-on-team shoot-off were the highlights of this event and a great spectator draw."

Billed as a Tactical event, SOF's surprise-stage concept appealed to the growing number of shooters who felt the practical side of practical shooting was being increasingly replaced by a more purely competition/sport philosophy. With no chance to walk through stages beforehand, SOF became distinctive.

"The semi- or full-surprise stage expectation prevented the 'choreographing' of the stage by shooters and required participants to remain somewhat fluid in their stage prep, rather than locking into some hard plan," Gangl explained. "This adds to the excitement and asks the real-world question, can the shooter think on their feet and improvise? Let us not forget that the common denominator among practical shooters is the addiction to the adrenaline rush."

More than anything, shooters who remember the old days of the SOF match continually refer to the stage design. Scoring rules implemented at the stage level for each specific stage, instead of across the board and for the entire match, enabled match designers to come up with stages unlike most shooters had ever seen before.

"Stage design and target designs were some of the most creative I've ever seen," Gangl said. "The scoring system was the foundation for the current Multi-Gun Association rules, with one fundamental difference. Where the multi-gun format today has become lock-stepped into a scoring system, due to the use of a program that accepts only predetermined values, the WC3G scoring system allowed for greater flexibility, with each range officer responsible for the design and proofing of their stage and free to use any type of scoring system as long as it made sense and was applied fairly to all. This may have been a basic time-only scoring system (based on raw time plus penalties in seconds), but, in some cases, it was a points system within some type of time restraint. The basic philosophy was to ask questions about real-world performance based not just on all-out speed, but on one's ability to manage their energy wisely and avoid mistakes under pressure. Whatever the raw stage results, the stage was converted to match points for the final aggregate."

USPSA Multi-Gun Nationals

By the late 1980s, the success and popularity of SOF had elicited an ironic effect. If one subscribes to the notion that SOF was founded, at least in part, as a tactical alternative to the "game" IPSC-style shooting had become, then the debut of USPSA Multi-Gun raised some eyebrows. From the onset, IPSC was formed as much to further combat pistol *doctrine*, as it was to establish the competitive arena in which to test and compare the competitors. But, as games so often do, the competition format itself, at least to some, had become more about pure competition and less about the practical side of the sport.

The popularity of the SOF match, to some degree, is no doubt owed to the "Tactical" style in which the competition was presented—physical and demanding, with full-surprise stages and combat-approved gear. However, if that been the only appeal of 3-gun, then the sport might have stagnated with just the SOF match alone. Instead, as this radical shooting sport gained popularity, a new form emerged under the auspices of the USPSA.

"In the early '90s, another multi-gun venue appeared out of the USPSA handgun format," Gangl said. "A small number of practical pistol shooters, with the influence of some who had shot in the existing SOF matches, decided to hold another national-level event under the USPSA rule set but modified to work with three guns. With the SOF match filling up by January or February of every year, there was a demand for another multi-gun match to accommodate the increasing interest in this sport. The first two of these events were held in Long Island, New York, and, for obvious reasons, moved to a more hospitable location, the Clark Shootout Range, in Shreveport, Louisiana."

Unlike SOF, where competitors "fought" their way through blind stages and used multiple firearm platforms within a given stage, USPSA Nationals set a limit of one gun per stage; ultimately, multiple Nationals champions were crowned.

"Initially, in order to work with the existing USPSA-type scoring system, the three guns were not mixed in any stage. The stages were all firearm-specific," Gangl said. "Also, there were no equipment classifications at the start, and most shooters shot in what would now be considered the 'Open' class, in which any gun configuration was allowed, as long as it was deemed safe.

"The first multi-gun match I attended personally was the second Long Island match," Gangl said. "I attended the 3-Gun Nationals every year after that. However, with my first opportunity to attend the SOF match, I realized there was another perspective on multi-gun competition altogether, one that attracted a much larger number of shooters who had a completely different take on the equipment and stage design. It was obvious that this was a more dynamic and pragmatic application of the multi-gun discipline, one that seemed to attract a highly dedicated and competitive group of people from LE, military, and civilian populations.

"Eventually, USPSA adopted equipment classes similar to the SOF/WC3G format, to bring those shooters under its tent and encourage them to shoot the USPSA-style events," Gangl continued. "These equipment classifications have now become one of the fairly consistent threads between most of these events."

Superstition Mountain Mystery 3-Gun

While SOF remained the preeminent 3-gun match in the country, a new form of 3-gun

began in the Arizona desert. In 1996, Superstition Mountain Mystery 3-Gun (SMM3G) debuted and, to some shooters, became everything SOF wasn't—and should have been.

Wide open and smoking fast, SMM3G established a new 3-gun philosophy based mostly on square-bay stages littered with some of the most entertaining and creative "props" seen in shooting. Combined with the allowance of Open-class race equipment, SMM3G quickly established itself as a new and exciting brand of 3-gun.

"The match has grown from 67 shooters, in 1996, to 275 shooters, in 2010," said Dan Furbee, SMM3G match director and founder. "I saw a need for a quality match. Prior to 1996, the only real serious 3-gun competition in the U.S. was the Soldier of Fortune match, in Las Vegas. SOF wouldn't allow competitors to use IPSC-style race guns or any other high-tech innovative gear, other than military or SWAT-approved equipment. By opening the competition field up to open-class shooters, the 3-gun competition as we know it today burst forward."

Superstition has proven to be a seminal 3-gun match in the history of the sport. The innovative thinking in stage design and the use of props had a major influence on the sport's awareness spreading through the shooting world. And ,with stages seemingly catered toward the use of race guns, a new style of 3-gun was born at Superstition, as well. However, one could argue that its influence on rules and scoring is the largest lasting impact of the Superstition Mountain Mystery 3-Gun.

"With a further simplified scoring system designed to expedite stage reset time per shooter, in addition to the elimination of the power factor concept and recognition of the most common equipment classifications, the SMM3G celebrates its seventeenth year with the 2012 event," Gangl said.

"The International Multi-Gun Association (IMA) evolved out of the SMM3G event, the intent being to establish a standardized set of rules and equipment divisions for multi-gun competition," Gangl continued. "Presently, North American multi-gun competition is shot primarily under IMA rules or USPSA rules (with some exceptions). The IMA model has become the most successful and widely used at this time. The IPSC world body has also become involved in multi-gun competition in countries that al-low the civilian ownership of the necessary equipment. However, while IPSC multi-gun is similar to USPSA, it only recognizes the Open and Limited divisions, with Limited requiring the use of iron sights only (i.e., no optics) on the rifle."

JP Rocky Mountain 3-Gun

By 2000, 3-gunners now had three established major national events in which they could shoot: SOF, USPSA Multi-Gun Nationals, and Superstition Mountain Mystery 3-Gun. The emergence of new matches proved the fledgling sport was finally experiencing growth. However, change was once again about to come to the world of 3-gun.

"In 2001, the SOF match split off from the *Soldier of Fortune* magazine and became the World Championship 3-Gun Tactical Match (WC3G)," Gangl said. "Colonel Robert Brown (Ret.), founder of the *SOF* magazine, then decided to run the SOF match at the NRA Whittington Center. Consequently, in 2001, 2002, and 2003, the SOF match was held at the Whittington Center and the WC3G remained in the original Las Vegas location.

The split brought about a bit of confusion, nationally, over what exactly was what. In Nevada, you had the continuation of the match that had been SOF. Meanwhile, at the Whittington Center, a new match under the same SOF name emerged, one with much of the former crew and shooters in place.

"In 2002, Kurt and Eric Miller (et al) were awarded a contract to run the SOF match for the magazine at the Whittington Center" Gangl told me. "The *SOF* magazine then decided that it no longer wanted to

John Paul Gangl, founder of JP Rifles, was instrumental in the formation of the JP Rocky Mountain 3-Gun Match sponsored by JP Rifles.

be involved with the match, and JP Enterprises, Inc., stepped in as the major named sponsor, engaging the existing match crew to run the newly named JP Rocky Mountain 3-Gun Championship. This match is unique, as it is designed and held in the natural terrain of the Whittington Center, as opposed to the typically well-developed square ranges competitors were accustomed to. The added dimension of a natural terrain match cannot be underestimated."

By 2003, the WC3G was no more. The Rocky Mountain 3-Gun match had effectively supplanted both the WC3G and the SOF matches, developing its own unique brand of 3-gun over the years, as match directors changed. Today, JJ and Denise Johnson successfully run RM3G, and the match is very much a reflection of their idea of what 3-gun should be.

"As IPSC and, later, USPSA matured and changed, some of the rules and divisional designations spilled over into 3-gun," Passamaneck said. "In the late '90s, several matches that owed their success to SOF grew larger and more popular than the original, which had ceased to exist after the final match, in 2002. However, there were several 3-gun matches born in the 1990s, and Rocky Mountain 3-Gun followed on the heels of the SOF matches with some of the past officials and competitors stepping in and running the match 'Under New Management,' thanks in large part to its title sponsor of JP Rifles."

Ultimately, the legacy of the SOF match lives on today, in some form, at Rocky Mountain, and with that match's survival,

and the success of Superstition Mountain, the stage was set for 3-gun growth on a national stage. All the sport needed was a catalyst.

Randy Luth and the DPMS Tri-Gun

With Superstition, Rocky Mountain, and USPSA Nationals, among others, becoming established 3-gun "Majors," the sport of 3-gun began to build even more momentum, with new local and regional matches popping up at range facilities that had never before hosted a 3-gun match.

Then, in 2003, an innovative AR manufacturer, led by its self-made founder and owner, jumped into the sport full bore. In doing so, DPMS changed the sport forever. Here you had a match sponsored by a gun manufacturer, which in and of itself wasn't unique, but the way in which Randy Luth and DPMS approached hosting a match changed everything. I covered that first DPMS Tri-Gun Challenge as a staff writer and editor for the National Rifle Association (NRA), and I remember walking the prize table with Luth shortly before the conclusion of the match. We both sort of stared out across the row upon row of AR-15s, upper receivers, lower receivers, and a multitude of parts, almost all of it exclusively provided by DPMS that first year.

"What do you think?" Luth asked, not really looking at me or waiting for my answer. "Yeah, it needs a little more," he answered himself. What do you think we should put out?"

"Some Low Pros might be

cool," I answered, shrugging my shoulders in complete disbelief that anyone could possibly give anything more away.

Luth turned to a DPMS employee, asked for some number of Low Pros to be brought out, and the prize table grew ever deeper, just like that. I don't recall how many tens of thousands of dollars in product Luth gave away that inaugural Tri-Gun Challenge. And I'm not sure he ever knew the amount himself, because it didn't matter. Randy Luth had decided to set the bar.

At this point, DPMS had assembled what amounted to one of the first fully sponsored 3-gun teams in the sport. The company backed up that investment by putting on what became one of, if not *the*, signature 3-gun match of the season—and, after that first year, it wasn't merely DPMS product on the prize table. DPMS reached out to the entire industry for support, even direct competitors, and the result was arguably the deepest, most lucrative prize table in the sport.

"We first got involved in promoting competitive shooting, when Al Greco introduced DPMS to Jerry Miculek at the Second Chance shooting event, in 1998," Luth said. "Al suggested we sponsor Jerry and some other shooters, based on the fact that we had been donating many rifles to the Second Chance events over the previous few years. It was through Al that we made some deals with Jerry and Bruce Piatt. In the meantime, we began donating products to the few 3-gun events that were starting up in the late '90s and early 2000."

As DPMS grew as a company, Luth continually supported competitive shooting events around the country, as do many gun companies at varying levels. But few company owners and presidents actually get out and shoot alongside the competitors and customers. Luth, though, was never your ordinary gun company president, and, in a refreshing take on "knowing your customer base," Luth got bitten by the 3-gun bug.

"One event we donated to was the Wily Coyote 3-Gun event, in White Bird, Idaho, put on by Evolution USA (rifle makers Edd and Leanne Woslum)," Luth said. "It was at that event that I was physically introduced to my first 3-gun. The two dudes that got stuck with me were Bill Sahlberg and Pat Kelley, and they were the ones who got me hooked. I had no equipment other than my rifle—they set me up with a pistol, shotgun, and gear to shoot my first match. As you can imagine, I finished in last place, but, from then on, we saw an opportunity to promote our products in a new arena that would generate some "brass"-roots marketing for our rifles and accessories, similar to what we had done with grassroots marketing at gun shows throughout the '90s.

As with any business, if the owner is active in the business at the customer level, then you automatically bring credibility to your product. It's sad to see so many firearms company owners who have no clue what's going on in their industry. My position was to get involved in 3-gun (and to use our products in the hunting arena, as well) to promote a new segment of rifle sales. If you want to

increase sales, then the best way is to go to a gun show and set up your table or booth and do one gun show a month for a year at different gun shows around the country—you will know *exactly* what's happening in the industry. Respect is earned by participation.

"We chose to sponsor 3-gun events to help promote our products in this new arena," Luth continued. "As a new competitor and owner, I felt that it was a great way to get shooters off the couch and involved in a fun and exciting venue, similar to what Dustin Emholtz had done with Zombie shoots at DPMS four years ago. Our industry has to adapt to the younger shooter, with new and exciting events and techniques for shooting guns. Our sponsorships to 3-gun was a win-win."

In short order, Team DPMS, with Jerry Miculek, Tony Holmes, Bruce Piatt, Dave Neth, Deb Cheek, and Randy Luth himself, became the top, if one of very few, full-fledged teams in the sport. With a top assembly of shooting talent competing at a high level that showcased the company's product in front of an emerging sport and customer base, Luth turned his attention to showcasing the sport east of the Mississippi.

"Our first Tri-Gun Challenge, in 2003, was a continuation of my interest in building new customers through the sport, plus, we had our own range to put on the event and a following of industry people we could tap into for sponsors, therefore we had a prize table that grew to over $200,000," Luth said. "It was great fun, as well as exposure for DPMS and our sponsors to help promote 3-gun."

For a lot people in and around the sport of 3-gun, it's hard to overemphasize the importance of DPMS' involvement in 3-gun. Never before had such a large gun manufacturer taken such an active role in the sport. The sponsored team featured many of the absolutely best shooters in the game, and the addition of the DPMS Tri-Gun match became a pivotal step in the sport's success.

The Tri-Gun brought major match access to roughly half the country, where before the sport had been mainly a Western phenomenon. Stages were fun and challenging, and the staff was top notch. Of course, the prize table became a lightning rod that sent shockwaves throughout the action-shooting community.

"People tell me that DPMS was a turning factor in 3-gun," Luth said. "I don't wish to take that credit, because there were so many people and matches nationwide that were as influential. However, we did put 100 percent of our efforts into sponsoring big and small matches across the country, putting the DPMS Shooting Team together in 2002 and beyond, with Jerry Miculek, Al Greco, Bruce Piatt, Tony Holmes, Deb Cheek, James Darst, Wayne Holloway, Kerry Dematos, part-timer Scott McGregor—all helped to bring awareness and credibility to the sport and to DPMS. All these factors helped to advance 3-gun."

"USPSA Nationals came after SOF in 1990, then SMM3G in 1997, RM3G in 2002," said Tony Holmes. "DPMS, in 2003, in its first year, had all of about 50 or more shooters that year. This is where I first met Randy

Luth and got his vision for what 3-gun/multi-gun should be and how the AR-15 had a place in it. Randy wanted and proved then that the DPMS Tri-Gun represented what all other 3-gun matches should be in regards to the quality of the staff and stages and the industry support for the game. He pushed and generated support for how the industry acts *today* in its support for 3-gun. If not for Randy Luth and DPMS Tri-Gun, along with Randy's persistence to make the industry stand up and take notice, I don't know if it would be where we are now."

Luth's impact on 3-gun goes beyond the obvious. Yes, his company made a great product

(top and left) DPMS and DPMS Tri-Gun Challenge founder Randy Luth eyes an aerial clay and prepares for a stage at the 2010 FNH USA Midwest 3-Gun Championship. (bottom) Luth takes on rifle targets during the inaugural Fallen Brethren 3-Gun match, in Texas, during the 2011 match year.

that was perfect for the sport, with options available to build a rifle essentially any way a customer desired. And, yes, Team DPMS went out and won match after match, so that Tri-Gun became the hottest ticket in the sport, with competitors from all over the country planning their work schedule, family vacations, and match calendars around the DPMS match. More than all this, though, it is the way in which Luth shared his position atop the sport that has had the most lasting impact. Instead of jealously guarding the enviable position his company had attained, Luth *pushed* rival gunmakers to get into the game right alongside him.

"Randy Luth has played a major part in promoting not only 3-gun, but shooting in general," said champion shooter Bruce Piatt. "Randy felt so strongly about the promotion of 3-gun that, even though he was the owner of DPMS, he called me, a sponsored DPMS shooter, and asked me to go to another AR manufacturer in an attempt to get another 3-gun match up and running—and now it looks like Ken Pfau, from FNH USA, has caught the same bug as Randy."

"I don't remember the details with Ken Pfau, but I am sure it was at one of the Shooting Industry Masters events that I encouraged him, as well as many other manufacturers, to get involved," Luth said. "Thank God they did. Tom Knapp and I also tried to convince Benelli to get involved in 3-gun four years ago or longer, and they resisted, but have finally seen the light. Our approach at DPMS was not isolationism or selfishness in order to protect our 'sandbox' in 3-gun, it was to get more manufacturers involved."

By 2007, the DPMS banner was flying higher than ever before. Now the second-largest manufacturer of AR-style rifles in the country, due primarily to the politically charged "black rifle revolution" that has swept the country, but also fueled by 3-gun sales, DPMS was acquired by Cerberus Capital Management, the same holding company that purchased Remington. Luth remained president of DPMS but, as with any sale of this sort, change was coming.

The most surprising change of all, at least for 3-gunners, came in 2010, in the form a disgruntled neighbor. After years of hosting signature matches of various shooting disciplines, a landowner adjacent to Randy's Del-Tone Luth Gun Club, home of the DPMS Tri-Gun, launched an all-out attack on shooting by challenging the Club's conditional use permit. Though to most it seemed a mere technicality,

FNH USA's Ken Pfau readies for a stage at the 2010 Blue Ridge Mountain 3-Gun match.

the challenge was upheld and the range was forced to cancel the Tri-Gun Challenge—a sad day for 3-gunners everywhere.

With Luth now retired from DPMS and the Tri-Gun match no longer in operation, one might think Randy's influence on 3-gun has ended. But that would be wrong, for the Luth ripple was just getting started.

FN Goes All-In

About the time DPMS was flourishing under Luth and the Tri-Gun was one of the major matches taking the sport to new heights, Ken Pfau set out to change the face of FNH USA—and he was going to do it in 3-gun.

Prior to Ken Pfau's influence, FNH USA had been many things to the firearms industry—but 3-gun wasn't really one of them. FN (Fabrique Nationale d'Herstal) itself was the legendary Belgian firearms manufacturer, steeped in history from John Moses Browning and his Auto-5 shotgun and Hi Power pistol to the legendary FAL full- and semi-auto rifles. More recently, the American arm of the company, FNH USA, had become a leading machine gun and rifle maker for the U.S. military. A student

Team FNH USA's Ken Pfau takes on pistol targets during the 2011 Superstition Mountain Mystery 3-Gun (below) and during the 2011 ARF-COM-Rockcastle Pro-Am (bottom).

of fine sporting arms or hard military weaponry would more likely have FN on their short list of in-hand brands—but not a 3-gunner.

But, just a few short years ago, Pfau launched Team FNH USA to compete in 3-gun and serve as a team of ambassadors for the company, the product lines, and the sport. FN followed up the formation of an action-shooting team by becoming the title sponsor of a major 3-gun match—first the Midwest 3-Gun Championships, in Missouri, followed up by the formation of a completely new major 3-gun event, in 2011, with the debut of the FNH USA 3-Gun Championship, in Glengary, West Virginia. Like DPMS a decade before, Pfau and FN had gone "all-in" with 3-gun—and they'd gone one step further by sponsoring a new TV show that sought to create a professional 3-gun tour—*3-Gun Nation*.

The 3-Gun Nation Effect

The sport of 3-gun was no doubt growing prior to the advent of *3-Gun Nation*. Matches such as the Fort Benning 3-Gun Challenge had pushed the sport in another new direction, as civilians leapt at the chance to compete in a match held aboard a military installation and get their hands on the "elite" firearms, vehicles, and gear normally used only by the U.S. armed forces.

Run by the U.S. Army Marksmanship Unit (AMU), the Fort Benning 3-Gun Challenge utilized the resources it had—soldiers—to staff and work an event in a way no other match could duplicate.

Stages were designed by AMU Action Team soldiers, and the competition was top notch. Finally, like the DPMS Tri-Gun, the prize table quickly became one of the deepest in the sport, attracting the top shooters in the game.

"After the demise of the WC3G event, in 2003," said Gangl, "a number of national-level multi-gun events have been organized and successfully run on an annual basis—the SMM3G, the JP Rocky Mountain 3-Gun, the DPMS Tri-Gun Challenge, the International Tactical Rifle Championship, in Gillette, Wyoming, the MGM Ironman event, in Idaho, the Fort Benning 3-Gun, and the

Deb Cheek runs her Open shotgun during the final Fort Benning 3-Gun Challenge in 2010.

new Blue Ridge Mountain 3-Gun match—with more being added every year."

Meanwhile, a movement away from square-bay matches was beginning to take hold, with the landscapes of the Midwest, Blue Ridge Mountains, and the Ozarks attracting an entirely new type of 3-gun shooter, much in the way the Rocky Mountains so brilliantly backdrop the NRA Whittington Center. The Blue Ridge Mountain 3-Gun match provided only the second major match east of the Mississippi, and match director Andy Horner's often brutally demanding and physically challenging stage designs struck a chord among many shooters.

The MGM Ironman presented yet another face for 3-gun, with stages bordering on the ridiculous, as round counts doubled or tripled anything seen at previous matches—anywhere. Physical, arguably maniacal even, the Ironman gave 3-gun a match that only the truly dedicated—or the insane—could call home. As such, 3-gun had its radical, no-holds-barred, renegade event, complete with the adjectives that once were reserved for only one match, the Soldier of Fortune 3-Gun.

Then, in 2010, *3-Gun Nation* threw gasoline on the fire. At the onset, *3-Gun Nation* was seminal purely for the fact that it gave the sport a home; any successful sport has immediate and continuous access in the form of TV. With the television show and the continuous coverage on 3GunNation.com, the sport had finally found its headquarters.

"In the mid-2000s, things really started to heat up in terms of major matches," Passamaneck said. "While there were not a lot of local and regional matches, by 2010, there were at least a dozen matches that many would call major. That year also saw a new entity enter the 3-gun frenzy, *3-Gun Nation*. Some of the competitors didn't know what this new thing was, nor what it would do to the sport we loved. Suffice it to say, *3-Gun Nation* helped to bring the sport to the masses more so than any prior attempt."

3GN also put in place the groundwork for what will be fully realized in 2013—the 3-Gun Nation Pro Series, the first truly *professional* sport in action shooting. Much like BASS or FLW Outdoors in tournament fishing, the $150,000 3GN Tour established cash payouts for the top competitors, with the 3GN Championship becoming the sport's ultimate prize. Win the Championship, the title of 3GN Champion, and take home a cash purse of $50,000—previously unheard of in 3-gun.

But, beyond the money going to top shooters, the increase in sponsored shooters, the deeper prize tables at matches where 3GN cameras were rolling, beyond all that the 3GN name is beginning to contribute to the most important increase of all—participation. Since *3-Gun Nation* first aired, in 2010, there has been an undeniable spike in the popularity of the sport. From the addition of more major 3-gun matches (FNH USA 3-Gun and Fallen Brethren, both in 2011), to the amazing surge in 3-gun participation at the local match level, the contemporary face of 3-gun is changing. New shooters

are jumping into the game in record numbers. Where previously new shooters had come almost exclusively from the world of action pistol, today's new shooters are giving 3-gun a try after merely watching it on TV or YouTube.

Even more impressive? A fresh crop of top talent has infused the game with new vigor, as young, fit, athletic competitors are raising the bar on the national stage. And, with the advent of a professional 3-gun tour and the chance at never-before-seen cash and prizes, not to mention a noticeable

increase in corporate sponsor-ship of shooters, these new 3-gunners are talented, well equipped, and hungry to make their mark on the sport.

Multi-gun was surely enjoy-ing some level of growth prior to *3-Gun Nation*, yet 3GN has become a major part of the equa-tion behind the recent explosion in its popularity. It is the latest step in the colorful history that is the sport of 3-gun.

"I've seen the shooting industry jump in with both feet and all of its support, and I've seen the black rifle make its case and prove itself as a legitimate sporting rifle to the general public," Tony Holmes said. "I've seen and used the new technology being intro-duced. I've seen the sport grow each and every year, and I've seen the birth of *3-Gun Nation* to the world and how it has brought 3-gun to TV.

"I wish I was 30 years old again and knew what I know now," Holmes laughed. "I'm just glad to have been a part of the explosion of 3-gun, past, present, and now into the future."

Todd Jarrett runs a stage during the final Fort Benning 3-Gun Challenge, during the 2010 match year.

Yamil R. Sued photo

CHAPTER 4

THE JOBS

Since the inception of 3-gun, in 1980, at the *Soldier of Fortune* match, the sport has rather evolved from the top down. Over the years, without any real system of local or regional matches to fuel demand, it was new *major* 3-gun matches that materialized across the country.

Some of these new major matches derived from the SOF match, while others sprouted in an attempt to offer something contrary to that very specific brand of shooting. In time, new matches were created, because it was becoming readily apparent that a real demand was building.

Today, 3-Gun Nation is building the foundation to meet that demand, with membership programs and club and amateur series points races that should help continue the increase in the sport at the grassroots levels—the very thing this sport has been missing. Meanwhile, at the top end, the 3GN Pro Series is taking the sport to a higher level than ever before—a professional sports league for 3-gun. But, even as the sport expands, it pays to remember that a big part of the soul of 3-gun will always remain in the Outlaw matches—the birthplace of the sport itself. Superstition, Rocky Mountain, Blue Ridge, Ironman—these matches were and are wide ranging in location, venue, and style, and all provide a distinct and unique face to the sport of 3-gun.

Superstition Mountain Mystery 3-Gun

The importance of Superstition on the landscape of 3-gun is arguably second only to SOF. While SOF established 3-gun as the renegade, anything-goes shooting sport on the periphery, Superstition brought real gun racing into vogue.

Held each year toward the end of March, Superstition has effectively ingrained itself in the sport as the unofficial kickoff to each new 3-gun season. Shooters from across the country converge on Arizona's Rio Salado Sportsman's Club, one of the finest action-shooting clubs in the country, some competitors dusting off gear that has been locked in gun safes for much of the winter off-season. The longest continuously running major 3-gun event in the country, SMM3G provides a fitting backdrop for the beginning of each new 3-gun season.

A large contingent of Open competitors drives in from the Western states, nearby in Arizona, or from as far as California, ready to put on a show at Superstition. Everyone loves the stage design at this match, but it's likely especially well suited for Open competitors, heavy on short courses and laid out wide

(left) Famous for its use of props, this stage at the 2011 Superstition Mountain Mystery 3-gun required competitors to hold a putter at the start position.

(below) A competitor braces against a prop "Jeep" during the 2010 Superstition Mountain Mystery 3-Gun.

open for shooting. Competitors from every division, probably here more than anywhere, absolutely *rip* through these stages, shredding paper targets and steel with three, four, and five pieces of brass in the air at a time, as they send rounds downrange.

The shooting sports have a long history of using stage props across many disciplines, but nowhere is this more prevalent than in action shooting. Probably the most unique use of props comes from the world of 3-gun, and, within that realm, absolutely no one uses stage props quite like the crew at Superstition Mountain. Roller coasters, helicopters, harnesses, cars, walls—if you can climb over, under, around, or through it, Superstition is likely to find a way to incorporate it into a stage. The unique use of props is as much of a signature of Superstition, as is the wide open shooting so thoroughly enjoyed by most of its competitors.

The sport of 3-gun, largely due to the success and ingenuity of several matches that have evolved into what are now considered majors, is currently experiencing an unparalleled explosion in popularity, considered by most industry experts to be the fastest growing discipline in the entire shooting sports. With no match more pivotal than SMM3G, and with it being the first major of the year, Superstition has relied on innovation and out-of-the-box thinking to keep it a favorite for 15 years.

"SMM3G is known as the match to attend," SMM3G match director Dan Furbee said. "We use the natural terrain of the Arizona desert on some of our stages to enhance the shooting experience. Our stages utilize great props and equipment, along with innovative and fun targets. We were the first to use the LaRue self-setting rifle target system. The SMM3G is also the first 3-gun match of the shooting season, and a lot of our dedicated shooters can't wait to get out of their snow-bound states to shoot in sunny Arizona. In addition to all that, sponsors such as DPMS, FNH USA, LaRue Tactical, Bushmaster, Patriot Ordnance Factory, JP Enterprises, Dillon Precision, Samson Manufacturing, Nordic Components, Trijicon, and SureFire, just to name a few, ensure fantastic prize tables that total more than $175,000 and make this the premier match of the shooting year."

Superstition also stands as a seminal match, due its overwhelming effect on the sport of 3-gun. Not only have stage design and target concepts been developed and proven in the Arizona desert, but rules and scoring doctrine that have influenced most of the major matches were developed by Furbee and his associates.

"SMM3G is the standard," Furbee said. "We developed the scoring system currently used in the 3-gun competition world. The International Multi-gun Association Rules (IMA) are accepted and used by most of the 3-gun competitions in the U.S."

Ultimately, the appeal of SMM3G derives from the fact that this is an event designed for shooters, by shooters. Understanding the wants and desires of the best pistol shooters in the country has evolved into a recipe that draws interest from shooters all over the country.

"All the serious 3-gun competitors are primarily competition pistol shooters who also happen to own these high-tech and very expensive rifles and shotguns," Furbee said. "We needed places and events where we could

Trapr Swonson takes on rifle targets through a "brick wall" barricade at Superstition Mountain Mystery 3-Gun.

compete with our other 'toys' and have a little fun. It's turned into a monster, and it's getting bigger! All any pistol shooter has to do is come to one of these matches and they'll be hooked."

Texas Multi-Gun Championship

Formally known as the Larue Tactical 3-Gun, match director Sheldon Carruth and his crew completely changed the face of this match and renamed it Texas Multi-Gun, in 2011. By all accounts the change was an emphatic home run.

Larue was retained as the major match sponsor, meaning there was no shortage of armadillo tactical bottle openers or barbecued pork from Larue's famous chuck wagon. More importantly, Larue provided an immense amount of support for the match itself, and the result was one that immediately elevated Texas Multi-Gun to become one of the premier events on the national Outlaw 3-gun circuit. Amazingly, nearly

400 competitors shot through the match—on time—during the 2011 Texas Multi-Gun.

"Match Director Sheldon Carruth and his team did a fine job with designing and running the match," wrote Bryce Towsley, in an article covering the event on 3GunNation.com. *"This is the first big 3-gun match on the relatively new Best of the West Shooting Range in Liberty Hill, Texas. The horseshoe-shaped range had all the stages close together for easy access, but each stage had plenty of room for a no-compromise design."*

The 2011 match had a World War II theme that, much in the tradition of Superstition Mountain, was nothing short of spectacular in the authenticity and creativity of stage props. Telephone poles were turned into palm trees, and trash dumpsters were transformed into Higgins Boat landing crafts. In short, the theme was carried out so thoroughly, the match had the unique backdrop of a World War II battle straight out of a John Wayne movie.

"While the match enjoyed excellent industry support, the main sponsor for the match was

Larue Tactical," Towsley wrote. *"In a unique and much appreciated gesture, they also supplied lunch and all the drinks. The theme for the eleven-stage match was famous battles of WWII, but this event clearly was designed by 3-gun competitors who understand the game. The stages were fast and challenging and laid out for trigger pullers. I didn't see any mind-game stages, hidden targets or procedural traps, just well thought out stages that challenged even the best shooters. The R.O.'s were all friendly and competent."*

Competitors left Texas amazed by the use of props, impressed by the staff, and blown away by the stage design. Message board forums all over the Internet lit up, singing praise for the new face of the Texas Multi-Gun Championship.

"I am completely amazed at how well the match ran and at the quality of the stages and props," said Team FNH USA's Dianna Liedorff. "In the past, I've heard shooters shy away from new matches or a change in direction of a match the first year, in order to let them 'work the bugs out,' but that certainly didn't apply to this match. It seemed like they have been doing this for years. The ROs were very skilled; each had a job, and together they worked like well-oiled machines."

Midwest 3-Gun Championship

Steel, steel, and more steel has become one of the interesting themes of Ken Flood's Midwest 3-Gun Championship. Great stages, with ample use of reactive targets littered across rolling terrain have contributed to Midwest becoming a favorite

Taking a page from Superstition Mountain, the 2011 Texas Multi-Gun Championship used an amazing assortment of stage props—all themed in World War II battles.

Vintage-looking World War II military props at the 2011 Texas Multi-Gun Championship set the tone for what was one of the most talked about matches of the season.

on the national 3-gun circuit, with Midwest enjoying explosive growth since its debut seven years ago.

"We started the match at the request of Randy Luth, former owner of DPMS, to have a sister match with the same rules as the DPMS Tri-Gun Challenge," Flood told me, going into the 2011 match. "We started with about 120 shooters and expect 230-plus this year."

Step to the firing line at Midwest, and it's pretty clear what's bringing more shooters to Missouri each year. Piles of spent brass litter a course of fire that stands as a solid mix of target presentations, from long-range rifle over vast expanses of real estate to built-up square range designs that challenge the top shooters in the world.

"The match utilizes both improved-type traditional ranges, as well as natural terrain," Flood said. "We put emphasis on rifle accuracy in the form of partially concealed paper targets, as well as steel out to 400 yards. We also like to feature a high round-count shotgun stage of at least 34 rounds. The most defining quality, in addition to our excellent range officers, is the challenge of each stage and their creative design and effective management."

Midwest was one of the original matches on the 2010 3-Gun Nation Tour. Today, along with most major 3-gun matches, the match is a 3GN-Affiliated event, where 3GN Divisional, Semi-Pro, Amateur, Lady, and Junior points are on the line. The venue and challenge combine to make Midwest a favorite among shooters.

"Our match is a good fit, because it's one of the top 3-gun matches in the U.S. and we are centrally located," Flood said. "We'll also draw competitors who will be attending the NRA Bianchi Cup, which is the week after our match and 20 miles away. We expect many international competitors, as well as many of the top U.S. shooters. We want to be a part of the 3-Gun Nation, because it's going to be the most exciting thing to ever happen to 3-gun and will certainly propel the sport into the limelight of the shooting world."

MGM Ironman

From giant slides to zip lines to funky firing positions to round after round after round of ammunition, MGM's Ironman is a multi-gun competition unlike any other. Win it, and most veteran competitors will consider you one of the toughest 3-gunners around. To do so, you must fire well over 1,000 rounds of ammunition from every type of conceivable firing position. You will shoot at sniper distances until your eyes grow weary, rip through CQB-type stages at a break-neck pace, and pound away with shotgun slugs at extreme range until your shoulder aches. Do all of this without breaking you or your gear, and you just might just survive the MGM Ironman.

"We came up with the idea for the match, because we like to shoot a lot," said MGM Targets company president and match founder Mike Gibson. "We like all our guns, and we like to shoot all of them every chance we get. Traditional 3-gun before our match would be a format of three stages of pistol only, three stages of rifle only, and three stages of shotgun only."

Debuting more than a decade ago, the MGM Ironman forever blew the traditional concept of 3-gun matches out of the water. Today, the Ironman is a grueling three-day marathon in the Idaho desert, where competitors shoot all three guns on each and every one of the Ironman's 10 or more eight-minute stages. In a word, the Ironman is, quite simply, intense.

"Most stages at any 3-gun in the country are over in less than two minutes, some in less than 40 seconds," Gibson said. "We have an eight-minute par time on each stage—and they're fun and crazy stages. Just go and Google "MGM Ironman 3-Gun." Shooting from the back of a moving pickup, shooting 32 birds launched from a trap house,

The zip line has become a signature stage at Ironman adding some truly unbelievable exhilaration to this already action-packed sport.

shooting your pistol and shotgun while you're driving a golf cart, shooting your pistol while you're sliding down a 285-foot zip line, shooting your rifle from a 20-foot tower, shooting two match-furnished full-auto guns on a stage (in addition to the three guns you brought with you), shooting bonus shots at 700 yards, a surprise stage that includes a 200-yard run, shooting three pepper poppers in a row with a shotgun, each of which launches two clay birds 30 feet in the air (so you have six birds in the air all at once), shooting 75 to 100 slugs out to 100 yards. Everyone will shoot at least 1,000 rounds at this match—assuming they hit every target with the first shot."

Sound nuts? Well, don't feel bad, because even the most experienced and accomplished shooters in the world require a deep breath before jumping into the Ironman.

"A shooter asked Taran Butler (a veteran 3-gun competitor with several titles) if he was coming back the next year," Gibson said. "Taran's reply was 'Hell no! After that match you have to buy three new guns!'"

Even without Butler, you can expect many top-ranked shooters back at the Ironman, as well as numerous non-sponsored shooters that come back to Idaho each year for the most challenging course of fire in the shooting sports.

"Shooters either come back every year, or they never come back," Gibson said. "Of the 150 shooters that we'll have this year, probably 70 of them have shot this match a minimum of seven or eight times previously. There is no other shooting discipline that creates an adrenaline rush like 3-gun, and certainly not one that lasts for up to eight minutes non-stop."

A thrill for many recreational and high-level competitive shooters alike, the MGM Ironman is also turning some heads within the military community. Due to its unique setting, challenging courses of fire, and its unrelenting demand on both the human body and gear used to compete, some U.S. soldiers are finding correlations between the Ironman and actual combat and are using MGM's brutal 3-gun event as training prior to upcoming deployments.

"Last year, we had five sol-

Outdoor writer Bryce Towsley breeches a door during the 2011 MGM Ironman.

diers from the U.S. Army 5th Special Forces Group, from Fort Campbell, Kentucky, come out and compete," Gibson said. "The sergeant major is right now on his eleventh deployment. They said this match was some of the best training they had ever had. This year, 13 guys from the Oregon National Guard, who are being deployed this Fall, are coming to shoot, using this match as one more component of their training. I don't think any of the other matches in the country are perceived as providing any significant training value to the military or law enforcement communities."

If it's a good enough test for the U.S. military, you can bet the Ironman is a worthy test of anyone's shooting ability. But, what sets this match apart is MGM's wicked idea of what a competitor must endure just

Team FNH USA's Dave Neth, with all three guns, runs one of the mammoth stages at MGM's brutal Ironman, which included negotiating some interesting props during the 2011 MGM Ironman.

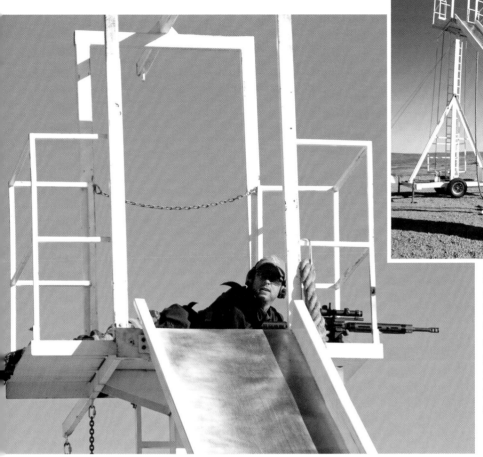

MGM Ironman is famous for its use of unique props—especially the Slide, where shooters take on long-range rifle targets. Competitors must clear their rifle and point it downrange before sliding down, where they reload and engage rifle targets all over again.

A group of competitors used a trailer to haul around the massive amount of equipment required to survive the MGM Ironman.

to take that shot, all 1,000 of them.

Northwest 3-Gun

Formerly run by R&R Racing's Robert Wright, the Northwest 3-Gun Championship was turned over to Scott Hawkins and Doug Hartley, in 2011, and, by all accounts, they have raised the bar even higher for the Pacific Northwest's largest major 3-gun match. And, while one stage can't make an entire match, it can sure put one over the top.

Such was the effect of the Crimson Trace Dark House stage, at the 2011 Northwest. With immense sponsor support, Northwest was able to provide a stage like no other for 3-gunners, much in the way the famous cave at Rockcastle is becoming that venue's signature.

"When Scott and I were planning this match," explained Harley, "I decided to do a dark house, because I really like them and most people don't get to shoot in one very often. Iain Harrison, from Crimson Trace, got wind of it and asked if he could set something up. I told him sure—anything to get it off *my* plate! Next thing I know, he has this whole plan of night vision goggles and SBRs (short-barreled rifles) with infrared lasers—I was *stunned*. For the folks who got to shoot this stage, it was a once-in-a-lifetime opportunity to use some very expensive equipment."

Crimson's Harrison designed and built wall panels, brought them to the facility on a flatbed truck, and assembled the house. Meanwhile, Peter Lesbo of I2 Technologies & Systems Integration provided night vision goggles, while Next Generation Arms provided the rifles,

and Hornady kicked in 3,000 rounds of free ammunition. The combined efforts resulted in an uncommon 3-gun experience.

"It's pretty timely that we ran this stage not too long after our guys got Osama," Hartley said. "I don't know for sure, but I'm willing to bet that the same technology we used on this stage was used to ventilate our No. 1 Most Wanted guy. It's not fair to the guys on the receiving end, but, as my buddy Scott says, 'If you're in a fair fight, your tactics suck.' Incredible technology with devastating effect—so cool you don't know what to say afterwards except 'Can I do it again?'"

JP Rocky Mountain 3-Gun

An offshoot of what many consider to be the founding match of 3-gun, JP Rocky Mountain 3-Gun (RM3G) continues a proud legacy that began with *Soldier of Fortune*. But RM3G is important not only as one of the forefathers of the sport, but as a challenging course of fire that utilizes the rugged New Mexico landscape to create a completely unique event.

For nearly three decades, *Soldier of Fortune* magazine sponsored its SOF match, which was later named the World Championship 3 Gun Tactical Match (WC3G). That SOF match held a special spot as the original competition in 3-gun. Yet, despite its overwhelming popularity, match support eventually waned.

"*Soldier of Fortune* magazine decided it no longer wanted to be involved with the match, and JP Enterprises, Inc., stepped in as the major named sponsor and engaged the existing match crew to run what we called the JP Rocky Mountain 3-Gun Championship," said John Paul, president

of JP Enterprises. "This match is unique, as it is designed and held in the natural terrain of the NRA's Whittington Center, as opposed to the typically developed square ranges. The added dimen-

Rocky Mountain 3-Gun challenges competitors with natural terrain at elevation in the New Mexico Rockies, along with plenty of long-range rifle shooting.

sion of a natural terrain match cannot be underestimated.

"Each year, different people took care of different parts of the match, but now it's run by us," said match director Denise Johnson, who runs the event with her husband, J.J. "The stages have always been very challenging, with long-range rifle shots as a staple. It has developed into

a match with more multi-gun stages, longer bonus targets, and more moving targets for shotgun, and the match overall has been at the forefront of gun transitions that are safe and speedy."

Set at an elevation exceeding 6,000 feet, Raton, New Mexico's NRA Whittington Center provides a fitting backdrop for a physically demanding match. More importantly, with the tremendous space provided by NRA's signature range development, JP's Rocky Mountain

(above) Few shooting ranges enjoy the backdrop that is the home to the Rocky Mountain 3-Gun. Held aboard the NRA Whittington Center's 30,000 acres, Rocky Mountain offers stunning views.

(below) John Paul Gangl runs a rifle course during the Rocky Mountain 3-Gun.

3-Gun delivers rifle opportunities not common in competitive action shooting.

"The thing that makes it unique is the ability to shoot in

natural terrain and use rocks and hills as part of each stage's design," Johnson said. "Although the altitude gives people's hearts and lungs a workout, there is no other match where you can have a deer being chased by a cougar dash by the stage briefing, or have a brief shooting stoppage, while a bear looks at your targets and lets you know what he thinks of you."

While the setting is panoramic, to be sure, it's the diverse stages of fire, long-range rifle requirements, and the physically demanding nature of the event that drives competitors to come back year after year. As such, RM3G remains one of the most popular and well-respected 3-gun events in the country.

"JP RM3G is one of the premier events of 3-gun and, in fact, has often been referred to as a World Championship match," Johnson said. "It tests more than just standing and shooting, including physical challenges, as well as mental ones. JP RM3G is unique and fun. It's a match that tests the well-roundedness of the shooter in the most unique setting in the world."

AR15.com-Rockcastle Pro-Am 3-Gun Championship

In 2011, arguably no 3-gun match received more hype, and no match was more anticipated, than the debut of the AR15.com-Rockcastle Pro-Am 3-Gun Championship. And with good reason, as, for the first time, internet forum juggernaut ARFCOM (AR15.com's nickname) provided massive support for a major match. Using its massive reach, word quickly spread about the first true Pro-Amateur 3-gun match.

Also contributing to the buzz was the venue, the Rockcastle Shooting Center, in Park City, Kentucky, a recreational resort that has quickly established itself as a premiere shooting venue. With approximately 2,000 acres of natural, rolling terrain, the Rock has the ability to put on a match that very few facilities can equal. Combined with its sporting clays, archery, golf, hotel, and restaurant and bar, the Rock provides the most unique shooting experience in the country, regardless the

discipline. Better yet, the Rock excels at hosting 3-gun matches, with the template already well established from hosting the Blue Ridge Mountain 3-Gun for several years, along with specialty events such as the Pan American IPSC Shotgun Championship in 2010.

Once the idea was established, NRA Board Member Joe DeBergalis, Rockcastle owners, brothers Nick and Nate Noble, industry leaders such as Brownells' CEO Pete Brownell, and, of course, the Avila family, who own and operate ARFCOM, began casting their wide net in search for industry support. The result was overwhelming, with pro clinics, side matches, and one of the richest Outlaw prize tables in the support, not to mention a second, separate match designed exclusively for amateur 3-gun competitors, many of whom had never competed in any shooting discipline at any level. Veteran 3-gunner Jeff Cramblit was brought in to create the format itself, and the result was two unique matches, one a challenging open course of fire for top 3-gun competitors; the other a slightly scaled back version, one where competitors with limited experience could still expect to successfully finish the match.

The matches themselves turned out to be entertaining ones, with the usual suspects dominating the top of the Pro match, while the Amateur match enabled a completely different set of shooters a moment in the spotlight. Ultimately, Daniel Horner dominated, Jerry Miculek survived, and Corey Schwanz held on by the slimmest of margins—three completely different ends to a remarkable weekend at the inaugural AR15.com-Rockcastle Pro-Am 3-Gun Championships.

In the Pro Tactical division, Horner (768.00) dominated a field of more than 170 competitors, winning five of eight stages on his way to the overall win. Taran Butler (719.36) finished second, followed by Kelly Neal (660.08), Chris Sechiatano (639.53), and Keith Garcia (638.73).

In the Open class, Jerry Miculek survived a tough back-and-forth battle with Clint Upchurch, James Darst, Mike Voigt, and Tony Holmes—all of which were in the hunt at some time to win the match. Miculek's 709.88 points secured the Open win, followed by Upchurch (679.61), Darst (660.32), Voigt (649.17), and Holmes (633.89).

On the Amateur side, Corey Schwanz (572.85) survived a nail-biter over Lee Pettross (570.05), winning by a mere 2.8 match points. Chris Cazin (564.67) took third, followed by David Schuster (563.42) and Patrick Kangeter (541.01).

"After looking at the scores for five of the seven stages, I knew it would be close," said Schwanz, who's a reloading technician for Sinclair International, a Brownells company. "I had been shooting fairly well, but after what happened to me on the final stage of the weekend, I thought I had lost too much time. I was surprised to hear my name called as the top amateur shooter."

Cramblit and his staff designed two separate matches,

with eight Pro stages and seven Amateur stages. However, they shared one common theme in that they were wide open. With relatively fast par times, most of the stages were fairly short in round count, as well, and required minimal movement compared to other natural terrain courses of fire. All combined to keep plenty of brass in the air, as well as smiles on the faces of the competitors.

"I liked the open stages of this match," Schwanz said. "Most of them had a variety of ways to shoot them, and we had to figure out what would be the best way for us. It fit with what I like to do in matches—try to find the shot or angle no one else saw and gain some time because of it."

The match format, which effectively served as two simultaneous matches, enabled approximately 350 shooters to compete over the three-day event. While the format itself was unique, with this Pro-Am being the first of its kind in the sport of 3-gun, the event also borrowed heavily from other successful firearm industry events to create a stellar weekend. Several companies provided support personnel and kicked in prizes for fun and challenging side shoots that ran throughout the weekend. Arguably, even more popular were the pro clinics, where top 3-gun competitors such as Bruce Piatt, Bennie Cooley, Jerry Miculek, and others held free clinics on different aspects of shooting 3-gun competitions.

"It seemed like everybody who was anybody in 3-gun was at this match and sponsored a side match," said Pro Match competitor Karla Herdzik. "Benelli sponsored a shotgun speed shoot. FNH had a P90 machine gun

stake shoot. Crimson Trace had a pistol run through one of Rockcastle's infamous pitch-black caves. LaRue Tactical was there with its new OBR (Optimized Battle Rifle), and its famous barbecue trailer! And there was a 3-man team stake shoot, too! The best part of all these side matches? All the proceeds went to benefit some great charities supporting the men and women who sacrifice their lives daily for our freedoms—the NRA Life of Duty Foundation, the Lone Survivor Foundation, and Task Force Dagger."

"The event in general was a blast," Schwantz said. "This was my first trip to Rockcastle and my first national-level 3-gun match. I really liked the Pro-Am format and the multiple days of shooting. The pro clinics were a great addition to the schedule, as well. The level of support this match received from all the sponsors was absolutely amazing. All of them deserve a big thank you!"

"The great folks of AR15.com, Rockcastle Shooting Center, Brownells, Sinclair, the PoliceStore.com, and Hornady joined in our mission to open up this competition to more competitors than ever before," said NRA Board Member and Match Chairman Joe DeBergalis. "Our event was unique and original in format. The emphasis was to provide an avenue for those wanting to become active within 3-gun, while simultaneously providing a challenging event for the seasoned competitor. Our Match Director, Jeff Cramblit, accomplished that task admirably. Our team at the Rockcastle Shooting Center, led by the Noble Family and General Jerry Humble (USMC, Ret.), did a good job ensuring that our facilities were in superb shape. Everyone was touched by their generous hospitality. As an NRA Board Member, I received great support from Wayne LaPierre, the NRA's executive vice president, and Chris Cox of the NRA's Institute for Legislative Action. We also introduced the NRA's Life of Duty Program, a mission-driven NRA initiative that benefited our acknowledged charities, the Task Force Dagger Foundation and the Lone Survivor Foundation. There was a vendors' row and demonstration area for our participating sponsors that enabled those competing and

The ARFCOM-Rockcastle Pro-Am utilized the Rockcastle Shooting Center's Cowboy Town for one of its 3-gun stages.

watching the opportunity to try the very same equipment and gear the competitors used during the match.

"We created an 'industry buy-in,' by inviting our friends in the industry to take stock in the match and enable us to provide for them a showcase of their products that could help grow the sport," DeBergalis continued. "For instance, we provided range access to those companies that wanted to display their products in real time. Our side matches allowed interested parties the opportunity to try LaRue Tactical, Spikes Tactical, FNH USA, CMMG, Crimson Trace, Bushnell, Benelli, and JP products, to name a few, during range conditions that allowed them instant point-of-sale opportunities. This

also allowed for instant branding and product recognition—much like the NASCAR adage, 'Race on Sunday, buy on Monday.' Well, based on the feedback from our participating sponsors, everyone there took that to heart!"

As word began to spread about the Pro-Am inaugural match, more and more companies decided get involved. For some, it marked their first entry into the sport of 3-gun.

"We are proud to say that we opened opportunities in 3-gun for those companies who had not yet been involved. Daniel Defense, Troy Industries, Alexander Arms, CMC Triggers, and Ritchie Leather were all first-time sponsors who had a great time and have already committed again for next year," DeBergalis said.

"Through the hard work and effort of all involved, we enjoyed welcoming a total of 61 sponsors to our event and team. And, when I use the word 'team,' I mean it. As I mentioned previously, their buy-in was integral to our success. Most importantly, each sponsor became a major part of the competition and now has a stake in the growth of our match for next year.

The Pro-Am delivered a home run on a scale seldom seen in any type of first-year match, a testament to the tremendous cast of supporters involved, and the Rock as the pivotal cog in the wheel. To that end, the online registration process took a matter of minutes for the follow-on match this year, with an initial waiting list numbering in the hundreds! It's fair to say the Pro-Am is here to stay on the Outlaw 3-gun circuit.

Ozark 3-Gun Championship

In 2009, following on the heels of successful new match introductions such as the DPMS Tri-Gun Challenge, Fort Benning 3-Gun Challenge, and the Midwest 3-Gun Challenge, another new major Outlaw match debuted in Missouri—the Ozark 3-Gun Championship (O3GC). Taking advantage of leased rural land near Columbia, the Ozark immediately became known for its rolling natural terrain and the good stage design woven in.

"The Ozark 3-Gun Championship is a natural terrain match shot in the hills of the Ozarks, in southern Missouri," said Kirk Broyles, match director, prior to the 2010 event. "It features fun and challenging stages for all levels of competitors. And now we have a new location with more than 1,000 acres at our disposal. There are some great stages."

Challenging long-range rifle stages, a tremendous amount of small, reactive steel pistol targets, and a massive all-shotgun stage have become signature at Ozark. With the second venue in 2011, a small lake enabled the added dimensions of rifle shooting from unstable platforms,

Rafael Esqueda takes on rifle targets during the 2011 AR15.com-Rockcastle Pro-Am 3-Gun at the Rockcastle Shooting Center in Park City, Kentucky.

The Ozark 3-Gun Championship is one of several major matches trending toward the use of small, knock-over steel for pistol targets.

such as a small boat. Also in 2011, Ozark was held on the weekend of September 11, the 10-year anniversary of the 2001 terrorist attacks. An active-duty soldier himself, Broyles dedicated the match to the memory of that horrific day, and every stage was themed after important battles or missions conducted by U.S. forces in the War on Terror.

Since 2010, Ozark has been a 3GN-Affiliated match, hosting two 3GN Shoot-Offs and now part of the 3GN Outlaw Division series, giving yet more reasons to shoot one of the top matches in Outlaw 3-gun.

"I'm very excited to be a part of *3-Gun Nation*. It's doing great things to promote the sport," Broyles said last season. "As the newest match of this size, I am extremely honored to host the first 3GN Shoot-Off of the 2011 season. And I look forward to a long, successful relationship."

FNH USA 3-Gun Championship

One of three new matches to debut in 2011, the FNH USA 3-Gun Championship didn't receive quite the hype as the Pro-Am, when the shooting season unfolded. This was understandable, as the Pro-Am had launched a completely new format and was publicized to the hilt on AR15.COM. FNH, mean-

while, quietly went to work delivering what the East Coast had never had—a premiere, major 3-gun match of its very own.

Rather than re-invent the wheel, as the Pro-Am had, FNH USA match director Larry Houck sought to perfect it. His vision was realized in an interesting blend of range bay and natural terrain courses of fire. The stages were constructed in a wide-open fashion, yet the most interesting stage philosophy was one centered on "shooters' choice." On these, competitors had varying degrees of selection by which targets could be engaged with certain firearms. The result was a wonderful blend of fast shooting and wide-ranging strategy, along with some demanding and technical mid- and long-range rifle shooting thrown in for good measure. Ultimately, for many who competed, the FNH USA 3-Gun Championship was the surprise hit of the 3-gun season.

"As a competitor, I love to have choices," Houck said. "It's no fun traveling to matches where everyone has to shoot a stage the same way. I also wanted competitors to play to their strengths. If you're better with a pistol than a shotgun, then shoot your pistol. No competitor can look back and say the stage caused them not to do well. Even more interesting, a tremendous amount of rain leading up to the match prevented us from getting all of the bays completed. So it actually made our match better, as we had a true mixture of ranges and natural terrain on which to shoot."

The match also marked the debut for one of our country's new-est range and training facilities. Sprawling across a vast expanse of West Virginia mountains, the new Peacemaker National Training Center, while early in its development, provided opportunities not available at a standard square-bay type range facility.

"This was the facility's first big match, so it was a huge learning curve and at a rapid pace, considering I was doing all the coordination from 1,900 miles away," Houck said. "The staff were great to work with, and I can only see better things in the future for Peacemaker National Training Center."

One of the highlights of the event was the unique use of FN firearms. Used as stage guns, with all ammunition provided by FN, the event gave competitors an opportunity to shoot products they might not ever have the chance to otherwise.

"We shot a PS90, suppressed SCAR 16, and an FN 303 Less Lethal Launcher," Houck said. "Most people will *never* get to shoot these guns, especially the Less Lethal Launcher, as it's not available to the general public."

Ultimately, the inaugural FNH USA 3-Gun Championship was a huge success, setting it up to be yet another must-shoot event.

"Expect exciting stages with choices," Houck said. "We want to make this a great experience for everyone involved, from the shooter to the range staff and especially our sponsors. We want to be the match that everyone wants to be involved with."

Robby Johnson takes on pistol targets placed among the trees during a stage setup in the woods at the Blue Ridge Mountain 3-Gun.

Blue Ridge Mountain 3-Gun

From the very beginnings at Big Bear, the driving force behind much of the innovation in major practical shooting competition has come out of the western United States. However, in 2008, Andy Horner founded the Blue Ridge Mountain 3-Gun Championship (BRM3G), giving the sport, at the time, only its second major 3-gun event east of the Mississippi.

"The BRM3G was begun in order to bring a major 3-gun championship to the eastern U.S.," said Horner, match director of the BRM3G. "With all of the matches except the Fort Benning 3-Gun Challenge (now defunct) being west of the Mississippi, there are many shooters who have not been exposed to the excitement of high-level 3-gun competition. Being able to talk with, watch, and compete against the best shooters in the world is introducing new shooters to 3-gun and is increasing interest in our sport generally."

While the eastern states may have been slow to develop major 3-gun competitions, Blue Ridge Mountain nevertheless hit the ground running under the watchful eye of match director Andy Horner, a veteran multi-gun shooter. Taking lessons learned from competing in major matches all over the United States, Blue Ridge utilizes a remarkable expanse of land at the new Rockcastle Shooting Center, near Bowling Green, Kentucky. As such, Blue Ridge utilizes the natural terrain features of Kentucky's western foothills, in turn delivering what are some of the most challenging stage designs in 3-gun competition.

While I haven't competed in every major out there, of the ones I've personally shot, the Blue Ridge has been my favorite thus far. For the same reason some top pros *don't* like the Blue Ridge, I think others are drawn to it. Physically demanding and technically challenging, the stages at Blue Ridge challenge equally with all three guns, while the venue itself provides a wild card. Targets are hidden behind trees, in bright sunlight one moment and then in contrasting shade the next—you *never* know what you will see at BRM3G. While some 3-gunners understandably prefer the challenge be equally applied to all at all times, I still think there is

Match director Andy Horner is famous for his challenging target placements—and sometimes hard-to-see unpainted steel—at the Blue Ridge Mountain 3-Gun.

something to be said for shooting a match where surprise is still an element of the game. This is, after all, a practical sport.

"The BRM3G has several characteristics for which it's known," Horner said. "First of all, being one of few major matches held over natural terrain, the match uses features of the land to create interesting and challenging courses of fire that test both the skill of the shooter and the effectiveness of their equipment. Stage design also sets the BRM3G apart. The stages are physically demanding and have a higher than average round count—this is *not* a stand-and-shoot match. We strive to create stages that require competitors to get out of their comfort zone and have their abilities tested.

The 2010 Blue Ridge Mountain 3-Gun redefined low-light shooting when it introduced the Cave Shoot to 3-Gun. Top competitor Dave Neth is pictured to the right.

This is accomplished through requiring significant movement, unusual shooting positions, unusual presentation of targets, and the occasional longer shots."

This blend of terrain, stage design, high round count, and demanding match tempo have instantly elevated Blue

Ridge to major status, one of only about 10 matches in the country to create such demand. In only a few short years, the competitor field, comprised of novice and veteran shooters alike, has grown exponentially,

"We have definitely been growing," Horner said prior to Blue Ridge 2010. "The first year we had 99 shooters, then 176, and this year the match is full and expecting 240-plus shooters."

While the Blue Ridge Mountain 3-Gun delivers an uncommon shooting experience, with a top-notch match, resort hotel and other amenities all in one location, what keeps the pros from all over the country coming back is the high-octane match itself.

"Again, the BRM3G is not a stand-and-shoot match," Horner emphasized. "Some folks love that type, some don't. Fortunately, 3-gun matches around the country each have their own flavor, and the BRM3G provides an opportunity for those who enjoy a more physical and technical match."

Fallen Brethren 3-Gun

The final new major 3-gun event to debut in 2011 was developed in an attempt to fill the hole in the match calendar voided by the demise of one of the top matches in the country—the Fort Benning 3-Gun Challenge. While the match had been continuously full, the prize table loaded, and the shooting always top notch under the watchful eye of the U.S. Army Marksmanship Unit Action Shooting Team, the match nevertheless was cancelled, apparently a decision by higher ranking officials.

After a group of soldiers sought to continue the match tradition at a new venue, the task

fell to Jim Smith at Spartan Tactical, a private training academy outside of Dallas, Texas. Smith built his staff, picked up the sword, and eventually brought in Sheldon Carruth and his team from Texas Multi-Gun for additional staffing and support. This proved to be a key move, and the result was a well-run, challenging course of fire over distinctive, Texas brush country natural terrain. Despite rain, fog, and extremely challenging footing at times, approximately 150 soaked and muddy competitors shot an entire 10-stage major match in 48 hours, and there likely wasn't a disappointed shooter in the bunch.

While several days of rain dictated a slower pace on many stages, making footing a challenge across the immense 10,000-acre facility, solid stage design and a strong crew of range staff pushed the field through the entire match in just two days. True, FB3G enjoyed a bit of luck, with a reduced field of 150 competitors, but completing such a match in just two days is virtually unheard of and a testament to the staff running this event.

For those who braved the elements, the payoff was an outstanding course of fire, highlighted by Stage 9, a long-range rifle course that required competitors to shoot from the side of a cliff down into a panoramic valley below to engage rifle steel at approximately 100 to 550 yards. This stage demanded calculation of angles of fire, calling the wind, and multiple target holds for a good run. In the Tactical Optics division, Kelly Neal outpaced Rustin Bernskoetter 824.46 to 791.03 to pick up the win. Burton Thompson (776.20), Adam Popplewell (750.74), and

Trip McIngvale (743.14) rounded out the top five.

Chuck Anderson narrowly edged out Tony Holmes 816.48 to 810.41 to win the Open division. Anderson put together a solid match, shooting early with the match staff on Thursday. However, Holmes almost certainly delivered the more impressive performance, battling adverse weather conditions, yet still commanding two stage wins on the final day. Holmes won Stages 2 and 3, after shooting them in their absolute worst conditions, an impressive feat. James Darst (759.41) finished third, followed by Jesse Tischauser (666.43) and Kelly Raglin (579.17).

In the Heavy Metal Optics race, Tate Moots announced his definitive return to 3-gun with an impressive victory, winning seven stages and scoring 886.85 match points. (Moots has competed in very few matches over the last two seasons while recovering from a back injury.) J.P. Gangl (726.49) finished second, followed by J.J. Johnson (653. 63), Vance Blackwell (556.56) and Shane Cuperus (437.13).

Kuan Watson (846.72) outlasted West Chandler (782.13) to win the Tactical Iron division. Michael Chambers (677.96) finished third, followed by Ben Zacharias (591.67) and Jeremy Moore (579.04).

As impressive as the top shooters were and despite the bad weather, the most notable feature to this first edition of the newly organized FB3G was the backdrop itself, Spartan Tactical. Run by former Army Special Forces operator Jim Smith, Spartan's massive natural terrain facility enabled gunsmith and range master Sheldon Carruth tremendous creativity in stage and course design. Major match sponsors Remington, Leupold, and DSG Arms, along with secondary sponsors Warne Scope Mounts, SureFire, XRAIL, Stag Arms, MGM Targets, and many more, contributed a solid prize table for a first-year event, one that promises to grow into a must-shoot event on the major match Outlaw 3-gun circuit.

USPSA Multi-Gun Nationals

The term "Outlaw 3-Gun" exists in overt defiance to what some in 3-gun believe USPSA represents. To be fair, much of the early work in Outlaw 3-gun grew in an absence of USPSA rules and definitions, as the pistol doctrine didn't always work for this emerging multi-gun sport. However, compared to all but a few of the major matches currently in operation, USPSA Multi-Gun Nationals has been doing it longer than most, and that deserves credit. And, while USPSA has its detractors, there is also a staunch, loyal following of competitors that travel the country to compete, officiate, and set-up USPSA events, including the Multi-Gun Nationals. As such, for some especially die-hard, high-level USPSA pistol competitors, USPSA Multi-Gun Nationals remains one of the top venues in the sport, a must-attend match on the national major 3-gun circuit.

In recent years, much has been made of the stage design at Nationals. To many veteran competitors, after years of lackluster opinions of the match, recent stage design has improved, elevating this event's stature. Under the watchful eye of former president Mike Voigt, a very vocal supporter of multi-gun within USPSA, the Multi-Gun Nationals

have indeed flourished in recent years. Today, USPSA is under fresh leadership, with newly elected president Phil Strader. A pistol competitor by trade, Strader nonetheless competes in 3-gun, as well, and, in fact, qualified for the 3GN Championship Finale, in 2012. What remains to be seen is how hard Strader will push for the continued development of USPSA 3-gun.

The Other Players

Shooting a major 3-gun event is a large commitment in time and money. Match fees are usually somewhere around $250. Add in travel costs, meals, and enough ammunition to get you through the match, and a major shoot can easily run a couple thousand dollars to attend.

"There is an enormous amount of time and energy that goes into training, preparing, and actually attending the matches," said Team FNH USA's Dianna Liedorff, who finished second in the 2011 3-Gun Nation Ladies Division. "The matches are pretty tricky to get into and require a lot of planning relatively early in the season. By February, I was already entered into every major 3-gun match I planned on attending for the year."

"For me, the time commitment is the biggest obstacle to overcome," said Open division shooter Clint Upchurch. "Having a full-time job, a family, and other priorities makes the preparation, training, and travel required to be at the top of the sport extremely difficult. There is a lot of time spent prepping gear, loading ammo, and training before you even talk about spending four to five days to travel and compete at an event. Trying to balance these factors without

neglecting other priorities seems almost impossible at times."

"There's a lot of gear and ammo required, and if you don't drive, you have to figure out the most economical way to get it there," Liedorff continued. "That requires a lot of planning. If I'm not driving, I've had friends that are driving take my stuff while I fly. Or I plan ahead with ammo and leave my bag/ammo on the FNH USA truck. Most major matches are three days long. That's a huge commitment of time away from work."

Luckily, there are several of what I like to call "regionals" across the country. While that's not an official designation, it does give a description for matches that are obviously larger in size, scale, and cost than a local club match, yet more affordable and more easily accessible than a major.

Compared to 250 shooters at a major, regionals run 100 shooters or more. Instead of a $200,000 prize table, there will be a much more modest selection of guns and gear to be won. The real prize here, most often, is in the shooting itself.

From Fort Smith, Arkansas, to Kentucky State in Owensboro, to USPSA Area 1 Multi-Gun in Parma, Idaho, some of the finest one- and two-day match schedules in 3-gun can be found at venues of this size.

For an affordable price, and within driving distance to where you live, chances are there is a once-a-year regional-type 3-gun event. If you're not quite ready to make the jump to a major 3-gun event, but want something more than your local club has to offer, a regional 3-gun match has the potential to really deliver a fantastic experience.

DIVI

CHAPTER 5

THE DIVISIONS

In the sport of 3-gun, available equipment encompasses a wide range, one with a vast spectrum of performance capabilities. Race guns in light calibers and loaded down for softer recoil perform entirely differently than full-power .308 rifles and .45-caliber pistols with military ball loads. As such, competing head-to-head with such diverse equipment is not a fair comparison.

Over the years, several different equipment divisions have been established and, for the most part, even standardized across Outlaw 3-gun matches. From the fast, accessory-driven Open division to the pounding big-bore guns in the Heavy Metal division, 3-gun's different equipment divisions are really a big part of what attracts shooters into the game and what sets it apart from other shooting disciplines.

Tactical Optics

By an overwhelming margin, often exceeding 75 percent or more at major 3-gun matches, Tactical Optics is the division in which most competitors play. Not only does it have the greater number of shooters by volume, but the majority of the very best of the talent pool play here. Daniel Horner, Taran Butler, Greg Jordan, Tyler Payne, Rustin Bernskoetter, and many other of the best 3-gunners in the sport call Tactical Optics home at every event in which they compete.

"The Tactical Optics division, casually referred to as 'Tac Scope' by many who play the game, also goes by the monikers 'Scoped Tactical' and 'Limited Scoped,'" said Patrick Kelley. "This is the division where the majority of competitors play, and for good reason. The equipment roster reads virtually word-for-word the same as it does for the Limited division, with the exception being your rifle optic choices. Whereas in the Limited division you are held to a magnification maximum of 1X for your scope (i.e., iron sight and/or red dot), in Tactical Optics, you can run any scope you desire. And many desire more power!"

For the most part, it's the allowance of the variable power scope, while still limiting the exceedingly expensive accessories that define the Open class, that maintains Tactical Optics as the standard bearer. That scope use, for the most part, is simply driven by the challenges competitors commonly face now, with targets, often within the same stage, varying in distance from a few feet to 400 yards or more.

"Over the course of a season, shooters will face targets on the long side of 400 yards," Kelley

explained. "Some match directors take it a bit further, challenging and perhaps frustrating competitors with engagements to 600 yards. Couple this with tough lighting conditions, wind, and weather, and having a 4X, 6X, or even an 8X scope on top of your rifle makes sense."

As such, the new breed of variable power scopes, with power ranges that begin at 1X or 1.5X and range past 4X and on up to even 8X, dominate the field. Leupold, Swarovski, Bushnell, Burris, and more all make rifle scopes within this niche. Designed with an eye toward military and law enforcement use, the 1X variable revolution has totally redefined what once was a division in which a 1-4X scope (of which many are still used effectively), previously dominated the equipment choices among the consistent match winners.

The gun platforms themselves are quite wide ranging, with no one brand leading the pack, but there are certain types that see more use than others. In rifles, AR-15s chambered in .223/5.56

are king. Stag Arms and Colt's now both offer out-of-the-box rifles ready for 3-gun, competing with those from JP Rifles and DPMS. DoubleStar is currently planning a dedicated 3-gun rifle, while Samson Manufacturing is rumored to be working on an entry, as well. FNH USA's model SCAR 16 has made a big splash, in large part due to the solid use by its own team members in competition. It's now becoming common place to see SCARs in rifle racks at major matches that don't belong to Team FNH USA

shooters, evidence of the gun gaining acceptance.

The most widely used shotgun among top shooters is most likely the Benelli M2, though the FNH USA SLP has made a major impact over the last couple of seasons and become a serious threat to Benelli's dominating presence in the sport. Mossberg's 930 has also seen some use since its debut, as has the VersaMax creation from Remington.

Pistols, like rifles, are really all over the place, even if the majority of veteran pistol shoot-

(left and top) During the Heavy Metal divison run at the 2011 Kentucky State Multi-Gun Champtionships Bryan Ray runs a single-stack 1911 on the pistol stage, and loads his pump-action Benelli Nova during shotgun action. This top competitor is shown dialing up his elevation knob on his Springfield M1A while competing in the Heavy Metal divison at the 2011 Blue Ridge Mountain 3-Gun (bottom).

Tom Carpenter, competing in Tactical Optics, engages long-range rifle targets from shooting sticks, as required during a stage at the 2011 Blue Ridge Mountain 3-Gun.

ers do use some form of the 2011 (yes, that's 2011, not 1911), most often an STI or Caspian build. But Glocks, Springfield XDs, Smith & Wesson M&Ps, and even the new FNH USA Model FNS are also popular choices among competitors.

"The overall equipment is virtually the same as one would use in the Limited division," Kelley said. "There will be an AR in .223/5.56, a self-loading shotgun in 12-gauge, and a pistol holding 18 or more rounds in either 9mm or .40-caliber. There are no comps, ports, or optics allowed on your pistol or shotgun. In the Tactical Optics division, you just bolt your favorite scope onto your rifle and you're ready to rock."

Ultimately, the Tactical Optics division really just represents the types of firearms that have the most widespread appeal across the greatest number of competitors. Affordable, easy to use, and with many dual-role purposes, Tactical Optics firearms and gear are most assuredly the products that best define the sport of 3-gun and those who shoot it.

"This is the division where most shooters start and stay," Kelley said. "The equipment is practical in size and weight and, as configured, are useful for other operations. Need a varmint whacker? Got it. Upland gun? Plug your shotgun's mag tube and you'll have a fast handling pellet spreader. Pistol for personal protection? Why not? Any of the battery of three could well defend hearth and home. Now *that's* practical. Heck,

maybe that's what it ought to be called—the *Practical* division!"

It's also the division where the top pros in the sport come to play. The 2012 3GN Pro Series marks the first year where all 3GN Series points—reserved for the shooters at the top level—will be earned exclusively in Tactical Optics. A television move, as well as a competitive one, the Tactical Optics-only format will once and for all settle the question as to who are the absolute top competitors in the game.

In years past, the sport crowned champions at each indi-

Ben Fortin, shooting in Tactical Optics, uses his Dueck Defense RTS sights to engage short-range targets at the 2011 Rocky Mountain 3-Gun.

vidual event in several different equipment divisions. This is a system that remains intact at Outlaw matches, as it should, but to mainstream America, this is analogous to putting NASCAR, Formula One, and Truck Series drivers, each running their different cars, all on the same track at the same time. So the 3GN Pro Series format finally puts and keeps all the top shooters in one division, going head-to-head, to determine individual match winners and crown a season champion. Regardless the division's name, putting the very best shooters in the world together, competing heads-up for the largest cash payouts in the sport, will be unquestionably exciting and may be just the spark 3-gun needs to elevate it even further into the limelight.

Open Division

In 3-gun, the Open division is just that—the no-holds-barred, anything goes, brass-in-the-air, high-speed division of practical shooting. Watching Jerry Miculek, Mike Voigt, or Clint Upchurch absolutely burn down a stage in this type of class is a sight to behold.

By comparison, all other divisions are ones that limit, in varying degrees, the firearms and gear. As such, the Open division is more gear-driven than any other, with a high emphasis placed on ammunition capacity and muzzle control. Increased capacity reduces time-robbing reloads, and highly modified compensators keep the muzzle flat, thereby increasing control and speed—the Open shooter lays on the trigger and lets it rip.

"Open looked like the most fun division," said Colt's Clint Upchurch, describing why he chose the Open division, when switching from USPSA pistol competition to 3-gun two years ago. "Having so many options

with the gear was appealing, and I thought it would be a more natural transition into 3-gun after a few years of exclusively shooting Open pistol."

In Open, high-capacity magazines—from SureFire 60-rounders on up the 100-round Beta-C mag—are used for running rifles. As it is in all divisions, .223-chambered ARs rule the day here, except that restrictions concerning muzzle brakes and compensator sizes go out the window. Bipods are also used to good effect in Open.

Open is also the division that allows multiple optics on rifles. Companies such as Warne Scope Mounts, with its RAMP mount, produce mounting solutions that provide for a traditional variable power scope on top of the rifle, while also incorporating a 1X reflex sight mounted 45 degrees from the scope and in line with the bore. The set-up enables shooters to sight the 1X for close-range paper targets, anywhere from 10 to 25 yards, while the main scope is used to engage

(top and left) Tommy Thacker runs his XRAIL-equipped SLP in the Open division at the 2011 Rocky Mountain 3-Gun, and rapidly engages pistol targets with an Open handgun during the 2011 Superstition Mountain Mystery 3-Gun.

(below) Tony Holmes runs an XRAIL-integrated Benelli in the Open division at the 2011 Rocky Mountain 3-Gun.

(above) Though he sometimes uses an XRAIL in competition, Jerry Miculek used only an extended magazine tube and speedloaders on his Open shotgun, during the 2010 Midwest 3-Gun Championship.

long-range targets. The combination, one now being copied by elite U.S. military units, delivers incredibly fast target acquisition at close range, while maintaining increased power setting for long-range engagement.

"My experience has been that you lose or gain the most ground in long-range rifle," Upchurch explained. "There is just more time to be wasted when you take a lot of extra shots with the rifle. Also, wind and lighting are more of a factor here. If you shoot shotgun and pistol under different conditions, those things won't make a big difference, but they can change things tremendously for the rifle."

Open pistols are almost universally of the 2011 configuration, with STI, Caspian, Infinity, and more showing up in high-speed holsters at major matches. Capacity is high, red dot optics are allowed, comps are huge, and any other manner of gunsmithing and accessories are used to squeeze the final bit of speed out of this 100-year-old 1911 design.

"A pistol can be anything you wish, so long as it's 9x19mm or larger," Patrick Kelley said. "Magazine *length*, not capacity, is restricted to 170 millimeters. Port it, comp it, hang crystals from the rearview mirror. If that makes you go faster, it's all good. Bolt on any sight system with the exception of projecting lasers. Kickstands and gas pedals are okay, too! Really! A kickstand, in this instance, is an arm sticking off the side of the pistol that props it up so you can get a better grip for those lying-flat-on-the-table starts. Gas pedals? Nope, not kidding, this speed part is for your support hand thumb to press down on and help control muzzle lift!"

Then there's the shotgun. In terms of pistols and rifle, it's mainly just different variations on the same theme that make up the primary differences in competitors' gear. Shotguns, on the other hand, are quite different, and they provide the one place within the Open division where individual preference makes its loudest expression.

"The difference from Limited to Open shotguns is in magazine capacity and the use of electronic sights and speedloaders," said Bruce Piatt. "A shooter can take his Limited shotgun, put a longer mag tube on it, install a bolt-on Armstec speedloader, mount a Burris SpeedBead, screw in a combination compensator/choke, and be ready to shoot Open—all without permanently modifying his gun."

"The Open division shotgun displays the biggest departure from the other divisions," Kelley said. "Whereas speedloaders are forbidden in all other divisions, in Open, these devices, including detachable box magazines, are virtually *obligatory*! An Open division shooter *could* live without comps, optics, or porting, but one would be hard-pressed to win without the ability to speedload the shotgun!"

Today, shotgun speedloaders come in three basic forms, stick types, detachable box magazines, and a singular product called the XRAIL, which is a self-articulating, rotary magazine tube system. At this point, it's hard to say which style is more effective, as each of the most consistent top shooters in 3-gun use a different shotgun speedloader system.

Clint Upchurch, winner of the 2011 3GN Open division, runs an R&R Saiga, a highly customized, box magazine-fed shotgun sys-

tem. Meanwhile, Mike Voigt, who Upchurch narrowly edged out, runs a traditional stick speedloader, as does Jerry Miculek. Miculek has also been experimenting with an XRAIL system in competition, the same system used by top Open shooters James Darst, a 3GN Shoot-Off winner, and Tony Holmes.

If you want to shoot in Open, you had either be heavily sponsored or have a heavy wallet, as Open gear is quite often the most expensive in the sport, especially the high-end race pistols that can exceed more than $4,000. An R&R Saiga shotgun can easily reach $3,500, while the XRAIL is pushing a $1,000 investment by the time you're completely geared up—and not including the shotgun itself. Thankfully, the rifle isn't that much more complicated than those used in most other divisions, though with high-end fore-ends, better barrels, and dual optics, you can still spend a lot of money here, too. For some, obviously, it's money well spent, and there is no denying the thrill of burning ammo at the rate so often enjoyed by 3-gun Open division shooters.

"If the guns of 3-gun were race cars, Open Division would be the home of the full-tilt, open-wheel F1 car," Kelley said. "While equipped with the latest go-fast parts, they can be a tuning nightmare, but in the right hands and running right, nothing is faster!"

Tactical Iron

Also known as "Tactical Limited" or "Limited," the 3-gun Tactical Iron division experienced a radical transformation during the 2011 season. A division

(top and above) Team FNH USA's Larry Houck shoots off a legal Open division bipod during the 2011 Rocky Mountain 3-Gun, and he ran an XRAIL on his FN SLP shotgun while competing in the Open division at the same match.

(right) SureFire's Maggie Reese, geared up for the Open division, readies for a stage.

(below) SureFire's Maggie Resse takes on long-range rifle targets with her Open rifle, during a stage at the 2011 Rocky Mountain 3-Gun.

clearly in decline, as more and more competitors switched over to the popular Tactical Optics division, one simple rule change breathed new life into it—and kept alive a division that, in many ways, perpetuates as one of the more accessible divisions for new 3-gun shooters.

At the end of the 2010 season, a rumbling debate within the 3-gun community was gaining steam. It seemed a growing number of competitors were asking match directors to consider allowing 1X optics, i.e., non-magnified red dots or tubular sights, in the Tactical Iron division. Normally, any type of red dot or optic would automatically place a competitor in Tactical Optics.

"While Limited has been the domain of the iron sight shooter, many matches have adopted permissions for 1X or non-magnified electronic or optical sights," said Patrick Kelley. "This change has been, for the

most part, welcomed by the 'old hand' iron sight shooters, not because they will change to optics, but because the addition of red dots or other optics with a maximum of 1X brings new blood to the division. Keep in mind that 1X power is what your eyes are when they're open."

Part of the argument for adding these limited sight accessories derived from the equipment list used by Tactical Optics and Open competitors. For years, both divisions had enjoyed the use of a secondary sighting system. In Open, competitors regularly use a 1X red dot as a secondary sight to a variable power optic. Mounted at 45 degrees from the main optic and in line with the bore, these optics are set up for 15- to 25-yard shots. In Tactical Optics, though, competitors have also long used iron sights as backup to a primary variable power scope. Like the red dots in Open,

Kurt Miller hammers close-range targets with his Tactical Iron rifle, during the 2011 Rocky Mountain 3-Gun.

in recent years it has become common practice to mount these irons at a 45-degree angle from the main tube and, again, in-line with the bore.

There were obvious parallels between the use of 1X optics and traditional iron sights already established in the sport, and a number of competitors felt that, if 1X optics could be used as a main sight, it could do much to help foster renewed interest in the Tactical Iron division, especially for older or other vision-challenged shooters. While a 1X optic has questionable overall advantages to irons, for those who can't pick up a front sight due to eyesight issue, the 1X means everything.

Many agreed, and the 2011 major matches across the country allowed competitors to use either a 1X optic or iron sights on their Tactical Iron division rifles. For some shooters, the move was controversial, for others a welcome change. Regardless, feedback was tremendous, and the division saw an immediate increase in participation levels across the board.

Ultimately, across the landscape of the major Outlaw 3-gun matches, both iron sight and 1X optic users did well. In fact, aside from a few new faces crashing the party, the top of the Tactical Iron division represented the usual suspects in 3-gun, proving once and for all its more about the skill of the shooter than the equipment he carries.

"It's funny, until last year, I was strongly of the opinion that I didn't want to shoot a rifle with a scope that wouldn't magnify up to at least 8X," said James Casanova, who finished second for the 2011 season in 3GN's Tactical Iron division. "Then, when I started to play with the 1X options out there, I began to realize how wrong I'd been about how the guys in this division were shooting.

"I had been of the opinion that, on the longer shots, out past 400 or so, they were just hosing the area until they hit something. I learned that was totally not true. It is a different kind of shooting for sure, but you can pick your shot and call your hit even with 1X. It's really satisfying to whack steel that looks like a pinhead in your sight picture.

"Now, there are some targets that are a bit tougher to score on, due to how those targets function. For instance, with a 1X, you can't see the bullet frag as it hits on some targets, so you do have to wait a little, but so does every

other non-magnified optics or iron sights shooter. On the plus side, the speed with which you can transition on shorter targets is excellent. Not having to think about what power I will shoot a stage with or where I plan to dial the scope are other advantages that make me smile. It's more about shooting and less about gear management on the clock."

"I personally like the feeling of accomplishment that comes from using iron sights," said Brian Vaught, who finished in the top 10 of the 3GN Tactical Iron Division using traditional iron sights. "No electronics, no fancy reticles, just knowing your rifle and how to hold on different sized targets at different ranges. When you hit a piece of steel that's way out there, it's worth the time you spent in preparation."

Clearly, both gear options have a place in the current Tactical Iron division. However, the choice of gear has ramifications well beyond bolting the accessory onto the rifle. Training regimen, shooting style, and even mental preparation to prepare for the upcoming sight picture are all affected by the choice of one's gear.

"My rear sight is a standard, bolt-on A2 aperture, made by Rock River," Vaught said. "The front is where individualism becomes apparent amongst iron shooters. I use a clamp-on JP A2-type gas block-mounted at the end of my barrel. My front post is a KNS 0.034. The JP base is solid as a rock, when clamped down, and having it mounted forward with the thin front post allows you to draw a fine bead on long-distance targets."

Iron sight shooters like Vaught typically mount the front sight as far forward as possible, increasing the sight radius between

the rear and front sights and maximizing accuracy potential at distance. Meanwhile, 1X optics users are free to run a lighter, more nimble rifle platform.

"Last year, I used the same rifle setup I would have if I'd shot Tactical Optics class, with the one difference being the Leupold Prismatic instead of a magnified scope," Casanova said. "The rifle was one of our builds for Carbon Arms, using a Firebird receiver set, a Nordic Components 16-inch stainless barrel with 1:8 rifling, an AR-Gold Trigger, Ace ARFX Stock, and a couple different comps over the season, including Henning's Thor .223, the Miculek comp, and an F2. Before the season got rolling and I was contemplating making the division switch to Limited/TI, I tested just about every red dot that fit the application. Then I got lucky, when my brother found a Prismatic on sale at the local Gander, and I figured, what the heck, let's give it a try.

"That Prismatic had the Circle Plex reticle in it, which is not ideal for this game," Casanova continued, "but of all the 1X options out there, I liked it the best. Then I heard that Kelly Neal—a veteran 3-gunner and top Tactical Iron competitor—was using the same scope with a different reticle. So, I contacted him, and he guided me toward the DCD reticle. I did give iron sights a try, but decided that, with the short amount of time I had to prep for the first match of the season, I didn't have time to set up a really good iron gun and get used to the sights. One of the really cool things about running the Prismatic is that barrel length becomes less of an issue, since sight radius is not part of the equation, plus you can swap the sight system back and forth between a magnified scope and the non-magnified without altering any other aspect of the rifle."

Most shooters were thrilled that non-magnified, 1X optics were allowed into Tactical Iron at major matches last year. But, as the 2011 3-gun season began to play out, it became clear that three distinctively different shooters might win the 3GN Tactical Iron Division, which is, effectively, the "Shooter of the Year" award for that specific division.

On one side was Kurt Miller, the legendary 3-gun veteran who had been competing in and running matches dating back to the days of the vaunted SOF match. Trying to knock off Miller were Kelly Neal, widely regarded as one of the most versatile competitors in the game, and James Casanova, who was having a major breakout year, in 2011.

If the personalities and competitors themselves didn't make for great storylines, the gear did. Both Neal and Casanova quickly took advantage of the new 1X rule, with each competitor running a Leupold Prismatic 1X (non-magnified) tubular scope. Meanwhile, Miller, the veteran who had shot iron sights for years, held onto traditional equipment. The debate was on—would Casanova and Neal have a gear advantage? Would it make a difference?

"Kurt and Kelly are both extremely good shooters and very seasoned competitors," Casanova said. "Kurt's preference for iron sights, I think, comes in part from being so in tune with the sight picture they give him over his years of working with them. He definitely proves that irons are not out of the picture in the

TI division. My impression of Kurt's shooting style is that he brings this knowledge with him to the line, and it shows through in the solid confidence he projects on every stage. The consistency of shooting the same sighting system for a long time gives Kurt the added advantage of not having to put conscious thought into his sight picture—his eyes know when things are right to let the round fly."

Casanova continued, "I haven't had the opportunity to shoot with Kelly much, so I really can't say I know anything about his shooting style, other than it's very effective. He was kind enough, when he had no idea who I was, to steer me in the right direction with the Prismatic reticle early in the season, so I am very grateful to him for that. The fact that Kelly has placed in the top three in every division at major matches over the last 10 years tells me that his fundamentals are rock solid, so it really doesn't matter what gear he's running, he'll be in the hunt. It may be partly because Kelly has shot so many different divisions in the past, his long experience has given him the itch to do something different in the form of running the Prismatic this year."

"You can't say that a guy like James or Kelly has an unfair advantage, because they would win no matter what equipment they shot," Vaught commented. "They are that good and have a strong game with all three guns. However, for those just starting off or coming up in the division, I believe the learning curve is a little less steep with a 1X optic than with true irons. I didn't like the addition of 1X at first, but it has expanded the

field of competitors, and the more shooters the better."

For new shooters interested in getting started in Tactical Iron, it's certainly not limited to just rifle shooting. Pistols and shotgun play just as an important role as they do in other divisions.

"I work mainly on sight focus," Casanova said, referring to his pistol practice. "What am I seeing with different kinds of shooting, and what am I getting as a result of what I am seeing? In 3-Gun, we get such a range of target types, sizes, and distances that having different sight/target focuses programmed so that they are sub-conscious is absolutely critical."

"Last year, my main focus was loading," Casanova said of his shotgun practice. "Over the winter, I worked on adapting a European style of loading two shells at a time, and developed with my brother and Mark Passamaneck a new shotshell caddie and clip system to support this loading method. Both products are now the core of our Carbon Arms TWinS loading system.

"I also put a good deal of effort into shooting slugs," Casanova told me. "I tested just about every make of slug I could get my hands on and found the ones that ran through my gun the best and were the most accurate. This year, I'm adding more shotgun shooting to my training in the form of sporting clays and other range drills."

This kind of fine-tuning aside, when it comes to the one key feature that sets the Tactical Iron division apart from all the rest, it is clearly the rifle.

"The pistol and shotgun are about the same as in other divisions," Vaught said. "If you want to shoot Tactical Iron, you really need to get out and shoot from some difficult positions and at the various ranges you're going to expect in a match. Know your holds out to 400 yards or so. Shoot some reactive targets out to 300 or 400 yards. Understand that the only way to confirm a 300-yard zero is to shoot your rifle at that distance. Don't let the first time you shoot at a

Kelly Neal, who finished second in the 2011 3GN Tactical Iron division, runs a stage during the 2011 Blue Ridge Mountain 3-Gun.

barely visible flasher be on the clock. When your squad gets to a stage and the targets are being painted, ask if you can shoot first. Every little bit helps."

Finding the right sighting option in Tactical Iron, for most competitors, will be through trial and error. Compared to the irons sights used by top competitors, the standard A2-type front sight post is too thick to reliably maintain the accuracy required at major matches. On the other

hand, all 1X optics are not created equal, with the reticle itself generally being the most important cog in the wheel. The only way for a competitor to know what suits them best is to get out and send rounds downrange with as many different sighting systems as possible.

"Get out and try every kind of 1X or iron sights you can get your hands on," Casanova said. "If at all possible, also try to find someone with competition-based iron sights. The typical irons that come with a lot of ARs are not a fair test of the system. Figure out what feels more natural for you and then stick with it. Take advantage of opportunities to talk with others who are more experienced with the same system you're using.

"Do your homework. Know whatever system you are running, what the sub-tensions of the different parts are at differ-

ent ranges, what your ballistics are," Casanova continued. "That kind of information will make you a lot more successful at all ranges. Try *everything*. Just because you're running one thing now doesn't necessarily mean something else won't work better. Work the fundamentals, too, like trigger control and cheek weld, which will help no matter what equipment you shoot. Test, test, *test*, and pay attention to what you see happening out on the range. Also, shoot as many matches, especially the bigger matches, as you can. There is no substitute for that experience."

Iron sight shooters, perhaps more than variable power scope users, understand the benefit of lots of rifle practice, especially in the awkward shooting positions from which stages will be shot. An iron sight shooter must know the ballistics of their bullets, where the impact will occur at every distance and, more importantly, what the sight picture should look like in order to break the shot.

"I focus mostly on knowing my sight picture at different ranges," said Casanova. "If I can hold the image in my head of the sight picture I need, then the position I am shooting a target from doesn't matter. I do practice positions, too, but not as much. A large part of the sight picture work I do includes working with my ballistics and knowing what a particular load is going to do in different conditions."

The reason for so much rifle practice is the target presentation itself. Iron sight shooters have long bemoaned the fact that long-range rifle targets at Outlaw 3-gun events almost exclusively put the platform at a disadvantage. The lack of contrasting backgrounds, changing light conditions in sun and shade, and the size of steel targets at distances ranging from 200 to 550 yards combine to make iron sight rife shooting an extremely tough endeavor.

"FNH was the best match for Tactical Iron last year," Vaught said. "Ozarks had the targets in plain view, but they were little and skinny. The only thing I don't like to see are stages where there is a great deal of variability in target presentation during different times of day."

Natural terrain matches are quite often the biggest offender, regarding long-range rifle target placement, with hills, trees, and valleys casting a wide range of sun and shade conditions, not to mention foliage and the hues present in forest or desert landscapes. Take an unpainted piece of gray steel, drop it in one of these backgrounds, and it seems to melt away. Too, a 100-yard range bay can be just as challenging when the sun sets behind the berm, placing the targets in darkness while shining the last available light directly into the competitors' eyes.

But, at the end of the day, for most Tactical Iron shooters, there's still value in shooting what was once a seemingly dwindling division. The challenge of ringing steel *without* using the latest and greatest in optics is a major draw to most of the die-hard Tactical Iron shooters.

"Matches need to keep Tactical Iron, because it offers those guys with a basic AR or patrol-type rifle with a dot a division to shoot in and not be under-gunned," Vaught said. "Plus, there are guys like me who just really get a bigger kick out of the basic principles of rifle-craft than they

do getting into a technology race.

"Shooters should consider the TI division, because it's easy to get equipment for and be competitive," Vaught continued. "It takes and builds on strong, fundamental shooting skills. Your rifle will not be burdened by one of those ugly tube-like things bolted to the top of it. Other

(top) Brian Vaught engages rifle targets on his way to becoming the 2011 Kentucky State Champion in Tactical Iron at the Kentucky Stage Multi-Gun Championships. Above, he runs his Tactical Iron rifle during, the 2011 ARFCOM-Rockcastle Pro-Am.

shooters will think it was luck, when you hit your first 300-yard flasher with irons—until you hit the next 10."

More importantly, the Tactical Iron rifle is the one many new shooters are most likely to own. Therefore, Tactical Iron remains an equipment division essential to the effort of keeping the sport of 3-gun accessible to the widest range of potential shooters.

"I shot a local match last month here in Kentucky," Vaught said. "Of 57 shooters, the largest division was TI. I think it could get deeper."

The Tactical Iron division most likely *wouldn't* be considered deep at most major 3-gun matches, despite the allowance of 1X optics. Nevertheless, the race for the 2011 3GN Tactical Iron Division Championship was an exciting one—a sprint to the final wire between Kurt Miller, Kelly Neal, and James Casanova.

With two matches left in the season, Casanova failed in his bid to pick up a pivotal second overall win for the season, effectively eliminating him from the title—yet, he would still have a say in who would win. At the final points match of the season, the FNH USA 3-Gun Championship, Casanova knocked off Kelly Neal, thereby giving the title to the division veteran and iron sight shooter Kurt Miller, who edged Casanova by a mere .63 for the season in the final standings and a score that was nearly 14 points ahead of Neal.

After all the hype, controversy, and debate surrounding the inclusion of 1X optics, the division still belonged to the iron sight shooters, though the availability of 1X optics had unleashed an infusion of new blood into the ranks.

"Limited division is really cool and the foundation of the game, at least as far as equipment goes," Kelley said. "It is the home of a diehard group that has mastered the fundamentals of marksmanship and firmly believes that, if they can see it, they'll hit it. It employs good, basic gear that is relatively inexpensive and easy to maintain. Still, until the inclusion of 1X optics, I would have said it was not a place for the new guy to get started. Iron-sighted rifles take more time and effort to learn to use well, and that learning curve can discourage the newbie from playing. But, bolt on a 1X optic, and the new guy gets better faster—and, as a 3-gunner, better and faster is where we all want to be!"

Heavy Metal

Diligentia, Vis, Celeritas.
Accuracy, Power, Speed.

This is the principle upon which practical shooting—combat shooting—was founded.

"Speed without accuracy is useless, as is accuracy without speed, and both together may not suffice without power."—*Marine Colonel Jeff Cooper, the Father of Practical Shooting*

By early in the 2000s, yet another sub-movement was beginning to take shape in the ever evolving world of 3-gun. In some ways, it mirrored the same type of thinking that had led to the first SOF match so many years before. This time, a growing number of shooters saw the need for a special division within 3-gun competitions, one that rewarded the use of true, combat-proven gun and cartridge platforms.

Much of the debate about

modern handguns and rifles in America has centered around one topic—power. In hunting circles, the debate took the form of .270 versus .30-06 and O'Connor versus Keith. In combat shooting, the argument matured into major versus minor power factor, or the formula derived to measure the momentum of a fired projectile (mass x velocity/1,000 = power factor). In basic terms, minor caliber in 3-gun competition most often represents the modern NATO chambering currently deployed by most nations—9mm double-stack pistols and .223-based AR-style rifles. Major power factor comes from the military guns of yesteryear, most often viewed through "Old Slabsides," the Govern-

ment Model 1911 in .45 ACP, along with the M14 (or Springfield M1As, in civilian circles), and its .308 chambering. While IPSC pistol or Bianchi Cup use the definition of power factor to achieve benchmarks in a slightly different way, in Outlaw 3-gun, power factor really only applies to Heavy Metal, meaning it's either Heavy or it isn't.

This debate has raged on from the time the U.S. military switched from the fabled M14, that wonderful battle rifle fashioned from wood and steel, to the much maligned, at least in its early years, M16 platform. In the 1980s, the iconic M1911 was replaced by the Beretta 92F, with the 9mm pushing the venerable .45 out of military use. "Power"

was indeed one of the founding principles behind combat shooting itself, as well as the original dogma upon which IPSC shooting was born. As such, as specialized race guns took over the winners podiums in practical shooting, it became only a matter of time before a strong push for a return of these founding principles returned. In 3-gun, that movement was realized in the form of the He-Man, or Heavy Metal, division.

"To the best of my knowledge, Pueblo, New Mexico, Police Department Captain Eddie Rhodes* coined the name 'He-Man,'" said Patrick Kelley, who is probably the most accomplished Heavy Metal 3-Gun competitor in the division's nearly decade-long

history. "He also proposed the equipment guidelines that called for a return to our founding principles. Rhodes' idea was to generate healthy competition by using full-power, heavy-caliber ammunition delivered from basic patrol car or home-defense gear. So, He-Man is a revisit to our combat roots and is *not* a retro or antique division. We have divisions for the low-recoil, go-fast guns. And, thanks to Captain Rhodes, we now have one for the power tools of the game."

"I came up with a concept that we now call He-Man," Eddie Rhodes said in an interview at the 2008 DPMS Tri-Gun. "It involved using a .308 rifle at a power factor of military ball, a .45-caliber handgun with a power factor of military ball, and a 12-gauge shotgun shooting buckshot and slugs only. We called it He-Man, and some other matches have called it Heavy Metal."

On the outside, Heavy Metal might seem like a difficult division in which to get started. In reality, for some shooters, the cost is likely to be much less than that it will take to assemble the more specialized gear seen in larger equipment divisions. The beauty of Heavy Metal, to many, is that the gear is indeed Spartan. A pump shotgun, a .45 pistol, and a .308 rifle will get you onto the playing field.

"The initial cost is less expensive than that of likely any other division," competitor Bryan Ray said. "A pump shotgun set up for 3-gun will cost less than half

Tate Moots takes on long-range rifle targets with his Heavy Metal Optics division rifle, during the 2011 Rocky Mountain 3-Gun.

that of a good semi-automatic. Almost everyone has a .45 ACP that can be used, but, if not, a Glock or Springfield XD in .45 can be bought for under $600. The rifle isn't much more expensive than any iron-sighted AR set up for 3-gun, whether the competitor chooses an M1A, one of the various .308 ARs, or even an FAL. The money saved by not having to buy an optic can go toward a lot of ammo. Guns using .308 ammo run roughly twice the cost of .223, but, if the competitor keeps this in mind, it makes a good sight picture just a little more important! I shoot almost all local matches in Tac Irons with a .223 AR and a 9mm or .40-caliber pistol so that I can save the expensive ammo for major matches."

Indeed, in a gear-driven sport, Heavy Metal (and, to be fair, Tactical Iron, as well), serves as the inclusive and accessible division for 3-gun. Gun guys and gals are creatures of habit, and so many of them who already have a .45 pistol are just as likely to have a pump gun and a surplus-type .308 in the safe. Or they may need only one of the trio to have what's needed to jump into their first match. This commonality, combined with some shooters' interest in military history and martial arms, makes Heavy Metal an obvious place for some to get started in 3-gun.

"My late father-in-law was drafted into the Army, in 1967, and was trained on the M14 in basic," Ray said. "After hearing him talk about how much he enjoyed the M14, I bought a Springfield M1A, around 1998, with intentions of shooting High Power matches. That never happened, so the rifle sat in my safe until 2008, when I signed up for

my first 3-gun match, the Blue Ridge Mountain 3-Gun. I studied the divisions to see what I could shoot without buying a bunch of extra gear. There was a Remington 870 Police in my closet, a single-stack 1911 I used in USPSA, and the M1A. I shot my first match with this gear, running out of shotgun shells on almost every stage, stuffing rifle magazines into my back pockets, and had the time of my life. I came in second at this match behind the late, great Eddie Rhodes and was hooked on Heavy Metal."

Heavy Metal, though often

the smallest division at many major matches, soon developed a small but loyal following, with competitors such as the late Eddie Rhodes, Patrick Kelley, and others putting big-bore action shooting on display. This is the division of loud, hard-kicking rifles and pistols, as well as the pump-action shotgun. The calibers are bigger, the recoil more pronounced, and the strategy—and most always the hardships—completely different than in any other 3-gun division.

"Heavy Metal is not for everyone," Kelley said. "You have

to be willing to put more effort into training than most any other division. The reason for this is torque and recoil. No matter the platform or the modifications, .308s produce more torque and recoil for the competitor to deal with than .223s. Same goes for the fixed-breech 12-gauge pump-action shotgun versus the recoil-mitigating auto-loader. Ammo management with these guns is a hurdle to jump, too.

Competing in Heavy Metal Optics, Jansen Jones conducts a magazine change, during a stage at the 2011 Rocky Mountain 3-Gun.

Remember, you, as a Heavy Metalist, have only 20 rounds per .308 magazine versus 30, 40, or more for the .223 shooter. This applies to your handgun, too, where you have just eight to 10 rounds in your .45 ACP of choice versus 20-plus rounds of .40 S&W or 9mm. I'm not selling this very well, am I?"

"This gear is *heavy*!" said Bryan Ray, who, at 165 pounds, has emerged as one of the country's top Heavy Metal competitors over the last couple seasons. "Between a 12-pound rifle, steel magazines, and the ammo, it's a *lot* to carry from start to finish on a stage. Shot-to-shot time with the rifle is a little slower due to the recoil, and, when targets must be engaged from some sort of wobbly prop (like the boat and dock at Ozark and reacquisition of the sights a little more difficult. Contorted positions while running the pump shotgun can get almost to the painful category. At Benning, in 2010, I remember shooting from within the Cooper tunnel, and while I'm working on the right-hand targets, it crossed my mind that I had never once practiced operating the pump shotgun support side, let alone while doubled up inside a tunnel. I still don't practice it, but now I at least know what to expect."

Despite the pain, Heavy Metal offers a place to play for those competitors who enjoy loud, big-banging guns. Nowhere is that more apparent than in the selection of Heavy Metal rifles, where modern-day renditions of World War II and Korea infantry guns still reign supreme, alongside specialized AR-10 variants and piston-driven rifles made for modern war fighters.

"Heavy Metal, unlike all the

other divisions is *not* ruled by the AR-15 platform," Kelley said. Major 3-gun events have been won with FALs, AR-10s, and the M1A rifles, placing additional truth on the adage 'It is the Indian, not the arrow.' For me, Springfield Armory's National Match M1A feels like it was born for this division. Accurate and completely reliable out of the box, sporting a 22-inch medium-weight barrel, match trigger, and excellent sights, expertly assembled and glass bedded to an oversized walnut stock, this rifle rocks! You might find more accuracy within the AR platform, but the M1A was built as a .308 from the ground up and was the original box-fed U.S. battle tested 'war club.' It lives up to this moniker very well indeed.

"Of the AR platforms, Armalite, DPMS, and POF-USA all make .308 rifles that are fully suitable as manufactured," Kelley continued. "Many competitors, when making the switch to Heavy Metal, are just supersizing their 'mouse' guns, giving them a potential leg up on those cross training to a different platform. As mentioned before, FALs win matches, too, and it's no wonder. The FAL has proven itself in harm's way all over the world and is the most prolific self-loading .308 military rifle in history. If you just want the best, the crew at DSA would be happy to outfit you, offering several models suitable for the Heavy Metal enthusiast. For the more budget conscience, one could get under way with less initial expenditure if you are willing to undertake a do-it-yourself project by assembling your FAL from surplus parts."

Today, more rifle manufacturers than ever before produce

.308-based AR-style rifles, giving 3-gun competitors tremendous options in that market. And new offerings, such as the SCAR 17, are just now being explored in competition. Better still, competitors no longer have to rely on surplus ammunition, as nearly every major ammunition manufacturer produces one or more match-grade .308 variant suitable for 3-gun.

"When I started competing, South African military surplus .308 is what I used, because it was available," Ray said. "As my supply ran out, I switched to Federal American Eagle 150-grain .308. It provides adequate accuracy through my rifle, with 100-percent reliability, and it's affordable for major matches at about $.55 per round. Most of the 168-grain loads are a little more accurate, but, with iron sights, I can't tell the difference between 1 MOA (minute of angle) and 2 MOA during the stress of a stage.

"My rifle is zeroed at 200 yards, because the trajectory is virtually flat from muzzle to 200 using this zero. I adjust the point of impact for elevation based on the stage either before the buzzer or after, depending on target distances. I prefer the same sight picture on every target, so I will dial elevation during a course of fire, if necessary. (I do hold for wind, though, rather than adjust the sight.) If there is a target at 225 yards and another at 275, I'll dial for 250 and shoot both with this setting, as the point of impact is close enough at both distances for a scored hit on an MGM flasher."

Jeff Cooper's Modern Technique, Gunsite, IPSC—nearly everything we associate with combat or practical shooting be-

gan with a single-stack .45-caliber pistol. As such, Heavy Metal is the only place a 1911-style pistol can still call home and remain competitive in 3-gun. However, the division is not limited to the original warhorse. Glocks, Springfield XDs, Smith & Wesson M&Ps, and more can all play in Heavy Metal, with ammunition capacity being the only real restriction regarding which models make the cut. It's that magazine capacity, generally eight rounds in a 1911 or 10 in a double-stacked pistol that becomes the game-changer for every competitor in Heavy Metal.

"When selecting a pistol, the

Heavy Metal division is *the* home for the single-stack 1911 in .45 ACP," Kelley said. "With either eight-round flush-fit or slightly extended 10-round magazines, this old yet ever-new combat- and competition-perfected pistol dovetails nicely into the fray. But, as much as I love that classic machine, when the event calls for 10 rounds on board, you'll generally find a Glock G21 in my holster. My reasons are twofold. First, all have passive safeties. Courses of fire require 'safety on' or 'gun empty' abandonment for the transition to long gun. Under the stress of time management, and with an immediate

Patrick Kelley is one of the most dominant Heavy Metal shooter in the history of the sport's division.

disqualification from the match for a violation of this rule, passive safeties are 'automatic.' Pick your flavor here—Glock, Springfield, or Smith & Wesson all play the game very well. Second, call it fashion sense, but extended 10-round .45 ACP mags and the 1911 just clash."

The limited round availability also creates a clash in stage design, as most match directors cater their stage plans around magazine capacities exceeding 20 rounds, meaning Heavy Metal shooters are subjected to twice as many magazine changes on high-volume pistol stages. To compete at a high level, the pistol game in Heavy Metal becomes more about accuracy and ammo management than the full-out speed seen in the Tactical Optics or Open divisions.

"You have only 10 rounds in the magazine, make each shot count," Bryan Ray said. "With the trend in 3-gun heading toward reactive pistol targets, it's easy to waste a lot of time reloading, if the shooter isn't getting hits. Practice doesn't have to be on an expensive plate rack, the head of a USPSA target works great, also."

The third level of Heavy Metal punishment comes in the form of the shotgun. While every other division in 3-gun allows an autoloader, Heavy Metal shooters are restricted to the pump-action. Still, the nearly universal choice for law enforcement, military, and even home-defense, the pump gun, then, could be considered the most "practical" of all the platforms currently used in the sport. Still, the pump gun is an interesting enigma. It is the most basic of all firearms used in this game, yet the pump gun is poorly understood and much maligned by many who don't use one. But make no mistake, in the right hands, a pump gun is a remarkable firearm on display. For the rest of us, running a pump can be considered the lost art of practical shooting.

"Sometimes I think the art is lost on me!" Bryan Ray said. "Just when a competitor feels real comfortable with the pump gun, they'll short-stroke it at the worst possible moment. I don't know how many times I've done that with an aerial clay at 12 o'clock. It's not much slower to operate a pump gun than an auto, if the targets can be shot from a standing position, but throw in a barricade to shoot around or under, and it can become challenging."

Compared to the complex, specialized race guns elsewhere in the sport, the pump-action shotgun is likely the most simple tool of the trade. Yet, for those outside the division, it might also be the least understood.

"When it comes to 3-gunning, shooters generally overlook the pump shotgun as a competition tool, and I understand why," Kelley said. "First, the poor pump lacks the important 'gee-whiz' factor the self-loaders have. And, for some of the 'cool kids,' it's better to look good than to shoot well. When you do see them, they are in the hands of the new guy—or in the experienced hands of the 'old dude.' Do yourself a favor here and watch out for that old dude, it might be me!

"Second, the pump is only as reliable as the person operating it, making the shooter a critical component. No matter the Internet bull, in human hands they don't cycle faster than an auto. To do that would mean cycling faster than 0.12 seconds between shots, and that is 500 rounds per minute, kids. That ain't happening!

"Third, the act of pumping is made even more difficult from awkward positions, and, fourth, the pump-gun transmits more recoil to you than does an auto! But, laying down a wicked-fast run that's met with a few hoots of approval is even cooler when the hooters never even *noticed* you were shooting a pump. Running a pump-gun at that speed is a unique experience and well worth the effort. That alone is reason enough to play. Heavy Metal, baby! Yea!"

It should also be considered that the mechanism that makes a pump gun, the physical act of running the fore-end through its entire range of motion, is a simple, yet overlooked, part of pump-gunning under the stress of match conditions. Inaccurate shooting, shooter-induced malfunctions, and unintentionally running the gun dry are common mistakes made by Heavy Metal pump-gunners—inexperienced and veterans alike.

"It's easy to miss a target, if you're thinking about operating the bolt while squeezing the trigger," Ray said. "Similarly, when the bolt slams back into

battery, the muzzle tends to dip a little. If you're too quick on the trigger here, the shots tend to be low. It's a little easier to miss a target with a pump gun than an auto, if the shooter doesn't take these things into account. Also, if the shooter loses count on the load, he usually doesn't realize the gun is empty until it goes "click," since the bolt will go forward on an empty chamber."

In Heavy Metal, the rifle is heavy and loud, it kicks harder, and the ammo itself is more expensive. The pistol, too, packs more punch, .45 costs more than 9mm, and the limited capacity makes stage breakdowns even more challenging. Finally, the shotgun is much more of a thumper; without the recoil-mitigating process imparted by the autoloader, the Heavy Metal shooter is subjected to extra foot-pounds of 12-gauge energy. These three gun types, taken each to their own in the context of Heavy Metal shooting, drastically changes the game. However, it's the full sum of its parts that paints the entire picture of what it means to play in this division. Heavy Metal is the land where big boys play, and where the meek are found wanting.

"As I stated before, Heavy Metal is not a retro or antique division," Kelley said. "It's a place that offers great personal reward for excellence in overcoming equipment challenges not faced in other divisions. It's a place closer to the roots of Practical Shooting. It's a place where you meet the challenge head-on with the tools, rather than adjusting the tools to meet the challenge, and it's a place where accuracy, power, and speed are points of pride. The Heavy Metalist must be consistently accurate, as capacity is limited. Power—and we generate much—is intrinsic to our weapons. To effectively demonstrate speed within this division means you have mastered technique."

"It's just another challenge within the world of 3-gun," Ray said. "The stages are the same as the ones all the other competitors shoot, but they have to be looked at a little differently, considering the capacity restrictions on the rifle and pistol—but, then again, it also gives the shooter a little personal satisfaction, when the range staff has to repair rifle targets after a .308 breaks them!"

As such, Heavy Metal caters to the 3-gunner who is a breed apart. To understand that is to realize we're talking about a niche within a niche, a sub-segment within a sub-segment. While 3-gun may be the fastest growing of all the shooting sports, within that body of shooters is a smaller, crazier, band of colorful characters who enjoy pain and relish thumping steel targets with a hammer bigger than anyone else's.

"I think Heavy is the division guys shoot because they sincerely enjoy the equipment they're using," Ray sad. "Some people compete in Open because they like to go fast, or in Tac Optics because they like to shoot against the most competitors, but most of the shooters in HM choose the division because they just want to shoot a big, loud rifle and a .45. It's sort of the cowboy division of 3-gun."

Today, Heavy Metal is actually two divisions, thanks to the addition of Heavy Metal Optics some years ago—a point of contention at some matches and one celebrated at others. As such, Heavy Metal Optics has perhaps the widest-ranging set of rules defining the approved equipment list for the division, including variances in pistol caliber and, amazingly,

Romero, normally a Tactical Optics competitor, jumped to Heavy Metal, in late 2011, to make a run at the 3GN Heavy Metal Division Championship—which he won by taking the final three matches of the season.

even shotgun type—pump guns at some matches, autoloaders at others. With the addition of 1X optics now allowed at some venues for traditional limited divisions such as Heavy Metal, the varying sets of rules that govern the sport become ever more complicated. Some have argued that Heavy Metal and Heavy Metal Optics should be re-combined on the national stage, which would, in theory, make one stronger division having a higher level of competition for all.

As it stands, and though Heavy in both its forms may be small, there are still plenty of mighty shooters who regularly shoot the divisions. Patrick Kelley has long dominated in Heavy Metal, and Rob Romero jumped into the mix, in 2010, to win the inaugural 3GN Heavy Metal Division Championship. Bryan Ray, in just a couple of years of shooting major 3-gun events, won two division titles last season and has become a real threat in Heavy Metal.

In Heavy Metal Optics, Barry Dueck and Adam Popplewell were a cut above the field in 2010, waging a season-long battle for the 3GN Heavy Metal Optics Division Championship that Barry Dueck won during the season's final weekend. Jansen Jones, Mark Hanish, and a host of other solid shooters also regularly play in Heavy Metal Optics.

"There are some terrific shooters in Heavy Metal right now," Rhodes said, in 2008. "Yeah, it's kind of a rough road to hoe anymore. You have the good shooters, and then you have the equipment that kind of beats you up a little more

than that in some of the other divisions."

In August 2012, Heavy Metal will receive another shot in the arm, with the debut of a new major match—the He-Man 3-Gun Championship, otherwise known within the 3-gun community as the "Big Johnson." The Big Johnson moniker is apt, a tribute to JJ and Denise Johnson, the Rocky Mountain 3-Gun match directors who remain vocal supporters of keeping rules in place that encourage participation in the smaller divisions, rather than limit them. To their credit, they are fierce protectors of everything "He-Man," the term originally coined by Captain Rhodes to describe the military ball division of a bygone American era—and maybe one that shouldn't be so bygone after all.

I don't believe just anyone could successfully put on a Heavy Metal-only match. However, the Johnsons are undoubtedly the most well suited of all the major Outlaw match directors to design and run such an event. First, and most importantly, JJ Johnson is a top Heavy Metal competitor, finishing fourth in the nation in the 3GN Heavy Metal Division. But, he and Denise are also intimately familiar with the venue, the NRA's amazing Whittington Center, in Raton, New Mexico. So, now a guy who knows the ins and outs of .308 competition has a match dedicated to the platform and 30,000 acres on which to test his ability to run it. The mix should provide for some absolutely wicked long-range rifle stages, a staple of the Rocky Mountain matches for many years.

Bryan Ray exploded onto the top ranks of the Heavy Metal division, in 2011. Here h loads his Benelli Nova during a stage at the 2011 AR15.Com-Rockcastle Pro-Am.

If successful, the He-Man 3-Gun Championship will become the most challenging test in the sport for how competitors handle power. In a real way, the crew who runs Rocky Mountain, the legacy of the original Soldier of Fortune match, is taking the sport of 3-gun back to its roots;

at SOF, in 1980, the winners used M1As, H&K 91s, and single-stack 1911s—some of which will surely be in plain sight in Raton for years to come.

"Dust off that pump gun and load-up that single stack," Patrick Kelley said. "Get your hands on a fine, self-loading .308 and join Club Torque and Recoil. I can tell you firsthand that victory is a little sweeter for the Heavy Metalist."

*The sport of 3-gun suffered a terrible tragedy, March 15, 2010, when, during a training run, Captain Eddie Rhodes, the father of the "He-Man" division, suffered a heart attack and passed away. Those in the 3-gun world who knew him best honor his memory—none more so than the staff and crew at Rocky Mountain and their new He-Man 3-Gun Championship.

"He was a fierce competitor, a warrior, and a man among men," said Patrick Kelley. "Those who shared the range with him are better for the experience. I know I am."

Wide-Open Shotgunning:
XRAIL vs. Saiga

The Russian Bear

Over the last few 3-gun seasons, no single gun design has changed an individual division more than the Saiga shotgun has the Open. What once took several seconds to load—whatever time it took a competitor to go to the speedloader multiple times—could now be achieved in a fraction of the time with a simple magazine change. While the Saiga 12 has been manufactured in Russia since the 1990s (it was previously imported by EAA, and now through Russian American Armory), it took a little American ingenuity to bring the Saiga to the point where it's made an impact.

For a multitude of reasons, the Saiga simply wasn't reliable enough to stand up to the demands of 3-gun competition. But seeing the potential in a box magazine-fed shotgun system, several gunsmiths went to work perfecting the system. One of the most successful of that group has been Robert Wright and his R&R Racing out of Oregon.

When one hears of the laborious process it takes to get a Saiga running reliably, you have to wonder why on earth a gunsmith would want to take on such a task. For Wright, it all started as a project of necessity, but one that's paid huge dividends in the long run.

"I switch divisions every two years and needed a mag-fed shotgun for Open division," Wright explained. "I knew that a mag-fed gun was the only way to go, and my plan was to buy a gun and the parts to build a gun. But nobody made any parts that were any good, so I started making the parts.

"One day, I was on the phone talking to my friend Paul from MSTN and told him about my gun project. He talked me into building him a gun—and then another. Things started taking off from there, and now I'm working on an FBI contract. I beat

out several companies to come up with a breaching gun."

Wright takes imported Saigas and completely overhauls the entire shotgun, hogging out material and machining many new parts—a multitude of processes are required to get the imported shotgun competition ready.

"It is easier to tell you what I *don't* do," Wright said. "I do seven processes on the barrel alone. The receiver gets about 15, while the carrier gets five. The dust cover gets three, and the bolt gets three. I bet that I go through more than 60 processes on each gun, and every gun is built the way I build my own. I will not cut any corner to save time or money. When you buy one of my guns, it is first-cabin all the way.

"I shorten the gas system so the gun will have enough gas to run the comp," Wright continued. "I also build my own pistons, op rods, op rod tubes, and gas plugs. The guns still say Saiga on the side, only because the ATF makes me leave it. But they are as far from a Saiga as you can get. The guns as they come to me are very crude and inconsistent, and that's why you see so many that don't work. Most people just move the trigger forward and add a stock."

Expensive and time consuming, Wright's overhauls turn a lumbering, Spartan import into a smooth, versatile machine. The proof, for Wright, is all measured in time—the name of the game in 3-gun.

"When I used to shoot Tactical, I could load a shell in a second from shot-to-shot," Wright said. "That was on a really good day, when the stars were aligned just right. Now I can load 12 rounds in under 1½ seconds. I shoot my gun like I shoot a Limited 10 pistol—when in doubt, put in a fresh mag. With a tube gun, you can't afford to miss a shot, because it will cost

you a second for a make-up shot. But, with a box mag, going from birdshot to slugs to buck is just a mag change. And you can stack rounds in the mag to go from bird to buck or slugs. Because all

the rounds are so close to the shooter, the box mag guns transition faster than a tube gun. In fact, my guns transition even faster than a tube gun with an XRAIL. Plus, when you pick up one of my guns, it feels like your AR rifle, so you don't have to think as much."

For shooters new to 3-gun, the Saiga represents an easier first step into the game, as one isn't required to learn the weak- or strong-hand reloading techniques employed in other divisions—not an overly complicated chore, but a time consuming one. The Saiga delivers a sys-tem readily familiar to most any shooter who can execute a magazine change.

Nowhere is that impact potential more apparent than in the 3-gun career of Clint Upchurch, a solid USPSA pistol shooter who jumped into 3-gun two years ago and right into the Open division.

"I felt that reloading the Saiga was *so* much faster," Upchurch said. "And the flexibility of magazine configurations al-lowed options that made the Saiga easier to manage than the other platforms. The controls of the R&R Saiga were very user friendly. I liked the left-side charg-

The Saiga had the big advantage of being one of the fastest reloadable guns ever made, but it's overall quality wasn't up to the rigors of 3-gun competition. Robin Wright has been one of just a few successful gunsmiths to overhaul this gun into the one every 3-gunner dreams of shooting.

ing handle, and the safeties and mag release were just like those on an AR-15. To me, it seemed easier to operate than a traditional tube-fed shotgun. It was definitely easier to learn the platform—mainly because of the AR-15 similarities."

Upchurch, after only two years in the sport, exploded onto the national 3-gun scene by winning six major matches and outlasting a late-season push from both Jerry Miculek and Mike Voigt to win the 2011 3-Gun Nation Open Division Championship. While Upchurch clearly has tremendous game in all areas of 3-gunning, he nevertheless acknowledges an advantage provided by his R&R Saiga.

"The Saiga proved to be advantageous on a many occasions," Upchurch said. "Anytime we shot the big field courses with lots of shotgun targets I had an advantage. On the quick, low-round count stages, the shotguns were pretty much equal.

The X-Factor

RCI's Mark Roth is "constant"—constant movement, constant talking, constant smoking—a man of perpetual motion and ideas. So when the 3-gun bug bit Roth several years ago, I suspect his mind and actions were constantly revolving around every aspect of the sport.

That's an over-simplified portrait of my friend, for sure, but it helps set up what happens next. A contractor by trade, one who had built a successful business in his Appleton, Wisconsin, home, Roth was talking with DPMS' Bruce Piatt, while their squad waited to shoot a stage at the 2006 DPMS Tri-Gun. As the conversation progressed, the two began discussing the idea of adding more capacity to a tubular magazine shotgun without extending the tube beyond manageable lengths.

Once turned onto the subject, I'm sure it was only a matter of time before Mark's mind found a solution for the problem. A few weeks later, Mark's thoughts become the XRAIL.

For those not in the know, the XRAIL (Xtreme Roth Auto Indexing Loader) is a self-articulating, high-capacity, magazine-tube extension for tubular magazine shotguns. Consisting of multiple auxiliary tubes, once all the shotshells in the first tube have been emptied, the XRAIL

automatically indexes the next auxiliary tube into place to feed the main tube. And, because it's self-indexing, one can load it full and shoot it dry without making any adjustments. Incredibly, the system increases magazine capacity up to 23 rounds, depending on the shotgun platform.

"The XRAIL consists of four magazine tubes that work off a central axis—one primary tube and three auxiliary tubes," Roth said. "The system is added to the end of the existing shotgun magazine tube in the same fashion as a traditional magazine tube extension. It does not change the function of your gun."

Once installed, shotshells are loaded into the gun in a traditional manner, right through the existing loading port on the shotgun.

"To load, simply load the primary tube full and manually rotate the tube housing to access the first auxiliary tube," Roth said. "Load the first auxiliary tube and rotate to the second tube. Repeat the process until all the tubes are loaded. When firing, once a tube is emptied, the system rotates to the next tube and so forth, until the gun is empty. The primary tube is the first tube loaded and the last one emptied, and it is also the only tube with a spring and follower that extends down into the receiver of the gun."

In competition, the interesting component of the XRAIL involves sequencing on stages that mix two different loads within that stage—most often birdshot and slugs. In whatever order the targets are engaged, the loading sequence must be reversed in order to come out correctly. For example, during a particular shotgun stage at Ozark, in 2010, FN's Tommy Thacker, who was running an XRAIL on his SLP, faced a stage mixed with 16 birdshot targets and four that required slugs.

"The way I set it up," explained Thacker, "is that I look at how I'm going to shoot the course of fire, and I lay my shells out exactly that way. Then I have to load them backwards, so that the round I want to shoot last has to go into the gun first."

Along with Roth himself, XRAIL as a company has begun to build a stable of quality shooters who are running the accessory in competition, including Nick Kalishek, Tony Holmes, Jerry Miculek, and

2012 3GN Champion Tommy Thacker.

"Since the introduction of our product, we have been fortunate to have the world's greatest shooters want use our product," Roth said. "We are very happy to see that our vision has been realized by others of such distinction. We are seeing that the great shooters such as Larry Houck, Tommy Thacker, and Tony Holmes are excited to use our product, because of the advantages they gain on a gun they

trust. Having shooters of this caliber trust and use our product is equivalent to having Tiger Woods use your golf clubs."

XRAIL units are currently available for Remington models 870, 1187, 1100, and Versa Max; Benelli Super Black Eagle, Super Black Eagle 2, and the M1, M2, and M2 Tactical; FNH USA SLP; Mossberg 930; and the Winchester Super X3 shotguns. Retail is around $700 for a full-sized unit, $650 for a compact model.

XRAIL inventor Mark Roth of RCI, demos the XRAIL during the 2010 Superstition Mountain Mystery 3-Gun.

Yamil R. Sued photo

CHAPTER 6

THE FILES

At many major 3-gun matches, the rifle becomes the difference maker, with long-range stages often becoming the one course of fire that separates the top shooters. However, rifle shooting certainly isn't *limited* to long-range targets in this sport. The rifle game is two or three games within the game, depending on your perspective.

It starts with close-range rifle targets. It might seem as though a target a mere few yards in front of the shooter would be simple, and, in truth, it is. It nevertheless requires some thought and preparation, and a working knowledge of mechanical offset and the rifle bullet's ballistics.

Most top 3-gunners, when using a scope in the optics divisions, run a rifle zeroed out to 200 yards, although there are certainly several using a 100-yard zero. Because an optic sits roughly 2.5 inches above the bore, and because the bullet trajectory has yet to climb to apex, the bullet will always impact low at close range.

At most any 3-gun match, stage designs will feature close-range paper targets set from a few feet out to 25 yards or so. To test a shooter's knowledge of mechanical offset and their focus to remember their holds under pressure, reduced-sized targets, or only the smaller "A" zone on an IPSC-type silhouette will be presented, giving a target area roughly the same size as a softball, at times. When the rifle is held center mass on this area, the bullet will likely impact low and out of the scoring area, due to mechanical offset. Knowing this, competitors aim high, often holding on the very top of the target, which delivers solid scoring hits.

Conversely, long-range targets test the other end of the spectrum. Here, and again in reference to Tactical Optics, a good reticle becomes important—one with mil-dots, descending stadia lines, or other means of holds below the center crosshair.

Running a 200-yard zero with a typical 55-grain match bullet, at 300 yards, that bullet drops down into the neighborhood of eight inches low. At 500 yards, it will likely be more than 50 inches low, depending on the bullet and load.

To complicate matters further, match directors, the evil monsters that they are, stra-tegically place long-range rifle targets at random distances such as 385 yards or 533 yards, distances that don't necessarily match the points of hold common in today's advanced reticles. For the shooter, this means testing each subtending reference mark by shooting match loads at every distance possible and creating a mental picture of what different target sizes and presentation look like, so as to provide cues on where to hold the rifle and break the shot.

Today, the rifle game at major 3-gun events is one that tests the full ballistic range of a competitor's rifle and load, along with the competitor's ability to get hits at extreme close- and long-range distances and everywhere in-between. Let's take a look at some of the guns and upgrades that are making the grade and winning matches.

Stag Arms Model 3G Competition

In 2011, Stag Arms, follow-

ing the formation of its first sponsored 3-gun team with 3GN Pro Series competitors Jesse Tischauser and Kalani Laker, debuted a rifle built specifically for the sport. Best of all, Stag listened to the feedback provided by its shooters throughout the development process. The result was a rifle that has garnered high praise from within and without the 3-gun community.

The 3G Competition features an 18-inch stainless steel barrel, rifle-length gas system and Stag's own 3Gun compensator to reduce muzzle rise. A Geissele Super 3-Gun trigger is a solid upgrade. A Magpul ACS buttstock improves upon the standard A2- or M4-type designs.

A Samson Evolution free-floating handguard, one of the

Stag Arms Kalani Laker shoulders the new Stag Arms 3G Competition, a rifle that made a tremendous impact when it debuted in 2011.

hottest selling fore-ends in 2011, provided a significant upgrade over M4-style handguards. Dueck Defense RTS offset sights are available as an option. Utilizing upgraded components commonly seen on custom builds or from high-end rifle makers has made the 3G Competition one of the most out-of-the-box-ready rifles on the market. While Stag Arms isn't the first company to market a rifle specifically for the 3-gun market, its first offering is nevertheless a solid example of a reasonably priced gun featuring a well thought-out collection of aftermarket accessories commonly used in the sport.

JP Rifles Lower Program

John Paul Gangl's JP Rifles is, without question, one of the original companies to throw its full support into 3-gun. Gangl, a veteran competitor of many disciplines and a solid 3-gunner in his own right, knows the game inside and out. So, it's no surprise that his company remains a leader in high-end rifles built specifically for the needs of the action-shooting competitor.

Browse the JP website or catalog and you'll find several different variants, all of which use some combination of parts from Gangl's own design, such as heat sinks, improved triggers, buffers, and more. You will certainly pay more for a JP rifle than you would buying a "Brand X" M4, but you'll also get so much more rifle.

Veterans of the game seem to drift toward JP rifles, and JP-sponsored shooters regularly win major matches across the country. I see JP as the company that provides rifles for the customer who already plays this

game and knows exactly what they want in a 3-gun rifle.

Continuing on that theme, one of the coolest options JP offers is the Lower Program. Here, customers can send in their stripped lower receiver for a semi-custom re-build, ranging from a fire control kit up to a complete reconstruction. As such, the Lower Program provides a more economical method to obtaining one of the coveted rifles on the 3-gun circuit.

FNH USA SCAR 16s

Bolstered by the competitive success of Team FNH USA, the ample coverage in the 3-Gun Nation Shoot-Off, and most definitely because of the association with the rifle's early trials in the SOCOM community, the FNH SCAR enjoys a certain mystique. In terms of 3-gun competitors, the SCAR is slowly building a following, showing up in more rifle racks at major matches each 3-gun season.

(above) Mark Hanish engages long-range rifle targets from a prone, supported position—as good a position as one is lucky enough to get in 3-gun—during the 2011 ARFCOM-Rockcastle Pro-Am.

(left) Open rifles are often tricked out with bipods, compensators/brakes and secondary optics.

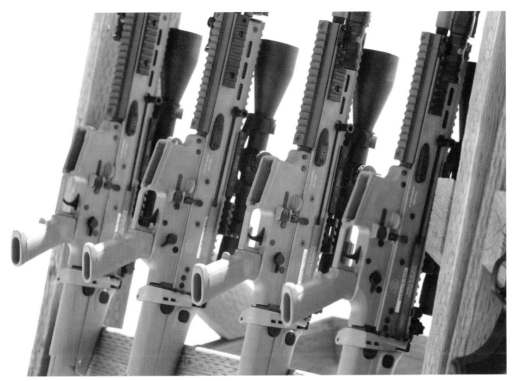

Since Team FNH USA began competing heavily in 3-gun, the SCAR has steadily gained popularity among 3-gunners.

While most competitors still, and likely will for some time, prefer the AR-15 design for 3-gun, Team FNH USA shooters are effectively making an impression with the SCAR. Two 3GN Shoot-Off wins belong to FNH shooters, including 2011 and 2012 3GN Champion Tommy Thacker. Meanwhile, Dianna Liedorff is one of the top female competitors in the game, and the entire team is competitive in multiple equipment divisions.

In practical terms, the SCAR, while possessing operating controls, chambering, and a magazine system in the AR-sytle, has a different platform that requires getting used to. The piston-driven rifle recoils differently, the reciprocating bolt handle requires a new manual of arms, and the overall ergo-

nomics are a touch unique. But the SCAR shines in short-range rifle applications, especially working in and out of port windows, due to its compact design. At the same time, it delivers more than sufficient accuracy for long-range work.

Colt CR Pro Competition

Timed with the company's first sponsored shooter in 3GN Pro Series competitor Clint

Upchurch, Colt's CR Pro Competition landed the company squarely in the middle of what 3-gunners like in a competition gun. As such, Upchurch, along with FMG's Scott McGregor, has sung high praises for the gun.

With a Geissele trigger, 18-inch barrel, SureFire muzzle brake, and fully free-floated fore-end, the CR Pro utilizes many top accessories normally associated with custom builds. Similar to the Stag, yet made in much more limited numbers, the CR Pro really delivers quite a lot and stands out-of-the-box ready for high-level 3-gun competition. More than any of that, though, the Colt CR Pro may

Taran Butler runs a lightweight AR-15 and on short-range rifle targets is one of the fastest shooters in all of action shooting.

prove most seminal if history remembers the rifle, along with sponsorship of Upchurch, as one of many first steps in the long-awaited return of the company's prominence and significance in the civilian market.

The small collection of rifles listed here only begins to scratch the surface of what's available, as one could easily fill a book writing about semi-automatic rifles on the market today—even by limiting it to gear well suited to 3-gun. The rifle market has exploded, as has the popularity of 3-gun, and never a finer match of timing and opportunity has been in the world of rifles fit for practical shooting.

As good as are the many rifles available straight from the manufacturer, the most common rifle in 3-gun isn't made by any of them. Commonly referred to as a "Frankenstein," these are the AR-15 rifle builds carried out either by a gunsmith or the rifle owner himself. Indeed, many veteran shooters simply build their own rifle for 3-gun, outfitting it with exactly the right parts to fit very specific needs.

Lower Receivers

Stag Arms, DPMS, Del-Tone, Spike's Tactical—there are way too many to name—all manufacture and sell stripped lower receivers. They are available through a variety of sources such as Cheaper Than Dirt!, Midway USA, and Brownells. The Brownells website goes a step further, with its awesome AR Builder software that enables users to scroll through Brownells entire inventory and then "build" the perfect rifle. Either way, this is a low-cost way to get into a good 3-gun

rifle—for example, a laser-engraved Stag Arms stripped lower retails for around $150—and it's a great way to personalize your own rifle build while fitting the parts to suit your shooting needs.

Uppers

Depending on a shooter's needs, uppers are available in a wide range of variations, ranging from completely stripped uppers on the least expensive end, to fully specialized uppers with barrels, fore-ends, comps, and completely tricked out models from the likes of DPMS, JP Rifles, and more.

Piston rifles have seen an explosion in popularity over the last half decade, and inclusion in 3-gun competition has contributed to that interest. Adams Arms' Evolution Ultra Lite Upper features the popular Samson Manufacturing Evolution fore-end, a three-position adjustable gas block, and a .625-inch (muzzle diameter) Melonite-coated barrel. For those who lean more toward M4-type gear, Ruger offers a couple variations on 16-inch upper assemblies. Each upper utilizes Ruger's new two-stage piston design.

Brakes & Comps

No 3-gunner worth his salt would attempt to shoot a match without using a good muzzle brake or compensator. The name of this game is time, and a good comp keeps the muzzle rise down, which in turn gets the shooter back on target more quickly and ready to break the next shot.

DPMS manufactures the Jerry Miculek comp, a hold-over from the days when Miculek was a sponsored shooter for

One of the first upgrades many competitors make to their rifle is the addition of a better muzzle brake, like this one from SureFire.

(opposite) Though you don't see it a tremendous amount, the kneeling position is nevertheless a skill every 3-gunner should have, as demonstrated by SureFire's Maggie Reese.

DPMS, and it's a very popular choice among shooters. The Lund/SJC was designed by Team FNH USA shooter Erik Lund and S&J Custom and is another favorite with top competitors, as is Benny Hill's Rolling Thunder compensator.

SureFire Muzzle Brakes

SureFire muzzle brakes, which also happen to be attachment points for SureFire FastAttach Suppressors, have generated a lot of favor among competitors over the last few seasons. Sponsored shooters Barry Dueck (who heads the SureFire Suppressor Division) and Mike Voigt deigned the brakes, which utilize SureFire's proprietary Impulse Diffusion design, where minimal gas blowback is directed into the shooter's face.

"When we score these events, it's based on accuracy and speed," said Voigt. "One of the tools that I use to hit targets faster is the SureFire muzzle

Taran Butler takes on rifle targets with a Stag 3G Competition during the elimination round of the 2011 3GN Championship.

brake. On an unsuppressed gun, you usually get a lot of movement up to the one to two o'clock area. When you put a muzzle brake on the gun, it reduces that rise. But, we've really tuned this brake to almost eliminate it."

"The bottom line with this is that, when I'm looking through the scope, I'm trying to acquire a target," Voigt said. "Once I fire, the target is right there again, it's waiting for me."

Stag Arms 3Gun Super Comp

Stag Arms, in conjunction with the launch of the new 3G Competition rifle, also developed a new compensator, the 3Gun Super Comp. I was the tackling of a new technology for the nimble AR manufacturer.

"It definitely wasn't easy," said Mark Malkowski, upon the release of the Super Comp. "We spent countless hours creating a muzzle device with the specific purpose of allowing a shooter to engage a second shot as quickly as their first."

The Super Comp utilizes cross drilling to vent gas upward, and a process called "nozzle technology" forms cones to propel the rifle back downward. At the same time, the weight balance allows gravity to counter muzzle rise.

Secondary Iron Sights

Ever since tactical and practical shooters began putting glass on rifles to serve as the primary sighting system, they began to search for better ways to back up the optics with iron

sights. In the tactical community, and in 3-gun events, flip-up iron sights became en

A competitor engages short-range rifle targets utilizing RTS sights from Dueck Defense.

Barry Dueck's RTS sights provide offset irons at a 45-degree angle from the main optic.

Open division shooter Mike Voigt hammers close-range rifle targets using a secondary rifle optic.

vogue—out of the way when you didn't need them, there in a flash when you did.

As Open shooters have known for some time, putting the secondary sighting system in a usable position is much more advantageous to the shooter. Today there are several different makes and models of sights hanging on seemingly every position in which one can be hung on an AR-15.

Dueck Defense RTS

Barry Dueck's Rapid Transition Sight (RTS) has become one of the more popular secondary iron sight systems in 3-gun. Dueck, a veteran of the Marine Corps and top 3-gun competitor, used his combined experience and took the old A2-stype sight from the M16 family, developed a mount to handle it at 45 degrees—just as Open shooters do with optics— and the RTS was born.

Because he used a military aperture and front sight post, the RTS is capable of accurate fire to surprisingly extended ranges. So, while the RTS is intended for use hosing closing-range targets, should the primary optic go down over any distance, shooters are still in the game with the RTS.

"A must-have for 3-gun shooting," said Practical Shooting Academy's Keith Garcia, a law enforcement officer and two-time 3-Gun Nation Shoot-Off winner. "The best back-up sight available anywhere. These sights are so sturdy I put a second set on my SWAT entry rifle."

Aftermarket Triggers

One of the first upgrades many shooters make to a stock rifle is an upgrade to the trigger system. JP Rifles, CMC, Geiselle, and AR Gold have all made good inroads in the sport, and their offerings come both as upgrade items on some rifles straight from the factory, or you can purchase them as aftermarket items. Brownells, Midway USA, and Cheaper Than Dirt! are all good sources for accessory trigger units. Depending on the model, some come as simple drop-in units, while others may need to be installed by a quality gunsmith.

Timney Triggers

One company making a push into 3-gun recently is Timney Triggers. Timney has built a solid reputation on its drop-in units that are a breeze to install. They drastically improve the trigger pull over a standard mil-spec trigger unit.

Modular in design, the completely "drop-in" unit from Timney is quickly gaining favor among 3-gunners.

For AR-15 designs, Timney's AR-15 Competition is pre-set to a pull weight ranging from three to five pounds. The Competition utilizes the rifle's original hammer and trigger pins. A true drop-in part, the Competition variant runs $210.

Due to the rising popularity of the FNH USA SCAR, Timney recently developed a SCAR variant built into an alloy housing and featuring a Teflon-nickel coating on the hammer. Also completely drop-in, the single-stage SCAR unit retails for around $310.

Ergo 2 Grip

One of the first parts 3-gunners often change out on a rifle is the grip. Top shooters swap out for better ergonomics, while other simply prefer different styles. Whatever the reason, Ergo Grips are one of the more popular aftermarket accessories in 3-gun.

The Ergo 2 SCAR Grip is designed specifically for the FNH USA SCAR, providing an over-molded, non-slip grip surface that improves upon the ergonomics of the standard grip. For AR-15 users, Ergo produces models in multiple styles and colors.

Grips are a common rifle upgrade by 3-gun competitors, such as this SCAR grip from Ergo.

(left) Samson Manufacturing's Upgrade Kit features offset iron sights, along with the company's extremely popular Evolution rail system.

Samson Competition Rifle Upgrade Kit

At a retail price around $550, the Samson Manufacturing Rifle Upgrade Kit is touted to contain everything a shooter needs to get their rifle match ready. The kit contains a 15-inch Evolution Rail, Quick Flip Front and Rear Sights, Enhanced Low Profile Gas Block, Evolution QD sling point, and Samson Field Survivor tool.

(middle right) John Bagakis takes on long-range rifle targets from an awkward firing position during the 2010 3GN Championship.

(right) Don Bednorz transitions out of a prone rifle position during the 2010 3GN Championship.

SHOT

Yamil R. Sued photo

CHAPTER 7

THE GUNS

Depending on the division in which one competes, there are several different shotgun platforms. In Open, for example, the box magazine-fed Saiga shotgun has become extremely popular, often heavily customized to achieve the desired results. Meanwhile, in Heavy Metal, where the pump-action is still king, Remington 870s, Mossberg 500s, old Winchester 1200s, and Benelli Novas all see good action. But the volume of shotgunning comes down in Tactical Optics, where the Benelli M2, FNH USA SLP, and Remingtons, both old 1100s and the new VersaMax, are all popular on the firing line.

"Remington and Benelli are top of the list," said Bruce Piatt. "FNs will be there soon, too, as will the Saiga box-fed shotguns.

"There are two main differences between Remingtons and Benellis," Piatt explained. "Remingtons are all steel, thus heavier, which can be good and bad. The extra weight sucks up recoil, but some say it makes it harder to handle or swing quickly. Benellis and FNs use alloy frames and are lighter, making them kick harder but swing faster. I guess it comes down to personal preference."

The shotgun game, for many beginning 3-gunners, is an eye-opening experience. Never before have most been subjected to loading a shotgun in this manner, under the stress of the clock. A first-time 3-gunner often

(right) A group of shooters pre-load their shotgun tubes prior to running a stage at the 2011 Texas Multi-Gun Championship.

looks as though they were leaving a trail of breadcrumbs to follow through the forest, littering the range bay with shotshells, as they amble through the course; then again, most first-timers are loading out of their trouser pockets or, at best, borrowed shell caddies, either way a nearly futile exercise without practice beforehand. But, that's okay, because I've heard some of the very best 3-gunners in the game relate similar stories about their first attempt at practical shotgunning (which means there's at least hope for the rest of us).

Shotgun use in 3-gun, and this varies depending on the venue, also includes several sub-games. It's not just load your shotgun and point it at every target you might face. Instead, there are subtleties that break down the shotgun game into distinct parts.

The most common component of shotgun courses is regular

(above) Brian Vaught runs an all-shotgun stage at the 2011 Kentucky State Multi-Gun Championships. Note the volume of shell caddies.

(left) Once the most popular shotgun in the sport, you still see a few Remington 1100s in the mix at matches.

old birdshot. The overwhelming majority of all targets faced will be engaged with standard No. 7½ shot, be it steel knock-over targets, steel poppers, Texas Stars, stationary clay targets, aerial clay birds, or clays affixed to moving target apparatus.

Distances vary, and so, too, will the chokes used to neutralize targets effectively. Improved Cylinder and Modified are very common, but others regularly use Light Modified and even Skeet. Their use varies from shooter to shooter, and it's a formula best arrived upon by the individual competitor's skill level and patterning the loads at distance.

Popular in both IPSC-style shotgun and 3-gun matches alike, buckshot, though not common, can be required. Slugs, on the other hand, have become a staple for many major 3-gun matches, with distances bordering on the ridiculous, out to 100 yards or more at some Outlaw matches. In any event, slug shots are very much a part of today's 3-gun game, and if you plan to shoot a major, and in some cases even a local club match, you had better know where your slug impacts out 75 yards or more to be competitive.

The biggest roadblock with the shotgun for new shooters is the act of loading. There are three common techniques employed today by top 3-gun shooters. They are the weak-hand reload, the strong-hand reload, and the two-by, or TWinS load.

Weak-Hand Reload

The weak-hand shotgun reload is, with few exceptions, the most dominant shotgun loading technique in the sport of 3-gun. While FN's Dave Neth is fast and furious, and AMU's Daniel Horner nearly unbeatable—both of whom load with the strong hand—weak-hand loading is still the winning technique most often used. Watch Taran Butler, Rob Romero, or Keith Garcia, and you'll see there is little doubt how devastatingly fast the weak-hand reload can be.

It all started with Kurt Miller, the "Father of the Weak-Hand Reload." Before he started dominating on the 3-gun fields—Miller is one of the most accomplished iron sight shooters in the sport—he served as a U.S. Marine, before taking a teaching position at Colonel Jeff Cooper's famed Gunsite Academy, in Arizona. It was there that the emerging practical shooter took a rigid defensive technique and refined it into what it is today.

"I didn't invent weak-hand loading," Miller explained. "It was a Gunsite technique, but they only loaded one shell at a time, stressing the need to keep the weapon on the shoulder. Eddie Rhodes was the first guy I ever saw who grabbed three shells at a time. From there, I practiced and got it to the level it is today."

As the sport evolved, so, too, did the importance of shotgun loading. Ultimately, shotgun round counts swelled in stage designs. While most top shooters often shot at similar speeds, the art of loading a shotgun within courses of fire began to separate the pack. When Miller began winning major 3-gun matches utilizing his 'new' loading technique, competitors took notice. Since then, Miller has taught nearly anyone who'll listen.

"I perfected it and designed the core of how to teach it, and then, of course, started winning with it," Miller said. "Being vocal about how good this system was got me to be the 'father' of the weak-hand load!"

When shooting a 3-gun match, you never know what match directors will throw at you. Shotgun targets can be pre-

(top) Ben Powell grabs shells while conducting a weak-hand reload.

(middle and bottom) Rob Romero conducts a weak-hand shotgun reload during the 2011 Rocky Mountain 3-Gun.

sented in all manners, and there are always many ways in which to attack those stages. Nevertheless, when a match director wants to put you in an alterna-

Kurt Miller, considered the father of the weak-hand reload, runs his Benelli during the 2010 Midwest 3-Gun Championship.

tive shooting or loading position, they usually have the means to do so. All this translates into the need to have many tools within one's shooting box. For shotgun loading, that means the ability to load from any position.

"Weak-hand loading is the most versatile and, in most cases, fastest method of loading the shotgun," Miller said. "It can be done with equal speed from any position, from prone, kneeling, sitting, standing, and on a dead run. It lets me see where I'm going and all the area around the gun instead of staring at an up-side down shotgun port."

The most impressive gain from using the weak-hand method is the ability to load while keeping the gun in the shoulder. I've seen shooters such as Miller, Jeff Cramblit, and Trapr Swonson actually continue to move with

the gun in the shoulder, while si-multaneously breaking shots and pulling shells from the caddy. It's awesome to watch a top pro run a gun this way. More important-ly, it shaves crucial seconds.

"For a 3-gunner, it's a very critical skill, in my opinion, to keep the gun at the shoulder during reload," Miller said. "It takes at least an extra 1½ to two seconds to drop the shotgun from the shoulder and, after loading, re-shoulder and re-index the tar-get—wasted time! The other part is, as you load, you can re-engage a missed target without having to stop your loading process. Just point the shouldered shotgun at the target and shoot it with your strong hand only.

"I saved myself three to five seconds at the Texas State 3-Gun match with just this tactic," Miller continued. "I was just starting to step out of a port to load and run to the next position, when I noticed the steel plate I'd previously engaged was not impressed by my pattern on it,

so, as I grabbed the four shells to load to the next position, I merely aimed the gun at the target one-handed, pressed the trigger, and got the plate while continuing my loading."

The weak-hand reload begins with the grab. By using the wall of the shellcaddy as a guide, shooters can establish a refer-ence point from which to build muscle memory, ensuring a clean, smooth grab every time.

"When you reach for the first shells, use your middle finger to reach down the side of the shell caddy closest to your weak side," Miller said. "Use it to start the grab by pushing it in between the amount of shells you are comfortable grabbing, which should be three to four. Next, your thumb drops around the top of the shell stack, you slide your middle finger right up along the side of the caddy and the shells stack into your hand."

According to Miller, many in-experienced shooters often make

(above) Kurt Miller, considered the father of the weak-hand reload, tops off his shotgun during a stage at the 2011 Rocky Mountain 3-Gun.

(left) Mark Hanish executes a weak-hand shotgun reload, the most popular style for shotgun loading in 3-gun.

the mistake of attempting to hold all four rounds flat in their hand. This usually ends in shells bouncing on the ground, with rounds coming out of their owner's grip, through the 'back door,' if you will.

"Shell retention is the key here, and too many folks try to keep all the shells flat in their hand, kind of like laying all four shells on the table," Miller said. "This is where most folks run into trouble. For shell containment, let the lower two fingers naturally curl in below the rims of the shells you just grabbed, kind of like if you were trying to hold three golf balls without dropping them. Now the shells

won't fall out of your hand, and they are much easier to roll into the loading port."

Finally, maintaining contact with gun during the interim between loading shells is critical to building speed. Having to reestablish the index point robs competitors of the smoothness exhibited by top pros such as Miller.

"When you get to the load, remember to keep your loading thumb in contact with the lifter or loading port," Miller said. "This keeps you from loading a shell and then dropping your hand away and having to build the index all over again."

In review, the weak-hand reload, as taught by Miller, has three main points.

"The three main points of weak-hand loading are to get a good consistent grab on the shells from the carrier, keep your loading thumb in contact with the shotgun lifter or loading port, and don't try to keep the shells flat to the gun!" Miller emphasized.

Practice, of course, is the key to building this skill set. However, Miller does not recommend spending hours on end of stuffing shells into your gun. Instead, 15 minutes of "good practice" will serve shooters better.

"Once you have the basic skills of weak-hand loading, dry practice with dummy rounds no more than 15 minutes at a time," Miller said. "This is the optimal time for letting your hand and brain learn the skill without overtaxing and fatigue. Anything more than this will actually hinder what you do. For most folks, a 15-minute session should be akin to loading around seven to 10 sets of eight shells—no more!

Strong-Hand Reloads

While Miller's weak-hand load is the most dominant method employed, it is by no means the only way to get the job done. For years, Bennie Cooley, a top 3-gun competitor, has utilized a strong-hand reload in competition. Dave Neth used a similar method for years, and his "tactical slide" method is one now copied by others in the sport.

Neth's technique calls for competitors to use the weak hand to position the shotgun butt on the shoulder with a clear view of the loading port. From there, one simply uses the strong hand to grab shells, either off a side-saddle carrier, an arm sleeve, or a belt caddy and load the shell into the gun.

"When I'm ready to load the shotgun, from the shooting position I turn the gun sideways and slide it up my shoulder," Neth said. "That allows me to control the muzzle with (my weak hand), and it frees up my strong hand. From here, I'll simply grab my shells off the side saddle and load."

If loading from the side saddle or arm band, shells are grabbed and loaded one at a time into the gun. While not practical from a belt-worn shell caddy, the proximity of the shells riding either on the gun or in a sleeve on the weak arm, make this move quick and competitive.

One strong point of Miller's weak-hand method is that it gives competitors the ability to load while keeping the gun in the shoulder. I've seen Miller,

Jeff Cramblit, and others execute this move while traversing a stage, going to the caddy and loading without ever bringing the gun out of the shoulder—an impressive skill. This cannot be achieved doing Neth's slide method, yet he remains one of the fastest competitors with a shotgun in all of 3-gun. With the tactical slide, Neth needs only to push the gun back off the shoulder to have it quickly returned to action.

"By pushing my support hand back out and pointing at the target, it brings the gun right off my shoulder and back on target," Neth said.

A second method for conducting a strong-hand reload, one often employed by Neth and used exclusively by Daniel Horner, involves taking the weak hand, which is already on the fore-end, and using it to simply roll the shotgun inboard. The strong hand is then used to acquire shells from a belt caddy and load the shotgun in a manner similar to Miller's weak-hand method.

"The other method I like to use is a strong-hand reload from a shell caddy off my belt," Neth said. "This requires you to grab four shells at once and bring them up. The shotgun comes underneath your arm, and you simply load one round at a time while keeping the muzzle pointed downrange and towards the target."

The Load-Two

The weak- and strong-hand reloads, while distinct from each

While the weak-hand is the most used, many top competitors such as Bruce Piatt still use a strong-hand shotgun reload.

other, are variations on at least a similar theme. However, the "two-by" or "load-two" technique is something entirely new.

During the 2010 Pan American IPSC Shotgun Championship at the Rockcastle Shooting Center, in a Level IV match that drew an international field, a fresh shotgun loading technique landed on American shores via the European contingent. Not only was it something radical and new to many American shooters, it was fast, especially in the hands of the Italians, who were especially strong in the match.

"Two of the Italian shooters would hold up their gun's loading gate and draw two shells at a time between their index and middle fingers, dropping one on the loading gate and thumbing it and the second one into the magazine tube, one behind the other," said Patrick Kelley, whose U.S. Standard Manual team took first place.

While several European competitors used a belt system to space out the rounds in pairs, others used homemade chest rigs that carried the shells stacked vertically. For several of the American shooters, the unique shell caddy turned heads first, but the loading technique itself was what really caught their attention.

"I did not get to see the so-called 'suicide bomber' vests in action, but three of the Italian shooters were using a technique that I found very interesting, and they were certainly fast," said U.S. Standard Manual team member Joe Satterfield. "They would pull two shells off their belt strong hand and use the nose of one to push the other into the magazine. I have played with it some since I got

A new type of shotgun load landed on American shores via Italy during the 2010 Pan American Shotgun Championships.

home and definitely think there is some potential there."

Word of the technique and new gear spread like wildfire through the 3-gun community. Within months, a couple different products were on the market, and now the technique is starting to find some favor with 3-gun competitors.

"It's a great way for newer shooters to learn to load a shotgun and be as competitive as seasoned professionals that are doing the weak-hand or strong-hand reload," said Noveske's Jansen Jones.

While many new shooters struggle with learning to grab four shells at one time and manipulate them into the shotgun, Jones and other 3-gunners have seen the European technique as an easier method to learn quickly. The load-two technique simplifies the loading process down into three easy steps.

"There are, in my opinion, three keys," Jansen Jones said. "Make sure you have the buttstock on your shoulder, the loading port at an angle where you can see it, and then get a nice, smooth grab. Watch the shells go in—the key is to not take your eyes off the shells. The first shell drops on the lifter, the second shell pushes it in."

The Drill

In 3-gun competition, winning with a shotgun, on most stages, boils down to loading skills. The shooter who does it the smoothest and fastest oftentimes wins the stage. The heavier the stage's round count, the more critical solid shotgun loading skills become. Here's a drill the pros practice to get themselves ready for a match.

When using a shotgun with an eight-round magazine tube, start by loading two rounds in the gun, one of those in the chamber. At the start signal, engage one target, and then begin covering ground to the next target. While moving, load eight rounds into the gun.

For most competitors, this drill requires going to their belt caddy two times, grabbing four rounds at a time. If using the load-two or TWinS system, the competitor will be required to make four moves to the shell holder. Remember, this isn't a tactical drill, so you don't have to keep your eyes downrange.

Find the caddy on your belt, and watch those rounds as you feed them into the gun.

"You already know what your footing is going to be," said champion 3-gunner Bruce Piatt. "The details of the loading process are what make you fast. Pay attention to how you get the shells each time."

Once all eight rounds are loaded into the tube, engage your second target (note that, if using a standard timer, the time elapsed between the two shots will give you your loading time). Change up the drill by going left to right, then right to left, forward and even backward—every type of movement will be thrown into a 3-gun stage at one point or another.

During a match, when working out a stage plan, loading a shotgun goes hand-in-hand with the number of shots that have to be fired and how much real estate needs to be covered until the next shot. The best 3-gunners manage to hit their reloads in that amount of space and time.

"In competition, if your feet are moving, you should be loading," Piatt said. "Keep it in multiples of what you can grab and load."

When moving, always know where downrange is and never break the 180-degree line, which would flag other competitors behind you. Not only is that extremely unsafe, it's an immediate disqualification from the match. So in practice, be conscious of where you're moving and where the gun has to be pointed—all while concentrating on making smooth, fast loads.

Load all eight and break the shots in 10 seconds and you've achieved a good benchmark of time from which to begin. Do it as fast as Bruce Piatt and other top pros, and you're going to be down in the five-second range or below—and that's *smokin'* fast.

Regardless the shotgun drill or practice you employ, most top shooters teach to go slowly first, building the muscle memory of the perfect load, not a fast load. Once the fundamentals are established, speed can be built from there.

"One of the things that's really important in 3-gun shooting is to practice your shotgun loading," said Keith Garcia. "I'll start off with the gun shouldered in position, drop it down to where I reload from, acquire my shells and feed them in, keeping my hand position where I want it, then shoulder the gun, seeing what it looks and feels like to do it right. That way, when I speed it up, my body already knows what it's supposed to be doing, I'm just going to try and do it faster. My objective at the end of a short training session is to put myself on the spot. I'm thinking to myself, *You've got one load, Keith—this is the one you've got to make under pressure for the match and pull it off.* That kind of load will win you stages."

The Guns

Let's talk for a minute about the individual guns playing a major role in today's game of 3-gun.

FNH USA SLP Mark I

Over the last couple 3-gun seasons, no shotgun platform has likely enjoyed more explosive growth in use than the FNH SLP. The Mark I variant is the model of choice in 3-gun, com-

ing ready right out of the box for high-level 3-gun competition.

Although the line was originally developed for the tactical community, and since so many practical and tactical features overlap, the SLP needs no after-market accessories or modifications to compete with it. With a 3-inch chamber, the gas-operated semi-auto reliably functions on 2¾-inch shells. Two pistons come with the gun, one of which FN claims is optimized to run on lighter target loads.

The eight-plus-one tubular magazine capacity is standard fare for running in all but the Open division, and a low-profile, adjustable folding rear sight blade, matched with a fiber optic front, is suitable for both slugs and shot. Simply raise the folded rear when a stage has

For the last few seasons, no other shotgun has gained ground on Benelli in popularity more than the FNH USA SLP.

slugs incorporated, and you can leave it up without worry to engage any birdshot targets that may be mixed in.

Weighing in at 8.2 pounds, the FN sits in the middle of typical 3-gun shotguns—heavier than a Benelli, yet lighter than a Remington 1100. It wears a 22-inch barrel, crossbolt safety, steel sling swivels, and a matte black finish for a package that has become ubiquitous in the racks of major 3-gun matches across the country.

SLP Mark I Competition

While the SLP was gaining traction within the 3-gun community, FNH went a step further last year with the debut of the FN SLP Mark I Competition. The same shotgun used by Team FNH USA and featured in the 3-Gun Nation Shoot-Off, the Mark I Competition features a blue anodized receiver emblazoned with "TEAM FNH USA."

The FN SLP is arguably second only to Benelli in terms of popularity on the national 3-gun landscape.

Benelli M2/Salient Arms Modified

The Benelli M2 has long been a favored choice among 3-gunners. The recoil-operated guns are extremely light and lively, and they just seem to flat out run. The only problem with it is that Benelli has seldom offered one straight from the factory that didn't need some extra work to make it competition ready—mostly in the form of an extended magazine tube. Yet, this did little to deter competitors from snatching up Benellis and sending them off to gunsmiths.

In 2010, Salient Arms, a California custom shop, made a lot of noise, when it started selling highly modified Benelli M2 shotguns. In truth, it wasn't that all the modifications employed on the Salient version were new, as gunsmiths such as Benny Hill and others had been turning out tricked Benellis for some time. But the Salient package had an appeal that launched a major wave in 3-gun.

Part of it was that, unlike those from some gunsmiths, the Salient versions were finely finished and looked as good as they shot. Another factor was the involvement of Taran Butler, one of the top competitors in the sport.

"Salient Arms International is a division of Salient Security Services, which is a diversi-

fied corporation that has been providing executive and personal protection services to VIPs and celebrities all over the U.S. and abroad," said Tony Pignato of Velocity Shooter, one of Salient's early dealers. "Rob Melhorn and Fred Lindley are the key members of the Salient Arms International firearms production division and have more than 30 years of combined experience in custom and competition firearms. Both Rob and Fred have been Taran Butler's gunsmiths since the beginning of his professional shooting career. Taran is also a professional consultant to Salient Arms, specifically for the competition firearms production. With his numerous years of experience and product knowledge, he was a perfect choice for USPSA/

Tricked out Benelli M2s are a favorite among many 3-gun competitors.

IPSC and multi-gun product development.

"My company, Velocity Shooter, was brought in to provide a link from the manufacture to direct customer sales. As Salient Arms International's primary source for product purchase, I also provide guidance on marketing and retail relations, based on my experiences with the competition and firearms industry," Pignato stated.

Within a matter of what seemed like months, top competitors such as Kurt Miller and Rob Romero joined Butler in running a Salient Arms Benelli. And why not? It had a collection of accessories and modifications that had become standard in 3-gun competition.

Salient upgraded the safety button, magazine tube and nut, and added an Arredondo oversized carrier release bar. Internally, the bolt carrier, extractor, trigger, and chamber were all enhanced or modified.

"We use a DMW (Dave Metal Works) magazine tube and magazine nut built to our specifications, because of the proven product performance and quality craftsmanship; the Benelli magazine extension clamp, because it provides quality, ease of removal, and integration into our performance platform; and Wolff magazine springs, because of their high quality and durability," said Pignato.

"The Salient Benelli M2 has a much better trigger pull, a match trigger," Butler said. "It's a faster loading gun—it's like glass, and your thumb doesn't get caught on that half-moon cutout the factory lift gate has. When the bolt recovers, because it's lighter, it doesn't dip

Ben Fortin runs his Benelli during a stage at the 2011 Midwest 3-Gun Championship.

the front sight at all. And, if the bolt is partly out of battery, you can still put a round in the tube without it getting seized up in the gun and causing a catastrophic jam."

Benelli Performance Shop M2 3-Gun

The effect of the Salient M2 must not have been lost on Benelli, which, by 2011, had finally jumped into the sport by sponsoring its first 3-gun team, with Taran Butler chief among it. In 2012, Benelli followed that up with the introduction of the Performance Shop M2 3-Gun.

Benelli's Performance Shop M2 utilizes a Nordic Components Speed Button bolt release and an oversized tactical bolt handle. An eight-shot magazine extension increases capacity to division standards, while a Teflon-coated magazine follower minimizes internal hanging or over-compression of the magazine spring. Additionally, the loading port is widened, with all sharp edges beveled; combined with the modified carrier, greatly enhances the ease of

loading. Weighing 7.2 pounds, the Performance Shop M2 is light and nimble, with a 21-inch barrel that utilizes a fiber optic sight suitable for slug use.

Now, hold your breath—the Performance Shop M2 3-Gun carries a suggested retail of nearly $2,700. But, considering the cost of a new M2, combined with the custom features included in this package, that price isn't nearly as obscene as it might look at first glance.

Remington VersaMax Tactical

The new Remington Versa-Max Tactical, though marketed toward law enforcement and home-defense, is nevertheless out-of-the-box-ready for 3-gun competition. Utilizing Remington's new "Versa Port" gas system, the VersaMax is billed as being able to handle any type of shotshell on the market.

"The heart of the VersaMax is the Versa Port gas system,"

said Brian Lasley, Shotgun Product Manager at Remington. "This unique gas system auto-regulates the gas pressure, based on the length of the shell being used, for flawless cycling of all 12-gauge loads."

An eight-plus-one magazine makes the VersaMax suitable for division requirements, while an oversized bolt release and button are also well suited for competition. However, it's the internal design that has received the lion's share of attention since the shotgun's release, as Remington claims the system requires little cleaning to maintain reliability.

"With its self-cleaning design, the Versa Port gas system stands ready to cycle hundreds of rounds with minimal cleaning, an amazing testament to its reliability," Lasley said.

Bruce Piatt, Robby Johnson,

and Daniel Horner are among a select group of 3-gun pros already running the VeraMax in competition. By all accounts, each of them plan on running one for some time to come.

(above) Daniel Horner readies with his Remington VersaMax, which made serious waves in the 3-gun world in 2011.

(below) The pump-action shotgun, this one a Mossberg 590, still has a home in 3-gun in the Heavy Metal division.

Mossberg JM Pro Series 930 Tactical Class

With Mossberg's release of the JM Pro Series shotguns, the company is attempting to leverage the winning name of top 3-gun pro Jerry Miculek alongside the solid design of the Mossberg 930 line of semi-automatics. By all accounts, that should be a formula for success.

The heart of the 930 platform is its dual-vent operating system that helps mitigate the forces of recoil in this gas-operated design. The anodized receiver incorporates a chamfered loading port, which should aid in loading.

The only major manufacturer to offer a 10-shot variant straight from the factory (along with a nine-shot version), Mossberg is clearly listening to Miculek as to what can help stand it apart from what is quickly becoming a crowded field of shotguns marketed for 3-gun competition. The 10-shot Tactical Class (nine-plus-one capacity) features a 24-inch vent rib barrel, while the nine-shot version (eight-plus-one capacity) wears a 22-inch vent rib barrel.

Benelli Nova

Likely the most common choice among top pump-action shotgun users in 3-gun, many shooters got a real treat watching the Italian team running these guns during the 2010 Pan American Shotgun Championship at the Rockcastle Shooting Center. Their Standard Manual team was extremely impressive with the Nova.

In America, Patrick Kelley has been thought of as this country's best pump-action shotgunner for several years. Kelley, who spent much of his shooting career running an out-of-production Win-

A competitor engages targets with a pump-action shotgun during the 2011 FNH USA 3-Gun Championship.

chester 1300 Camp Defender in Heavy Metal matches, switched to the Benelli Nova last season as part of his new sponsorship from Benelli USA.

Though Benelli markets a Tactical model, in truth, most Heavy Metal shooters pick up a used field model and then customize it to suit their need, most notably with a magazine extension tube from Nordic Components and other accessory makers.

Remington 870 and Mossberg 500

While more veteran shooters may use the Nova, sheer volume still belongs to the Remington 870. That, as much as anything, is simply a reflection of the market itself. Also in the mix is the Mossberg 500. Each of these shotguns has been produced in countless variations over the years, and there is a wide mix of customized former field models and factory-fresh tactical variants from both brands currently enjoying good use in 3-gun.

Box Magazine-Fed Shotguns

The holy grail of shotgunning is the absolutely reliable, yet affordable box magazine-fed shotgun design. In the imported Saiga 12 shotguns, there is certainly affordability, with guns retailing from Russian American Armory for around the price of a new polymer-framed pistol and even some pump-action shotguns. However, to make one run reliably enough for competition, the Saiga's price balloons into one more closely represented by an Open-style 2011 pistol.

Nevertheless, customized Saiga shotguns from R&R and Firebird Precision, among a select few others, have grown steadily in use among Open shooters. Firebird also unveiled a new twist on the box magazine-fed shotgun at the

2012 SHOT Show, when it introduced its highly tuned version of the Akdal MKA 1919, a Turkish import manufactured by Akdal Arms. Externally, the Firebird's improved 1919 is all AR-15, in terms of button and controls, which will sit well with most 3-gunners. Internally, the 1919 more closely resembles a Remington 1100, which has been successful in 3-gun since the days of SOF. Amazingly, the Firebird 1919 retails for $1,800—if this guns runs anywhere close to as reliably as a tuned Saiga, and for a fraction of the cost, the balance of power in Open shotguns could be at the beginning of a major shift.

(right) The MKA 1919, after being worked over by Firebird Precision, could seriously challenge the Saiga in the Open division.

(below) Kay Miculek, competing in the Open division, runs a Saiga shotgun during a match.

(opposite) Heavily customized Saiga shotguns, from makers such as R&R, are very popular in the Open division.

PIS

Yamil R. Sued photo

CHAPTER 8

THE TOLS

For many of the sport's very best competitors, action pistol shooting is where they cut their teeth. Though that trend seems to be shifting a bit, with more shooters coming straight into 3-gun than ever before, pistol shooters still make up the majority of the talent. One reason for that is access. More local clubs, for a much greater time period, have run pistol matches on a consistent basis. They're easier to staff, easier to set up and take down, and even for the competitors themselves, a weekend pistol match is more affordable and convenient.

"I think the sheer fact that someone has excelled at USPSA pistol shooting shows that they are well grounded in the basic fundamentals of shooting," said champion 3-gun and pistol competitor Bruce Piatt. "Combining shooting, reloading, moving, and negotiating obstacles or complex courses of fire, all while balancing accuracy and time on the clock, is the foundation to a great shooter—no matter what the sport. If you had the drive and ability to learn to do all those things in a course of fire, then you have the ability to adjust to any shooting situation."

Pistol shooting remains the hardest skill sets to master within 3-gun. Sure, shotgun loading is a difficult and foreign task for nearly every new 3-gun shooter, and long-range rifle has a science to it that can only be understood with time on the range. Yet, pistol shooting maintains the highest degree of difficulty, simply because it's the least forgiving tool of the trade. It's often said matches are won with rifle shooting or shotgun loading—and they can only be lost with a pistol.

At matches such as Superstition Mountain Mystery 3-Gun, the pistol game is a wide open, blazing-fast affair.

"The way most matches are presented now, you can't win a match as a result of pistol," Piatt said. "If the match staff presents a lot of small distant targets with a lot more no-shoot penalty opportunities, then a match could be *swayed* by the best pistol shooter. I doubt it will ever come to that point, though, because if it was that difficult for the top guys, imagine how the middle of the pack is going to feel driving home after such a match!"

Obviously smaller and lighter by comparison to rifles and shotguns, and with a drastically decreased sighting radius, a competitor is forced to be more solid in the fundamentals to run a pistol well. Long-range rifle, in terms of 3-gun shooting, certainly requires discipline in breathing, position, and trigger control, but shooters seem to be able to apply that skill set more quickly with a rifle. Jerk the

trigger on a pistol at close-range paper, on the other hand, and an "A" hit turns into a "C." And a bad trigger pull on even close-range steel? That's likely to be a miss altogether.

"Having the ability to consistently hit your target, no matter what the conditions, is what will make someone a successful 3-gun pistol shooter," Piatt said. "Now, if you can do it with speed, then you'll be a *great* 3-gun pistol shooter.

"Get to the range and experiment. Don't be afraid to change something every time you practice. Doing the same things over and over without experimentation will usually get you to a plateau. Change your grip pressure or trigger finger placement, anything. You might go right back to what you're doing now, but you would have learned what works and doesn't work for you."

At the highest level of compe-

Static knock-over steel is becoming a popular pistol target at major 3-gun matches, forcing competitors to shoot more deliberately than they might close-in paper targets.

tition, there is often very little that separates the winner from the rest of the pack. To that end, each match must be approached differently, depending on the challenge presented by the match director.

"Depending on the match, with smaller targets at distance, the most *accurate* shooter with the least misses is usually going to gain some ground," Piatt said. "When there are big, close targets with movement, then the *faster* shooter is going to take the lead. I just go out there and do my best, no matter what the challenge."

The latest trend challenging competitors is the use of small, reactive steel targets, often placed at extremely long-range pistol distances. While this type of stage design serves several purposes, it has one monumental effect—it forces competitors, sometimes right in the middle of an all-out run-and-gun stage, to slow down and get a good trigger press for accuracy.

Piatt agrees. "Yes, that has been the trend lately," he said. "I think the match directors were initially trying to minimize the logistics of buying targets and the labor of scoring paper. You have to remember that, especially if it's a rainy day, using bags over paper targets and keeping the hole pasters on the targets can add hours to a match. Rain, snow, or wind don't have too much effect on a piece of steel. Cost-wise, compared to buying targets, tape, and sticks for every match, the initial larger cost of the steel will pay for itself over the years. But whether or not it's about cost, this type of target presentation lends itself well to a shooter with more of an accuracy based foundation."

Like most 3-gun competitors,

Piatt, a New Jersey law enforcement officer and family man, has the same time constraints that limit most folks' time on the range. Because of that, his pistol training is focused, deliberate, and efficient.

"First of all, considering my work and family schedule, my practice sessions are few and far between," Piatt said. "I'll always start off with a zero check, then move right into some distance shooting. I'll shoot out to 50 yards, focusing on groups or hitting an eight-inch plate. Then I'll do some speed shooting on bigger targets, working on split times and target transitions at 10 and 15 yards. Then I'll continue the same drills, but do them on the move."

"I'll shoot a couple mags one-handed and weak-handed," Piatt continued. "No matter what I do, I'll always finish up my practice session back where I began—shooting some accuracy groups from distance, so that I leave the range with trigger control fresh on my mind."

Few are more qualified to speak on the intricacies of pistol shooting than Piatt. He's a five-time NRA Bianchi Cup Champion, the 2006 World NRA Action Pistol Champion, and a 17-time USPSA National Law Enforcement Division Champion, not to mention numerous championships in 3-gun and other disciplines. So I asked him, out of all the aspects of pistol shooting—stance, grip, trigger press, sights, splits, transitions, and on and on—what was the most important item one should focus on to make improvement for 3-gun? For Bruce, it all comes down to one thing—get the hits.

"As you mention, getting really good at split times and target transitions will shave tenths of seconds from your time," Piatt said. "Being accurate and missing less is going to shave *full* seconds off your time!

"A lesson I learned many years ago came from a discussion I was part of with a group of well-known shooters, including the then-current winner of the Steel Challenge, Angelo Spagnoli," Piatt continued. "We were quizzing each other on how he pulled off the win, and he claimed, and I will quote it as best I can remember, 'I didn't shoot faster than anyone out there, I just missed less.' That statement stuck with me, and I still follow that rationale to this day.

"Case in point was the 2010 3-Gun Nation Final Shoot-Off. I had to shoot against the likes of Jerry Miculek, Taran Butler,

While the Weaver stance and grip were the founding principals of action shooting, today's top competitors utilize more of a thumbs-forward grip and a forward-facing isosceles-type stance.

and Daniel Horner, knowing all the while that every one of them is faster than me 90 percent of the time. Following this 'miss less' mind-set allowed me to remain calm and just stick to what I know I can do, and that is be accurate. It worked for me. I finished second behind Horner and took home $10,000 to prove it."

Practical Pistols

With the surge in all things black gun and concealed carry, the pistol market, much like those for AR-15s and tactical-style shotguns, has never been stronger. But, for one interested in getting into 3-gun, walking into a gun shop with a wad of cash in the pocket can be intimidating.

"My advice for new 3-gun shooters trying to choose a pistol is not to rush it," Piatt said. "Come shoot with whatever gun you already have and are comfortable shooting, be it an out-of-the-box 1911 or one of the myriad plastic frame, striker-fired defensive guns. Just get out to the range and shoot some 3-gun. Pay attention to what others are shooting, and don't

be afraid to ask if you can try somebody's gun. That way you will invest your money wisely or find out what you already have will do just fine."

The 2011

For the guys and gals who play this game well, a majority have invested heavily in their pistol. Highly customized 2011 pistols most often fill the hands of match winners. You by no means have to run a 2011 to be competitive in 3-gun, but it's futile to argue that most top shooters use something else.

STI is likely the leader in this category, with varying levels of double-stacked 9mm or .38 Super models, and even guns in .40 S&W seeing use in competition. Caspian Arms, with its signature cast frames, are a favorite among some custom pistolsmiths, and companies such as Infinity, Bedell, Freedom Gunworks, and Accurate Iron are just but a sample of the many custom shops currently turning out quality 2011s suitable for 3-gun competition.

For those not ready to make the investment—some builds are in the $4,000 range—a quality polymer-framed pistol can still be had new for $500 to $600. Used models, of course, go for even less. And just as it is with 2011s, there is no shortage of smiths available to tune up these duty-style pistols to anyone's competition standards.

(top left) Junior shooter Katie Harris runs her 2011 pistol during the 2011 Rocky Mountain 3-Gun.

(top right) Tasha Hanish executes a pistol magazine reload during the 2011 Superstition Mountain Mystery 3-Gun.

(middle) Bruce Piatt runs a Caspian pistol at the Blue Ridge Mountain 3-Gun. Caspian's cast receivers are a popular choice for many custom pistolsmiths.

(bottom) Custom 2011-style semi-automatic pistols from makers such as STI, Infinity, and others are extremely popular in all but the most limited divisions of 3-gun.

Glock 17/34

As it is in law enforcement and civilian sales, chances are the Glock is also the most-used handgun in 3-gun. Okay, maybe not necessarily among elite shooters, as most top 3-gunners use a 2011 or are tied to a particular sponsor, but definitely for the majority of other competitors. The Glock is a very popular choice.

Most Glocks you see on 3-gun firing lines are model G17s or G34s, both chambered in 9mm, the most common pistol chambering at Outlaw matches. At USPSA Multi-Gun Nationals and pistol competitions, where the power factor comes into play, the .40 S&W certainly cuts into 9mm use, making the G35 a popular choice for competitors who play in both arenas.

What can you say about a Glock at this point that hasn't already been said? Known for incredible reliability, Glocks are generally accurate enough to be competitive, yet affordable enough to be accessible to most shooters. If I were buying one today for Outlaw 3-gun competition, my choice would be the G34. The 5.31-inch barrel is superior to that of the G17, and the standard magazine capacity is an ample 17 rounds, while 19- and even 33-round magazines are available. Moreover, there is no shortage of aftermarket parts, holsters, and custom gunsmiths ready to work on the Glock.

FNH USA FNS

FNH USA launched a new striker-fired pistol during SHOT Show 2012, highlighted by the finalists using it in the 3-Gun Nation Championship Finale on January 18 (the same

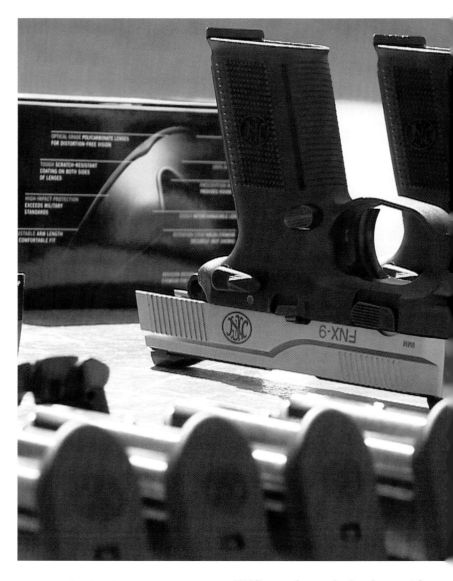

time as the SHOT show). During that week, the FNS made quite an impression on the SHOT show floor, in the competition, and during a Smoke 'N' Hope stage set up for media and industry professionals prior to the Championship.

"The new FNS series was designed to be the most operator-friendly semi-auto pistols available, and intended to give America's law enforcement officers a decisive edge," said Ken Pfau, Senior Vice President of Law Enforcement and Commercial Sales for FNH USA. "After five years of design development and nearly a half-million rounds of testing, the

FNS stands ready for duty with any agency, large or small."

Rumored to be working on a five-inch competition model, as well, the early FNS has proven to be well suited to the 3-gun game, as demonstrated by members of Team FNH USA in competition. As such, a low bore axis makes the pistol easy to control, while interchangeable backstraps enable a semi-custom fit for each user.

The FNS features fully ambidextrous controls, while low-profile three-dot night sights are standard. In 9mm, the magazine capacity is 17 rounds, while the FNS-40 holds 14 rounds. A polymer frame and

stainless steel barrel and slide round out the package.

Springfield XD(M) 5.25 Competition Series

Like Glocks, Springfield XD pistols have enjoyed a good amount of popularity in action shooting, including 3-gun. They are affordable, they shoot well, and they're consistently reliable, even under hard use.

The 5.25 brings some custom house-type touches to a factory offering. Lightning cuts in the slide reduce slide mass for faster cycling, while fully adjustable sights and fiber optic front enable shooters a better system with which to zero loads, as compared to the standard model XD.

(left) FNH USA FNX-9 semi-automatic pistols staged prior to a 3-Gun Nation Shoot-Off in 2010.

(below) Polymer-framed, duty-style semi-automatic pistols in 9 mm are very popular choices in 3-gun competition.

Internally, a match-grade steel barrel with a Melonite finish employs a fully supported ramp. In 9mm, the 5.25 delivers a 19-plus-one capacity.

Smith & Wesson M&P Pro

At a suggested retail of $670, the M&P Pro line, like the Springfield XD(M) 5.25, is billed as an enhanced model of the company's already successful duty-style line of polymer-framed pistols, in this case the M&P. As such, the M&P Pro is built to deliver many custom shop-type enhancements, yet maintain "stock" definitions for practical pistol shooting.

While those requirements are non-existent in 3-gun, the M&P Pro is nevertheless becoming a popular choice, simply because the pistol delivers a number of solid upgrades for a good price.

Upgraded fiber optic Novak sights, a five-inch barrel, and an improved trigger make the striker-fired Pro series competitive. The M&P Pro 9 has a magazine capacity of 17-plus-one, keeping it in line with other comparable pistols in this category.

(top) Running and gunning the pistol portion of 3-gun requires reloads on the move.

(right) Taran Butler, one of the top pistol shooters in 3-gun, rips though a stage at the 2011 ARFCOM-Rockcastle Pro Am.

(top) Jeff Cramblit takes on pistol targets during the 2010 3GN Championship in Las Vegas.

(middle) Barry Dueck runs his pistol while competing in the Heavy Metal Optics division at the 2011 Rocky Mountain 3-Gun at the NRA Whittington Center in Raton, NM.

(left) Mike Voigt runs his Open pistol in competition.

Yamil R. Sued photo

CHAPTER 9

THE OPTICS

Over the last few years, no area of 3-gun equipment has enjoyed as much technical advancement as has rifle scopes. With greater ranges of magnifications now available on scopes that deliver true one-power (1X) magnification at the lower end of the variable spectrum, rifle scopes have never been more well suited for 3-gun use.

The Weaver 1-5X delivers 1X at the low power end yet still magnifies out to 5X for long-range shooting.

Models with increased zoom range from Leupold, Swarovski, Bushnell, and others deliver top-end magnifications beyond the previous threshold of 4X on scopes that featured 1X at the bottom end. While monster top-end magnifications have been available for many years, it's the 1X that's the important part of the equation, as the sport of 3-gun demands the ability to shoot extremely close-range paper targets with a rifle.

Indeed, range bays themselves can be limited, making close-range targets a necessity, simply in order to get a sufficient amount of rifle shooting in. Moreover, fast-action close-range rifle, or "hosing," as it's referred to, is actually very much a part of the game. Trust me, there a few things more fun than getting on the trigger of a SCAR or AR-15 as fast as you possibly can, while running past a bank of paper targets 10 feet away.

Where scopes once maxed out at 4X, now 5X, 6X, and even 8X models are available, and they still include true 1X viewing. These bigger scopes are a boon in competitor's hands for long-range rifle shooting—a bigger boon for optics companies wanting to sell to tactical and practical shooters alike, as this is the hot trend in tactical-style optics.

The One-Powers (1X)

In 2010, new rules took over the Limited divisions of Outlaw 3-gun, with once-prohibited 1X optics suddenly approved for Tactical Iron and Heavy Metal in an effort to boost otherwise shrinking equipment classes. It worked, especially in Tactical Iron, at least in part because it immediately provided a new way to play the game. But, the development also benefited from the fact that there have never been more quality one-power optics.

Today's field of optics suitable for either secondary use on an Open gun or primary use in Limited divisions is dominated by reflex sights, including red dots, open-style reflex sights, and holographic sights. More recently, the conventional tube sight has been redesigned in the form of the Leupold Prismatic. Knowing the strengths of each, when combined with the primary duty of the shotgun, they can help shooters get the most out of sights that are diminutive in size but deliver big performance.

For nearly 10 years, the firearms industry watched as reflex sights turned from a curious anomaly to a staple of our soldiers' gear, with several makes and models used to good effect in Iraq and Afghanistan. Open competitor Mike Voigt is often credited for being one of the first, if not *the* first, to use a secondary sight on an optic in the sport of 3-gun—prior to similar use by the U.S. military.

Matt Burkett's Offset Sight Mount is suitable for mounting secondary optics on an Open rifle.

Aimpoint's Comp M4 has served with distinction with the military and has been used in 3-gun for years. A couple years ago, that technology was miniaturized into the revolutionary Micro series. A 1X red dot with unlimited eye relief, the Micro features a 4 MOA reticle and runs seemingly forever (five years continuous use at position No. 8, according to Aimpoint) on one three-volt lithium battery. Constructed of extruded aluminum and garbed in anodized black, the Micro is rugged.

The Micro weighs a scant three ounces and measures only 1.4 inches high, which keeps it

(left) The new Burris FastFire III is one of several reflex-style sights common in the Open division.

(below l. to r.) Leupold DeltaPoint, EOTech, Leupold Prismatic, and Aimpoint Micro H1—Examples of 1X optics used in 3-gun.

(bottom) Reflex-style sights such as the Aimpoint Micro H1 are commonly used as secondary rifle optics and as primary shotgun and pistol sighting systems in the Open division.

low to the receiver and out of the way. It also comes set-up to mount directly to a Picatinny rail (common on most tactical shotguns), or easily added as an aftermarket accessory.

For a fraction of the price, Bushnell markets the TRS 1X25mm. I was pleasantly surprised, when I ran this optic atop a Ruger 10-22, shooting multiple steel targets at a Bushnell writer's conference. The TRS features a 3 MOA dot, multi-coated optics and an amber, high-contrast lens coating.

While the Micro and TRS are diminutive optics, the open-style reflex sights made famous by Docter are even smaller. In 3-gun, they dominate the field for secondary optics in Open division, with models by JP Enterprises, Trijicon, and Burris all popular. One of the newest entries into this field is Leupold's DeltaPoint, which has received excellent reviews from shooters in competition.

The DeltaPoint features a wider design compared to the lens housing common in most of its contemporaries. Leupold claims

Variable power scopes with a low power setting of 1X, such as the Burris 1-6X XTR, are popular in 3-gun.

this delivers up to 56-percent more usable field of view. Motion-activated, the DeltaPoint also continuously samples light conditions and uses that information to optimize reticle intensity. The DeltaPoint employs adjustment numbering to 120 MOA. The unit rides in a magnesium housing and is shockproof and waterproof. Weighing a mere 0.6 ounces and measuring 1.6 inches long, you'll never even know the DeltaPoint is there—that is, un-til you see the red dot on target.

One of the hottest 1X optics recently introduced has been the Leupold Prismatic. I used the Prismatic often on M4 carbines as student in tactical training courses. The Prismatic is lightning fast for acquiring close-range targets, and top pros such as Kelly Neal and James Casanova have proven how accurate they can be at long range.

With the Prismatic, there is

The Leupold DeltaPoint is a great choice as a primary sighting system for any pistol or shotgun, or as a secondary rifle optic in the Open division.

(above) James Casanova hammers close-range rifle targets running a Leupold Prismatic in the Tactical Iron division.

much to make it stand apart from other reflex sights. First, it features the thickest main tube Leupold has ever built. The Prismatic also accepts a removable illumination module that delivers a red reticle with eight brightness settings, and an

etched glass reticle lies within the 1X14mm scope, as well. When the illuminator is running, it superimposes over the existing etched glass, so, if a battery dies or the illuminator breaks under duress, there is always the etched reticle there. A competitor running a Prismatic is never out of the game.

The Leupold Prismatic delivers 1X capabilities in a tube design.

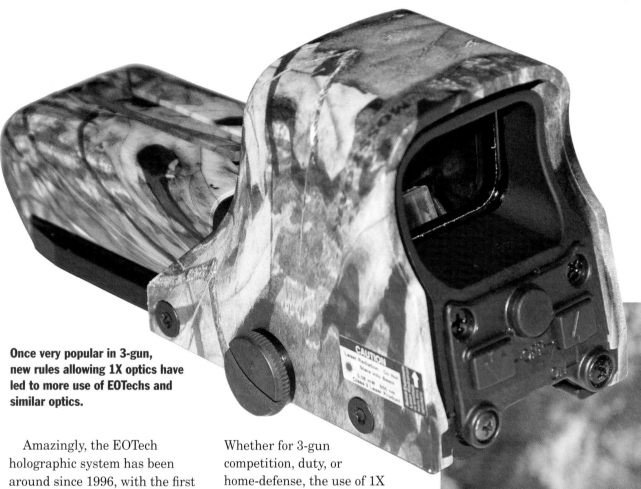

Once very popular in 3-gun, new rules allowing 1X optics have led to more use of EOTechs and similar optics.

Amazingly, the EOTech holographic system has been around since 1996, with the first military/law enforcement model HWS produced in 2001. The EOTech works by projecting a holographic image back to the shooter. This system enables the unit to function even if the actual display window is broken. The technology of holography delivers all information required to reconstruct the image to every part of that window. As long as any part of it remains intact, unobstructed by mud, etc., then that reticle is visible and usable.

EOTech produces several variants today, both for tactical and sporting markets. Compared to the Micro or the DeltaPoint, EOTechs are much larger and heavier. Still, the system is lightning fast, the unit runs on simple AA batteries, and my unit is as close to indestructible as anything I've ever ran.

These are but a sample of the myriad options available today.

Whether for 3-gun competition, duty, or home-defense, the use of 1X optics on long guns is a growing trend. Bolt one on your shotgun or rifle, urn some ammo, and you'll know why.

Swarovski Z6i 1-6x24 BRT

No rifles cope made a bigger impact upon 3-gun than did the Swarovski Z6i, in 2011—it simply took the sport by storm. At the end of 2010, as these scopes were beginning to trickle out, they were extremely hard to find. Yet, I will never forget walking to a rack of rifles at Superstition, in 2011, where an entire squad had just placed their rifles in the rack. Out of 10 rifles staged there, eight of them wore the brand new Z6i—and there wasn't one sponsored shooter in the squad—amazing!

(right) One of the most popular scopes in 3-gun in 2011 was the Swarovski Z6i.

The Swarovski Z6i features a BRT reticle with multiple aimpoints past the initial zero.

The Z6i is attractive, in my opinion, and I shoot one for two major reasons besides its good looks, those being the reticle and the field of view. With the power knob wrenched down to 1X, the field of view, listed at 127 feet, is incredible. Where the competition is looking for individual targets, you are looking for entire arrays with the Z6i. The second really attractive feature is the BRT reticle, a combination of mil dots and vertical bullet drop compensation lines that offer an easy, basic formula for taking on targets out to extended ranges and which delivers five hold points beyond zero.

The BRT illuminated reticle features an illuminated dot, with both day and night settings. Also, Swarovski's website features an online ballistic calculator pre-programmed for standard .223 16-inch or 20-inch barrels and numerous factory loads, although you can put in handloads, as well. The calculator can also compute a competitor's drops from roughly 100 to 600 yards, with a typical load.

Leupold's new 1-6X should become a popular scope among 3-gunners in the near future.

Leupold Mark 6 1-6X20mm

Leupold's new Mark 6 1-6X20mm M6C1 debuted at SHOT 2012 to much fanfare, and with good reason. It delivers a lot of features sought by 3-gunners, but at a fraction of the price of much of the competition.

With its 6X zoom range, the Mark 6 delivers plenty of top-end magnification for most long-range targets. A wide field of view promotes fast target acquisition, especially at 1X. Available reticles include the CMR-762 and CMR-W 5.56, giving all optics divisions in 3-gun, including Heavy Metal Optics, a solid option.

"Whether you're on the battlefield or in a 3-gun competition, our new Mark 6 1-6X20mm rifle scope packs all the optical performance and versatility you need in an extremely compact, efficient package," said Kevin Trepa, Vice President, Tactical Division for Leupold & Stevens, Inc.

Weaver Tactical SPR 30mm Mount

The Weaver Tactical SPR (Special Purpose Rifle) 30mm Optics Mount places optics at an optimal height on AR-15-style rifles and is designed to fit the 30mm scope tubes prevalent in 3-gun competition. Constructed of 6061 T6 aluminum and hard-coat anodized, at $100 the SPR represents a significant value in this product category.

MGM Switchview

If 1X is the gas pedal stomped to the floor, and 6X is slowing down for accuracy, then the

MGM Switchview is the gear shifter to your rifle shooting. The MGM Switchview is a lever that enables you to quickly change the magnification of your scope. These are great for 3-gun rifles and long-range rifles alike. Being able to look for a target and then zoom in on it, in less than three seconds and without taking your head off the gun, is a huge advantage.

The MGM Switchview has an MSRP of $59.95 and is available to fit models from Leupold, Vortex, Burris, Millet, NightForce, Schmidt-Bender, Trijicon, and IOR Valdada.

Warne RAMP

Popular with Open and Limited division shooters alike, the Warne RAMP, for Rapid Acquisition Multi-Sight Platform, is a cantilever-style mounting solution designed to deliver proper scope height on AR-15-style rifles. The RAMP also features 45-degree offset rails, one on each side, for mounting secondary optics—perfect for Open shooters. For other divisions, these rails can be removed.

Warne RAMP mounts are constructed of 6000 series aluminum and feature No. 8 Torx fasteners. The RAMP is available for one-inch or 30mm scope tubes.

The RAMP Mount from Warne Scope Mounts features Picatinny rails at a 45-degree angle from the main optic—perfect for mounting a secondary optic.

The Weaver SPR Mount is a solid mounting system that is suitable for 3-gun use.

Yamil R. Sued photo

CHAPTER 10

THE ITION

The bane of every 3-gunner's existence is ammunition. For the most part, anyone who gets into 3-gun is a serious trigger-puller anyway. But, 3-gun is a new kind of "illness" that can only be treated again and again with ammo. As such, most veteran shooters handload their own rifle and pistol ammunition, in an effort to keep down costs. Say what you want about tuning loads to match the gun and all that. Not in this sport. For most 3-gunners, handloading is only about saving money.

Shotshells, on the other hand, are generally purchased in the form of factory ammunition. For the most part, whatever bulk pack of No. 7½ birdshot you can find on sale at Wal-Mart is plenty sufficient to shoot even a major Outlaw match. Some matches will call for buckshot from time to time, which does increase expense, but buckshot round counts for match play are almost universally kept on the low end. And, while there are maybe three guys in the sport, somewhere, who load their slugs (I haven't met them yet), with the cost of slugs added to some major matches, where trends are toward increased slug use and ridiculously long shots with them, handloading slugs may be brilliant after all! But, until then, loads such as Remington Managed Recoil will likely remain popular.

For those who don't like to handload (and there are a surprisingly significant number of 3-gunners who do not), factory ammunition for pistol and rifle use is most often ordered in bulk instead of purchased from the local gun shop or box store. Especially for competitors running duty-style pistols, plenty of Winchester white box, Remington UMC, Blazer, and other discounted brands are readily available and very much present on the firing line. Most Glocks, M&Ps, XDs and the like are pretty reliable with a wide range of pistol ammunition, unlike the tighter-fitting

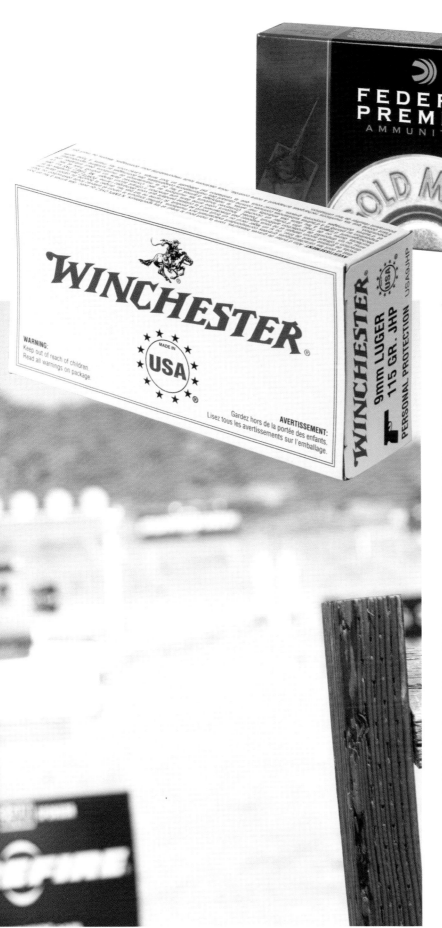

(above) While many shooters reload for practice, others still buy quality rifle ammunition such as Federal Gold Medal Match for game day.

(left) Value-priced ammunition is available from most major ammunition manufacturers, such as this 9mm load commonly referred to as "Winchester White Box."

(opposite) Federal Shotgun ammunition staged prior to a 3-Gun Nation Shoot-Off.

custom 2011s, which generally require better ammo for reliable operation.

Most competitors spend the majority of their ammunition allowance on quality rifle ammo. Even if they load or shoot lower-grade rounds for practice, many still purchase factory match-grade rifle ammunition for game day. These shooters continuously scour Brownells, Cheaper Than Dirt!, and elsewhere, looking for bulk deals or sales on their favorite loads. Following are a few affordable versions commonly seen in 3-gun competition.

American Eagle .223 Tactical is a solid factory choice for most AR-15 users.

Hornady Steel Match Ammunition

Utilizing coated steel cartridge cases, instead of traditional brass, Hornady Steel Match Ammunition costs as much as 40-percent less than brass cased match ammo. However, Hornady loads these rifle rounds with Match bullets and the pistol loads with HAPs, delivering accurate, yet affordable, ammunition designed specifically for competition.

Steel Match is available in .223 and .308, as well as 9mm, .40 S&W, and .45 ACP. The .308, .40, and .45 loads, though loaded to moderate velocities to reduce recoil, meet IDPA and IPSC/USPSA Major power factor.

Hornady's new Steel Match delivers pistol and rifle ammunition at a reduced cost, with steel cases being less expensive to manufacture than traditional brass.

Federal American Eagle 55-grain FMJ

Available in 1,000-round bulk packs, Federal's American Eagle 55-grain FMJ is a solid all-around load for 3-gun. While some competitors prefer a heavier bullet for long-range shooting, 55-grain bullets are most likely still the most common bullet weight used.

Loose-packed for added value, this load delivers a muzzle velocity of 3,420 fps. A 1,000-round bulk pack retails for about $370, but can be found marked down online on occasion.

Remanufactured Ammo

Another way to save money on ammunition is through factory-loaded, remanufactured ammunition. Here, ammo companies acquire spent brass, often through military and law enforcement channels, then re-load it to certain specifications.

Remanufactured ammunitions are most often used as training rounds, with competitors still electing to use match-grade factory ammo for competition. Black Hills, Atlanta Arms & Ammunition, and others offer both pistol and rifle loads suitable for sending a large volume of practice rounds downrange.

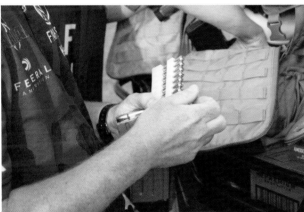

(above) Hornady .308 Match is a popular load for Heavy Metal shooters.

(left) Competitors go through a lot of rifle rounds at a major 3-gun match.

(below) Major 3-gun matches are conducted as "lost brass" matches, meaning competitors are prohibited from picking up the empty casings they just fired. A volunteer-driven sport, the lost brass often is given to the range officers and staff, while other ranges sell used brass.

Yamil R. Sued photo

CHAPTER 11

THE GEAR

The sport of 3-gun is about as gear-driven as any shooting sport gets. Nowhere else do competitors need the sheer and wide-ranging volume of firearms and accessories in order to not only shoot a match, but to actually get all your possessions to the range in the first place.

Beyond the rifle, shotgun, and pistol, there are numerous products a competitor has to have, along with several more that just make match life easier.

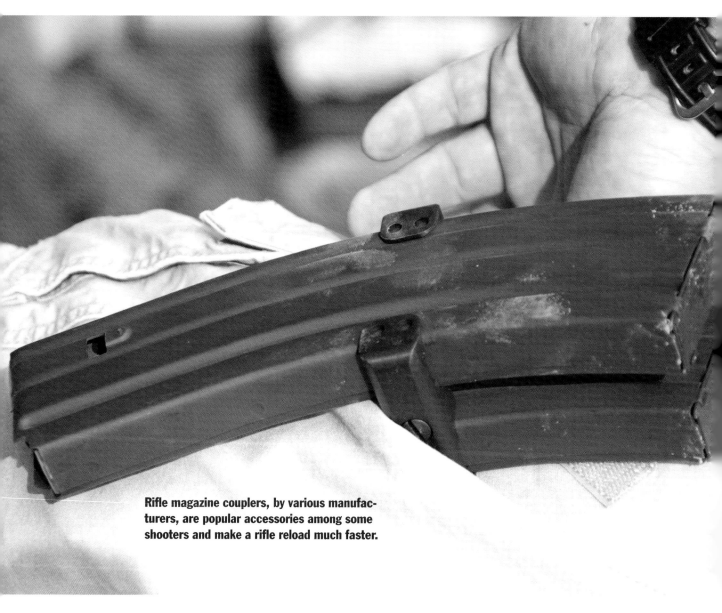

Rifle magazine couplers, by various manufacturers, are popular accessories among some shooters and make a rifle reload much faster.

Rifle Gear

If shooting an AR-15 or similar rifle, three to five magazines are fairly common in most range bags. Magpul, Troy, and Lancer are all popular aftermarket brands, while the new SureFire 60-rounder is highly sought after. While not as durable or reliable, a standard GI mag will do fine, and the Brownells version with the improved follower

is even better. One belt-worn rifle magazine pouch should be enough, as courses of fire generally begin with one magazine in or around the rifle.

Chamber flags are required on most ranges these days, but they are not all created equal. You will also want a sling in your bag at all times, as matches such as Blue Ridge and Rocky Mountain routinely require their use.

Tactical-style slings, like this one from Armageddon Gear, are a requirement for both shotguns and rifles at some major 3-gun matches.

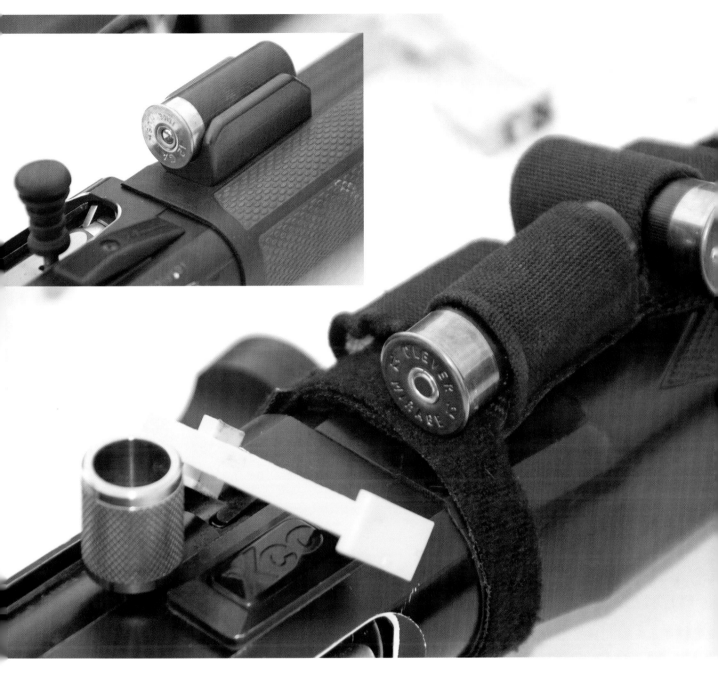

Shotgun Gear

A full assortment of chokes, along with the accompanying choke tool, is recommended for most matches, as you never know when the match director will put a tiny piece of knock-over steel out at 30 yards. Chamber flags for shotguns are also often required, and it's good to have a shotgun sling available.

Shotgun shell caddies are an important part of the 3-gun game, and their use is directly related to how much real estate you have available on your belt. The smaller you are, the less room there is for shell caddies, which should be a consideration when deciding between four- and six-shell caddies, or even AP Custom's new 4X4 that holds eight shotshells. For open shooters who run speedloaders, a pouch is needed for those tools, while Saiga shotgun users need pouches for those massive box mags.

Many veteran 3-gunners use single- and/or double-shell carriers near the ejection port to quickly reload a shell in case the shotgun is run dry.

Pistol Gear

A retention holster is most recommended for 3-gun. A race holster may be critical for straight-out pistol games, but that's not normally the case in 3-gun. Any time lost on a draw stroke is usually inconsequential in the grand scheme of things. There's a lot running and jumping in this sport, and much evil use of crazy shooting positions. If the pistol should unintentionally come free in the course of all that rigorous movement, that shooter is going home disqualified. This makes a solid retention system the better choice for 3-gun.

When running a typical high-capacity pistol platform such as a 2011 or Glock, a competitor needs three to five magazines to get through most major matches. If shooting a single-stack gun, more magazines are naturally in order. Belt-worn magazine pouches are standard equipment.

In divisions without prohibitions on ammunition capacity, a rifle or pistol magazine extension can dramatically increase capacity and reduce magazine changes.

The Belt

A sturdy belt is required for 3-gun—'cause there's gonna be a *lot* of stuff hangin' off it! Double Alphas are common, and Uncle Mike's has a new version of its inner-outer belt combination, one linked by hook-and-loop fasteners—these make life much easier than when having to use a duty or rigger's-style belt. Safariland's ELS system is a variation on that theme, providing a full system of interchangeable attachments that make reconfiguring holsters, mag pouches, and shell caddies a snap. A lot of top shooters have gone to the ELS over the last couple seasons.

Safariland's modular ELS belt system has become a preferred choice among many top shooters.

Bags & Cases

When traveling by plane, you will need an airline-approved travel case in which to ship your firearms. Be sure to check both airline and TSA regulations concerning the volume of ammunition allowed and pay close attention to regulations concerning packaging.

However you get there, once on site you'll need a good way to transport your long guns. Brownells and Safariland make excellent 3-gun bags, while Eberlestock packs are also popular. Most competitors also carry another, separate range bag. Brownells and Blackhawk, among many others, offer range bags in various sizes and configurations. Beside the firearms and belt, you have at least a

couple hundred rounds of ammunition, eye protection, hearing protection, shotgun chokes and tools, cleaning kits, chamber flags, rifle and pistol magazines, a multi-tool, lens wipes, etc., to cram in there. Add in a few water bottles and a protein bar, and man do you suddenly have one heavy load!

3-Gun Gear Best-in-Class

There's plenty of good gear out there, more than you can shake your three guns at, but there are always a few specific pieces that stand out from the crowd. What follows is a short list of some of the best-in-class gear making appearances at today's major matches.

Noveske Shooting Team 3-Gun Holster

Not completely satisfied with holsters available for action shooting, Noveske Shooting Team's Rob Romero designed one to fit a very specific criteria. The Noveske Shooting Team 3-Gun Holster, developed in collaboration with Ready-Tactical, has a lot to offer.

Romero sought out to design a holster that provided reliable re-tention without sacrificing speed during presentation, in other words, a holster fast enough for pistol competition, but one that would hold onto your gun during the rigors of 3-gun competition. When it comes right down to it, though, this is a 3-gun holster, and that means retention over-rides speed, especially on the natural terrain courses of fire or stages heavy with prop obstacles. As such, the pistol locks into place with an audible "click" and requires a definitive pull to bring the gun out of the holster. Retention is adjusted via the covered top retention screw only.

An interesting feature on this holster is the full hood designed to protect the rear sight from being hit, bumped, or damaged during use. With the wide range of terrain, stage props, and positions shooters are now required to maneuver over, through, and around, gear that rides on a competitor's belt takes quite a bit of abuse. The hood feature should go a long way toward protecting the rear sight during a competition—welcome insurance against the possibility of losing zero.

Finally, Noveske claims the dropped, offset design better enables the competitor to get in and out of shooting positions. During testing, I found the Noveske 3-Gun Holster comfortable on the belt. After getting used to the new position of my pistol, I found the holster conducive to presenting the pistol faster than with similar Kydex-

Designed by the Noveske Shooting Team, the Noveske Holster provides retention and protects the rear sight of the pistol.

style holsters that require the retention system be defeated via a thumb-break or button.

One thing we see continuously on the 3GN Tour, from veteran and rookie 3-gunners alike, is stage and/or match disqualifications when pistols come out of holsters and drop to the ground while a competitor is negotiating a stage. This most commonly occurs with race-style Open gear, but also Kydex-style holsters, which have little or no retention built into them. You can't win if you go home early, which makes a reliable holster an essential piece of any 3-gunner's gear.

"Whether running around barricades on a stage or diving hard into a prone position for long-range targets, this holster provides enough protection for the pistol, specifically the rear sight, to eliminate any worries of damaging the handgun," said 3GN Pro Series competitor Bryan Ray, who recently began using the Noveske 3-Gun Holster in competition. "Lacking mechanical retention, there are no devices to manipulate before the draw, but the holster holds the gun securely, while I'm running through a course of fire."

Uncle Mike's Reflex Holster

With its Integrated Retention Technology, Uncle Mike's Reflex Holster provides solid pistol retention in an amazingly simple holster design. The beauty of the Reflex is in the deactivation of the retention system. Instead of thumbing a button or tab to break it, retention is defeated by twisting the pistol inboard, a gross motor-skill movement that's simpler to commit to muscle memory.

The movement requires very little practice to become proficient with, though it must be noted that the pistol will not pull free unless this simple twist of is applied. It's a very basic principle, but one that translates well to 3-gun, where the stress of the clock and the pressure of the situation itself can work heavily on a shooter's nerves.

The Reflex is available for Glock, SIG Sauer, Springfield XD/XDM and 1911 pistols.

Karla Herdzik engages rifle targets from the prone position. Shooting positions such as this make a good retention pistol holster a must in 3-gun.

California Competition Works Speed Stripper

For all but Open shooters, some type of shotshell caddy is a necessity in 3-gun. For most competitors, that means an assortment of belt-worn four- or six-round caddies. California Competition's 12-gauge Speed Strippers are ubiquitous at 3-gun matches, accommodating 2¾-inch and 3-inch shells.

Constructed of plastic and using a stainless steel belt clip for attachment purposes, the CCW is among the most basic and affordable shell caddies on the market and an excellent choice for beginners and veterans alike.

AP Custom 4x4 Shell Carrier

If you shoot a major Outlaw match, or even if you have a fairly sadistic local match director, eventually you're going to need more shotshells than you can carry. With the massive shotgun stages seen at matches such as Rocky Mountain and Midwest, shooters were looking for a way to increase shotshell carrying capacity. The AP Custom 4x4 fills the bill by effectively carrying eight shells on the same belt space most caddies carry only four or six.

The AP Custom 4x4 is constructed of CNC-machined aluminum, is hard-coat anodized, features a spring retention system, and can be fitted with Tec-Lock or Safariland attachment systems, which follows trends from other makers of like products. What sets the AP apart is the arrangement of those eight shotgun shells.

Instead of eight vertical shells, which has been done previously, the 4x4 stacks shells in two rows of four, providing an immense savings in belt space, while also being less inhibitive to movement.

AP Custom's 4X4 shell caddy doubles the amount of shotgun shell carry capacity without taking up any more valuable real estate on a shooter's belt.

Safariland 3-Gun Competition Case

The Safariland 3-Gun Competition Case features a large dual handgun/accessory pouch, with individual hook-and-loop enclosed storage areas, along with four pistol magazine pouches long enough to accommodate extended mags. Constructed with closed-cell protective foam padding, the case is 46 inches in overall length, yet incorporates a unique barrel expansion slot for guns measuring up to 51 inches. Rugged ballistic cloth protects the exterior, and the case can be carried via an adjustable, padded shoulder harness or with adjustable backpack-style straps that can be tucked away in a storage compartment when not in use. Assorted accessory pockets are inside the case, along with heavy-duty lockable zippers and two adjustable accessory pouches are located outside the bag.

Safariland's 3-Gun Bag is a popular choice of competitors to tote their firearms to and from the range.

SureFire High-Capacity Magazines

Because a 60-round magazine eliminates the need for a magazine change on virtually every rifle stage a 3-gunner will encounter, the SureFire high-cap mag is a game changer—and its dimensions make it even more attractive. Not much longer than a traditional 30-round magazine, the 60-round version will fit in many of the magazine pouches used in 3-gun competition.

SureFire's HCM magazines, this one a 60-rounder, became a hot gear item in 2011. Double the capacity of a standard GI magazine, the 60-rounder nevertheless fits in several mag holders designed for standard magazines.

TRA

Yamil R. Sued photo

CHAPTER 12

NING

Talk to any top competitor and they will likely tell you, without even dropping into a dramatic whisper, that the secret to their 3-gun success is practice. Brutally and painfully obvious as that might be, I can't overemphasize just how much some competitors put into this game. Yes, some veterans have refined their game to a point where they don't put in countless hours on the range each day anymore, instead boiling down their regimen into a series of live-fire and dry-fire drills that involve a minimum investment of time, while still allowing them to maintain a high level of competency.

But make no mistake, whether a competitor shoots nearly every day or employs a compacted, efficient regimen of 3-gun training, the shooters that consistently win matches have accumulated the repetitions necessary to make it to the top.

"Practice, practice, practice," said FNH USA's Dianna Liedorff, when asked how competitors already at the top of their game can improve. "You have to put in the time to improve at anything."

"Good, old-fashioned hard work," echoed Rustin Bernskoetter. "Identifying my points of weakness. Shooting until my fingers bleed. Staying up until two o'clock in the morning reloading ammo so I can do it all again the next day."

Rustin Bernskoetter elevated quickly up the 3-gun ranks and is one of the top shooters in the game. He credits dedicated training to his rise.

The sport of 3-gun is difficult to master, simply because there is so much going on. Because of that, it can take years to really boil down what is effective in training from what isn't nearly as worthwhile. Still, there is a way to get ahead of the curve.

For those with little to no experience in shooting, chances are your local range provides basic shotgun, pis-

Advanced training is available at academies and sometimes at your local range from experienced competitive shooters.

tol, and rifle courses, with many ranges offering classes taught by certified NRA and NSSF instructors. Too, many of the top competitors in 3-gun regularly hold training classes specific to action shooting and 3-gun. Champions such as Daniel Horner, Bruce Piatt, Jerry Miculek, Taran Butler, Kurt Miller, Mike Voigt, and others either host classes at their home ranges or travel to conduct action-shooting classes across the country. For those wanting to take their 3-gun to a higher level, but who don't want or can't afford to travel to courses, there are training materials in the form of webcasts, books, and videos from several sources.

Jerry Miculek Practical Rifle DVD

It could fairly be said that no other competitor in practical

Students participate in a local 3-gun course at the Blue Grass Sportsman's Club, in Wilmore, Kentucky. Local classes can provide a lot of bang for the buck.

shooting has a resume to rival that of Jerry Miculek. The most famous revolver shooter of all time, Miculek has won championships in a multitude of shooting disciplines, including 3-gun.

Miculek has compiled those decades of experience into a three-volume DVD set specifically geared toward practical rifle shooting, and it is a perfect training aid for those trying to up their 3-gun rifle game. Featuring more than two hours of instruction, it covers topics including rifle set-up, stance, grip, and trigger con-

Jerry Miculek has spent nearly three decades perfecting the art of the rifle for action shooting.

trol. Advanced subjects include movement and target acquisition, multiple target engagement, and shooting positions.

"I've been competing for 25 years, and I wasted the first 10 years doing it wrong," said Miculek. "I put these videos together so other shooters don't have to waste that time."

Produced by Brownells studios, in partnership with Miculek's Bang, Inc., company, the *Jerry Miculek Practical Rifle* DVD set is available from Brownells.

Noveske 3-Gun Outlaw

The Noveske Shooting Team, consisting of Rob Romero and Jansen Jones, saw the need for

a volume of instruction aimed specifically at 3-gun and decided to make one themselves. The result is a how-to guide on shotgun loading, load management, stance, transitions, movement, shooting positions, and more.

"The popularity of the weak-hand reload video we put on YouTube was really the main reason for this video," said Jones. "People came up to Rob and me at matches all over the country and said things like 'You guys taught me how to reload a shotgun!' We talked about this DVD for months and finally just decided to make it. To our knowledge, there isn't another dedicated 3-gun DVD

out there, so we thought we'd give it a shot."

Similar to the courses the shooters teach at ranges all over the country, *3 Gun Outlaw* is unique in that it approaches all the instruction with how the skill sets and practice relate to preparing to shoot a 3-gun match.

"We tried to incorporate as much match footage as possible, not just to show some of the techniques under match conditions, but also as a way to say 'Thank you!' to all the match directors who put on these great matches," Jones said. "Without their venues, our video would be pretty shallow."

The video was produced by Pete Brown, the Executive Producer of *3-Gun Nation*, and contains match footage captured by the *3-Gun Nation* crew.

"We could not have done this project without the help of Pete Brown," Jones said. "We knew that, with his background producing *3-Gun Nation*, he was the perfect choice for our DVD. Overall, Rob and I are very happy with the way the DVD turned out and hope shooters find it helpful and see their scores improve at matches."

Airsoft and .22 Training

We all love burning ammo. But the cost of sending rounds downrange can get prohibitive, especially when you put in the kind of practice common to some 3-Gun Nation Pro Series shooters. To win, one has to maintain time on trigger, so something has got to give.

A growing trend among 3-gunners is to use Airsoft guns for training. Unlike the toys more commonly seen, a high-end

Airsoft trainer—conversion kits for the actual firearms used in competition—enables competitors to get a tremendous amount of time on the trigger without an over-expenditure of cash.

Inexpensive compared to centerfire ammunition, rimfire rounds provide another avenue to increase your number of good trigger pulls without spending a lot of money. A

The Noveske Shooting Team 3-Gun class prepares students to compete in a major 3-gun match—complete with walking a prize table.

recent increase in dedicated .22 uppers and complete rifles make .22 rimfire practice more popular than ever before.

"You need to practice a lot to build up muscle memory," said Keith Garcia, who is sponsored by BAM Airsoft, a company that specializes in trainers for action shooting. "I like to do a number of things. I'll dry-fire, and I practice with my Airsoft guns at home. I go to the range and do a lot of repetitions with .22 conversions just to build up those repetitions, but also to do so at a more economical cost. If you look at the cost of ammunition for your centerfire rifle or your handgun, a case of .223 would be about $300, a case of .40-caliber about $250. I can shoot 5,000 rounds through my Airsoft gun for about $20. Through my .22 conversions, a thousand rounds of ammo is about $35. All I do is take off the lowers of my competition guns and put on the conversion uppers. The guns feel the same, but now I'm shooting .22 ammo, and I can shoot that for about $.02 a round."

Regardless of whether one is practicing with an Airsoft, a .22, or their game-day equipment, the old adage remains true: practice doesn't make perfect, perfect practice makes perfect.

(left) 3-Gun definitely requires some training and practice, as you never know what you will face next.

(right) With conversion kits and dedicated .22 rifles and pistols that feel like their bigger brothers, .22 rimfire can provide excellent training at reduced cost.

"For me, the key is consistency," Garcia said. "You want to do one thing every day to improve your shooting. That's the way you're going to get good."

Physical Fitness

The final point I'll make about 3-gun training regards physical fitness. A 3-gun major takes three days to complete. Range days have long hours, sometimes in less than pleasant weather conditions, where you'll be shooting targets, setting steel, and traversing, with a considerable amount of gear, over a large expanse of territory—especially when talking about natural terrain matches. By the end of the weekend, a major Outlaw match can really take its toll.

This is a game of both speed and stamina. Speed is exhibited on the stages themselves, and it takes stamina, not necessarily to make it through an event, but to maintain the highest level of performance possible over an extended period of time.

While there are some larger folks out there who can still out-shoot most of the field after a lot of years in this game, the majority of wins seem to go to competitors who are younger, faster, and stronger. That said, it absolutely pays to work on being in the best shape you can be, regardless your age or years of experience.

A group of students works on pistol fundamentals under the watchful eye of instructors. Academy training is a great way to learn the basics of good shooting.

Yamil R. Sued photo

CHAPTER 13

A Nation of 3-Gunners: 3-GUN NATION

While the sport of 3-gun had been branching out and growing since the original SOF match, in 1980, the idea for a national points series, unbeknownst to the principals at *3-Gun Nation*, had been building through the mid- to late 2000s. Mostly among competitors and a few match directors, talk had been bubbling around the idea of some loosely formed affiliation and points series that would tie all the Outlaw 3-gun majors together, name champions in each division, and distribute prizes.

Yamil R. Sued photo

Around that same time, I was in the middle of my career with the National Rifle Association, where I'd worked up to the position of Managing Editor at *American Rifleman*. Along with various duties on the magazine, I eventually assumed a key role on *American Rifleman Television*.

As I began wading into the process of doing what I could to improve NRA's signature television show, a new production company came in to shoot, coproduce, and edit the show—Boss Productions. It was a stroke of luck, for me, for it was then that Pete Brown and I got teamed up for the first time, and we went to work improving *ARTV*. He and I thought a lot alike, with regards to what was good and what was terrible in outdoor television production. Though we had no budget to improve things in the way we really wanted, we nevertheless did what we could. In short order and, to be fair, with a lot of hard work from the entire staff at *Rifleman*, NRA Pubs, and other team members at BOSS, *ARTV* turned a corner; Pete's efforts in production quickly earned the show two Golden

Yamil R. Sued photo

Moose Awards for excellence from Outdoor Channel.

Because of our work for NRA, at different times, Pete and I were both exposed to 3-gun. Ironically, the DPMS Tri-Gun was the match that likely made the biggest impact on both of us. I was lucky enough to cover the inaugural match, even shooting a few stages, for the NRA publication *Shooting Sports USA*, while Pete filmed a couple later matches for *ARTV*.

Enamored with the game, we both began to wonder why the sport of 3-gun, at least in our eyes, was marginalized within the shooting sports. To us, it was far and away the most exciting brand of shooting on the planet, and this was from two guys who had seen it all at the top levels: Bianchi Cup, Camp Perry, USPSA Pistol, IDPA, clay sports, and on and on. While many of these disciplines enjoyed aspects of what was seen in 3-gun, no shooting sport put it all together and delivered the sport of action shooting quite like 3-gun.

Then, in 2008, during a long road trip from Portland to Bend, Oregon, to film for *ARTV*, we finally put the idea together: take the tournament formula

Yamil R. Sued photo

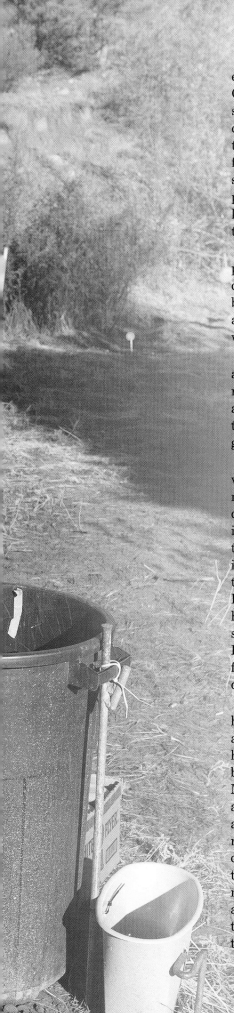

established by BASS and FLW Outdoors and replicate it in the sport of 3-gun. It was really quite a simple plan. We'd take the best shooters in the world, face them off head-to-head in some type of exciting fashion, put a bunch of money on the line, and then look out, because the fireworks would start!

In short order we put pen to paper, forming the original concepts of what would ultimately become the 3-Gun Nation Tour and the television show that would launch it, *3-Gun Nation*.

With our concept formulated and some basic marketing materials created, in 2009, we began actively searching for the one thing we desperately needed to get started—a sponsor.

The first person I turned to was Randy Luth at DPMS, a natural choice for all he and his company had done for the sport in recent years. But we were too late. Had we developed the idea a year or two sooner, prior to Luth selling his company, DPMS quite possibly would have been the original title sponsor for the show and tour. But things had changed, and for whatever reasons, it just didn't happen.

Next, I found what I would have presumed to be an unlikely ally in SureFire. While on a hog hunting trip, in Texas, I sat in a box blind with SureFire's Derek McDonald. For hours, we talked about 3-gun and what a show about the sport, if done correctly, could do for shooting, the competitors, and the companies that supported them all. Many months later, Pete and I sat in a meeting with Derek and his team, selling them on the idea that would later become *3GN*.

Meanwhile, Pete had estab-lished a solid contact at FNH USA and, over the course of several months, found his way to Ken Pfau. That's when everything changed. While I had worked with FN for several years during my time with the NRA, I'd worked mainly with the PR firm that handled the account, and I couldn't fathom that FN had the level of support for the sport that we needed to launch our project—and I couldn't have been more wrong about that. After many months of talks, ideas, and back and forth, at the SHOT Show 2010, just two months prior to the Superstition Mountain Mystery 3-Gun major match and the launch of 3GN, Pete and I shook hands with Pfau. FNH USA had agreed to become the title sponsor of *3-Gun Nation*. In short order, Pete and I founded a company and named it the National 3-Gun Association.

That same week, meetings with SureFire (little did I know then how important that conversation while hog hunting had turned out to be, for our association with SureFire gave us immediate access to its pro shooters Barry Dueck and Mike Voigt, whose competitive experience would prove invaluable, as we planned the first *3GN* season), Federal's Jason Nash and Kyle Tengwall, and Brownells' Larry Weeks, the companies that, along with FNH USA, became the original four sponsors and ensured we had the minimum amount of support to launch our endeavor. Soon after, FNH rallied support from Leupold Tactical Optics as well, including its amazing $25,000 grand prize to the 3GN Champion, and the 3-Gun Nation Tour was born.

CHAPTER 14

MAKE IT OR BREAK IT The Inaugural 3-Gun Season

We debuted at one of the most respected, well-known 3-gun venues in the country, the 2010 Superstition Mountain Mystery 3-Gun. I'll never forget that week, as we witnessed the full gamut of reactions to the signage and the buzz we'd created, while we set up for that first event. A few were truly excited about the prize money and the television coverage and welcomed us with open arms, but many more weren't quite sure what to think of us. Some were even dismissive, and, in defense of those skeptics, there had been failed attempts in the past by other groups to take 3-gun "mainstream" and the like. Their mistrust of this new media company invading something they all held so dear wasn't completely unfounded.

Many there that first event told us we put on a good show. With a crew of videographers larger than most outdoor television shows ever bring to a competition, we at least *looked* the part. In truth, we were a disorganized mess, and we had no clue about what we really needed to do to capture the story of 3-gun.

The 3GN Shoot-Off, the signature stage we used to culminate each event, was (luckily) another matter. In FNH USA, we had found Tommy Thacker, who proved worth his weight in gold that first season and beyond. A veteran pistol and 3-gun competitor, Tommy helped us develop a solid plan based on other competitions he'd been to over the years. What we came up with was to take the top eight competitors from several very different equipment divisions, use sponsors' guns to level the playing field, and put them through an exciting man-on-man format, with cash for the winners. MGM Targets' Travis Gibson stepped in and offered immense help, creating with Tommy the 3GN Shoot-Off course of fire.

Superstition Mountain Mystery 3-Gun 2010

Game day arrived. The MGM steel was set, Pete and his camera guys were geared up, sponsor guns and ammo were positioned and ready, and I took the microphone before a very reserved crowd and called out the very first 3GN Final 8: Mike Voigt, Taran Butler, Patrick Kelley, Glenn Shelby, Chris Sechiatano, Keith Garcia, Adam Popplewell, and Benny Hill. The group represented an extremely talented, experienced collection of 3-gunners, with Voigt and Butler delivering some decided star power.

In the very first bout of the 3GN Shoot-Off, I'm sure nearly everyone expected Taran Butler, one of the best 3-gunners in the game, to wipe the floor with Patrick Kelley. But they would be wrong. In a thrilling display, Kelley rocked the rifle, standing off the barricade to take down a six-plate MGM plate rack, before he then destroyed the shotgun array, and was solid enough on the pistol to hold off a late charge by Butler. The crowd *erupted* into sound at what was an exciting and entertaining upset of Kelley over Butler. From my point of view, watching the reactions of the crowd and seeing the people come to life, finally responding to the atmosphere of the moment, that first run was indeed seminal for 3GN. For in front of a very partial 3-gun crowd made up of all levels of 3-gun experience, the Shoot-Off was delivering—the first hook had been set.

Ultimately, that first event belonged to Keith Garcia, a law enforcement professional from California, and a sponsored shooter for Practical Shooting Academy and others. Garcia ran though some heavy hitters that day, eliminating Adam Popplewell and Patrick Kelley before facing off against uber-champion Mike Voigt in the finals.

Garcia was solid on the rifle, laid down a smoking shotgun run, and finished strong on the pistol to knock over the crossover stop plate first and win the inaugural 3GN Shoot-Off and $5,000 from U.S. P.A.L.M.

"I got to the shotgun and laid down what I thought was a pretty good run, and then I got to the handgun just a little bit before Voigt, and luckily the handgun came together for me," Garcia said following his win. "It's a good feeling. I just have to thank FN, SureFire, and all the other sponsors. It was a well-

Keith Garcia celebrates after winning the first 3GN Shoot-Off at Superstition Mountain Mystery 3-Gun, in 2010.

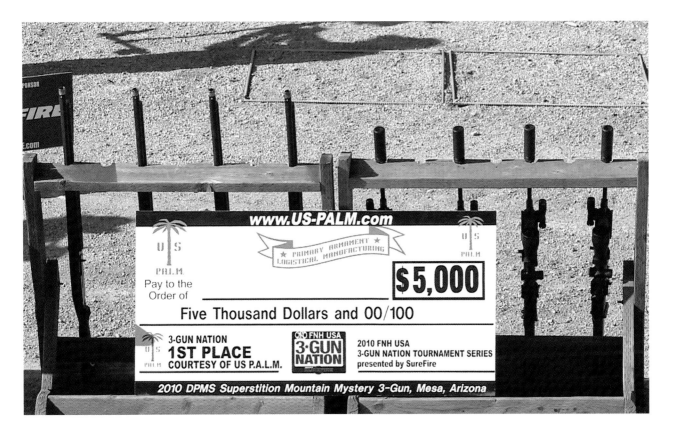

The first check presented by 3-Gun Nation at the inaugural 3GN Shoot-Off following the 2010 Superstition Mountain Mystery 3-Gun.

run event. The Shoot-Off format is awesome, and Team FN was very gracious. The sport of 3-gun is going to explode as a result of this. The publicity, the notoriety, these great Shoot-Offs—people are going to get excited. And I'm going to have to go train more, because now we're going to get a lot of new shooters to 3-gun and I'm going to get beat!"

Prior to winning that first Shoot-Off, Garcia was already a known, established shooter within practical shooting. Yet, in talking with him months after that first event, we were both in a little bit of awe at the first proof of what I like to refer to as the "3GN Effect."

"There is no denying that getting name recognition through the Shoot-Off and the TV show has helped me attract new sponsors," Garcia said. "Great companies like JP Rifles, Hornady, Swarovski, Tactical Solutions, Warne Scope Mounts, and BAM Airsoft have given me the chance to represent their products."

It didn't take long, maybe even before any of us at 3GN, for Garcia to understand what winning the Shoot-Off could do for his already promising competition career. Arguably his finest finish to date in a major 3-gun competition, the impact on Garcia was clear just moments after holding the first "3GN Big Check."

"The money, the publicity, and this new tournament style are going to be a big plus for everybody involved in shooting," Garcia said. "In this case, it was a big plus for me, not only because of the prize money, but also because I'm able to represent my sponsors in front of a bigger audience."

Fortunately, that first final eight featured some phenomenal shooters, and there were dominating performances, lots of high-level shooting on display, and, maybe most importantly, an upset or two. Of the upsets, none were more pivotal than Kelley's win over Butler. In that one run, a likeable dark horse 3-gunner, at least for TV, was found in Kelley, the non-sponsored veteran competitor who shoots what some would consider to be a marginal division—Heavy Metal. That Butler, who had the most dominating season in all the sport through much of 2010, could possibly go down in the first round—well, that established this format as something you just had to watch.

Blue Ridge Mountain 3-Gun 2010

One month after the success that was Superstition, potential disaster came at Blue Ridge

Mountain 3-Gun. At the beginning of the match, it looked like anything but failure. We were blown away with how challenging and demanding—and how cool—Andy Horner's stage designs were that first year we were at Blue Ridge. They had it all—difficult natural terrain, obstacles, high round-count stages, woods runs—you name it, Andy had found a way to truly push the competitors.

The first day of filming at Blue Ridge went well, really well. But the next morning brought a challenge none of us at 3GN had ever figured into the plan—dangerously bad weather. Severe thunderstorms, including tornadoes in the area, forced the cancellation of the Blue Ridge Mountain 3-Gun on day two, and only a small sample of the stages were completed.

For the competitors, this was a tough break, as many had spent a lot of money in match fees and travel, taken time away from work and family, and now their match was done. But, for us and the fledgling *3GN*, an unfinished match represented a world of problems. How would we give series points to the competitors? How could we determine the top eight competitors for a Shoot-Off? These were questions we didn't have immediate answers to, but, even worse, if the weather didn't break, and we couldn't get those things done, what in the hell were we going to do about it?

"Once that weather rolled in, we had to make a decision about what to do with the match," Horner said. "An option was to attempt to finish the match on Sunday, but it would have been midnight before the awards were completed. Therefore, we made a decision to call off the scored portion of the match and shoot for fun on Sunday. With the tornado warnings, severe thunderstorms, hail, and lightening, it was just too dangerous to continue Saturday afternoon."

After a long Saturday evening full of heated debate, where we listened to the opinions of a few key veteran competitors, match director Andy Horner, and the concerns from our sponsors, Pete and I basically locked ourselves in a room and pounded out a solution: it would be a random draw for 32 slots, with the field chosen from anyone who had notched a top 10 finish on any stage. The expanded field ensured at least a few top shooters would get into the mix, while the random draw served as the best plan we could arrive at since none of the squads had shot the same stages and there couldn't be any match leaders established, much less any winners.

Sunday morning broke warm, sunny, and clear, a gorgeous Kentucky spring day—and an absolute God-send, considering how contentious the previous night's debates had been. It was a good day for the largest shoot-off in the history of the sport, put on by *3GN* in only our second event!

After scrambling to come up with a bracket, set the stage, and even a frantic last-minute search to ensure we had enough ammo to run the sponsor guns (remember, we'd originally planned for an eight-man shoot-off), 32 competitors, including two women, stepped to the firing line that morning. And, just as it had been with Superstition, the level of competition, the drama that unfolded with the ebb and flow of each run, the dominating performances, the upsets—all

put on another amazing show of shooting and sportsmanship. Once again, the sport of 3-gun had delivered.

In the end, Taran Butler defeated Erik Lund to take home $5,000 from Leupold Tactical Optics. Competing in his second consecutive 3GN Shoot-Off, Butler seemed determined to fare better than his one-and-done finish at the Superstition Mountain Mystery 3-Gun that past

March. Lund, meanwhile, had looked equally dominant in his four wins, as he'd advanced past James Phelps, Joe Wong, Larry Toney, and Jason Wong in route to the finals.

But Butler, who took out Robert Romero, Adam Popplewell, John Bagakis, and James Darst, found his rhythm first in the final Shoot-Off against Lund, finishing off the rifle plates with a comfortable lead. Meanwhile, Lund accelerated through the shotgun plates, broke two clay birds, and closed the distance, as he headed into the final pistol targets. Ultimately, Butler's lead proved to be too much, as he cleaned his pistol rack and was first to knock down the crossover stop plate, earning him his first win 3-Gun Nation Tour win.

While Butler was well on his way to earning a spot in 3-Gun Nation's traditional eight-man shoot-off, the severe weather that rolled into the area had two interesting effects: First, it regrettably cancelled the match. Second, it propelled a whole cast of competitors—shooters who might otherwise not have qualified—into the 3GN Shoot-Off.

Taran Butler celebrates winning the unprecedented 32-man 3GN Shoot-Off at Blue Ridge Mountain 3-Gun in 2010.

The result was an intriguing mix of big-name pros, non-sponsored shooters, family members, and even one of the Blue Ridge range officers, Bryan Ray, a local shooter from nearby Elizabethtown. The draw also provided the first two women to make a 3GN Shoot-Off, DPMS shooter Deb Cheek and FNH USA's Tasha Hanish. A pair of family members, Jason Wong and his uncle and shooting mentor, Joe Wong, represented JP Rifles.

The "Joes," or unheralded, non-sponsored shooters, held their ground against some of the best pros in practical shooting, with North Carolina native Alex Hawkins and Kentucky's Bryan Ray delivering especially strong showings. In the second round, Hawkins shot well, pushing Mark Hanish to the end, while Ray was extremely vivid, notching wins over Matt Hood and Jamie Foote before falling to DPMS' James Darst on a foot fault. Amazingly, he was leading the veteran Darst through the shotgun portion when the fault was called. (And, despite that loss, Ray would in very short order go from unknown to 3-gun household name by winning the Heavy Metal division at successive matches and competing in future 3GN Shoot-Offs.)

The ladies also held their own, and though neither Deb Cheek nor Tasha Hanish were able to notch a first-round win, each pushed a couple 3-gun veterans to the limit. In fact, Cheek laid down an impressive rifle rack, before her opponent Adam Popplewell was granted a re-shoot due to an optic getting knocked out of alignment. And, after Hanish started slowly during her rifle run, she found a groove and made a mad dash to run down R&R Racing's Robert Wright, coming up just short.

Ultimately, the day belonged to Taran Butler, who shot extremely well over the entire weekend, a fact not lost on the crowd of spectators and shooters present during the drawing. The last name pulled for the Shoot-Off, with it an audible moan was heard throughout the crowd, as all recognized what Butler's presence meant for the competitors—it was game on.

"I'm glad I was in a position to get in the drawing, when the match points concluded on Saturday," Butler said. "The Shoot-Off went better than I could have dreamed. If you can stay smooth and not get ahead of yourself, you can cruise and still win."

Midwest 3-Gun Championship 2010

Two major matches down, and here came the third, where rain and mud were the themes again, as the 2010 3-Gun Nation Tour moved onto to Fayette, Missouri, for the FNH USA Midwest 3-Gun Championship. The second now common sight was the performance of Taran Butler, who won Tactical Optics in a 3GN-Affiliated match for the third consecutive time to qualify for yet another 3GN Shoot-Off. Basically, everywhere we had been in 2010 at this point, Butler was there making noise in the Shoot-Off.

This time, though, Rob Romero, who Butler had knocked out at Blue Ridge, was waiting and motivated to have a better showing than he'd had in Kentucky. Romero had a tough road to the finals, drawing veteran 3-gunner Kurt Miller in the first round, but moving on and taking out Glenn Shelby in the semi-finals. Then Romero gained a measure of payback in the finals, upsetting the vaunted Butler for a 3GN Shoot-Off win and a check for $5,000 from FNH USA.

"The reason I got into this sport, I was watching professional shooters on TV one night, and I said 'I got to try it,'" Romero told me. "I've always been into guns, but I've never had a sport that I could actually come out and try. Seeing those guys on TV, Taran and Kurt and Miculek, that was the real appeal. And being able to rub shoulders with them on these big stages? To me it's a big accomplishment for them to even know who I am."

While Romero's upset of Butler in the finals was big, what turned out to be one of 3GN's early signature moments came in the first-round match-up between Butler and legendary 3-gunner Jerry Miculek. At this point in 3GN's short history, we had already seen some amazing runs by top shooters. Mike Voigt had made a run into the finals at Superstition, and Butler already had his first 3GN win. But when Butler squared off against Miculek, 3GN had its first true "wow" moment.

It was quite amazing, that period of time leading up to the run. From the moment they drew each other for the first round match-up, to when they walked to the firing line and prepped their guns before stepping into the start box, the entire atmosphere on the range changed. The crowd seemed to be suddenly charged with electricity, and there was a rising hiss of excitement as the moment drew near.

To the delight of the crowd, the two titans of practical shoot-

FNH USA
WWW.FNHUSA.COM

DISTINCT ADVANTAGE

$5,000

ROB ROMERO

Pay to the Order Of

Five Thousand Dollars and 00/100

3-GUN NATION
1ST PLACE
COURTESY OF FNH

2010 FNH USA
3-GUN NATION
TOURNAMENT SERIES
PRESENTED BY SUREFIRE

2010 FNH USA MIDWEST 3-GUN CHAMPIONSHIPS, FAYETTE, MO.

ing were dead even coming out of the rifle portion of the Shoot-Off, before Miculek surprisingly opened the door during the shotgun run, and Butler laid down a blistering pistol rack to seal the victory.

"I think he's done stuff that no one will ever do on this planet," Butler said. "Jerry is obviously the best revolver guy ever, and he shoots semi-automatics fantastically, too. Plus, he does some wild, amazing trick shooting that no one will ever duplicate—you can try all day long, and it ain't gonna happen. So he's going to go down in history as an epic, one-of-a-kind shooter of all-time."

MGM Ironman 2010

In June, the fourth stop on the inaugural 3GN Tour landed at what has to be the most unique event in all of 3-gun— the MGM Ironman. Aptly

named, the Ironman is a grueling test of everything that can possibly break—be it physical, mechanical, or psychological. The insanely high round counts, in a harsh environment made more extreme by wind and a fine, gritty sand, tests your body, your gear, and your mind. In many ways, winning Ironman isn't about being the best shooter, it's the one who best survives the challenge presented.

In 2010, that person was unequivocally Team FNH USA's Dave Neth, who showed a singular determination at that event, one driven by a unique situation just starting to take hold. By Ironman, the first opening was presented that might possibly show the effect *3-Gun Nation* might be having. Because Ironman was the first event that hadn't already been sold out at the time of *3GN's* debut at Superstition, within a matter

Rob Romero celebrates his 3GN Shoot-Off win following the 2010 FNH USA Midwest 3-Gun.

of time after that Superstition, competitors got a chance to see what *3GN* was and the prize money on the line. Once they did, a wave of top sponsored shooters signed up for Ironman. Seemingly overnight, the talent pool got deeper, and Dave Neth was suddenly very aware that it was going to be more difficult for the local competitor to claim what had become his "home" match.

But Neth was on absolute fire that weekend, and the seven-time Ironman champion took high law enforcement honors and won the Tactical Optics division, before rounding out the weekend with the 3GN Shoot-Off victory. With his son and father among a crowd full of friends and other locals who cheered spiritedly for Idaho native Neth, a fan favorite,

Dave Neth and his son celebrate his 3GN Shoot-Off win in front of a home Idaho crowd at the 2010 MGM Ironman.

the champion shooter defeated John Bagakis and Mike Voigt, before cruising to victory in the finals over Chuck Anderson to win the check for $5,000 from Warne Scope Mounts.

"It was huge," Neth said of the win. "Having my little boy there helping out all weekend, and having him watch it—that was better than anything, to be able to have my dad and my son there. Three generations of sportsmen and shooters, now that was fantastic."

With his son, Riley, at his side all weekend resetting steel, pasting targets, and grabbing gear, the veteran 3-gunner was forced to complete extra stages on Thursday and Friday in order to finish the match and report to work early Saturday morning. A couple hours after his shift ended, Neth battled the likes of Bagakis and 10-time USPSA Multi-Gun National Champion Voigt, before the final showdown with Anderson.

There were also a couple cool "firsts" at Ironman, as the first active duty U.S. military member and first junior qualified for a 3GN Shoot-Off. Ben Fortin, an Army sergeant first class out of Fort Campbell, Kentucky, squared off against 17-year-old Kyle Jameson. Qualifying out of the Limited division, Kyle narrowly won the division, beating out the second-place finisher, his father, Kirk Jameson.

Rocky Mountain, Robby Johnson, and the Return of Daniel Horner

There were a lot of great storylines throughout the debut season of 3GN, and even more great shooting by some amazing competitors. But there was one noticeable absence in the sport.

Regarded as the most dominant competitor in the game, Daniel Horner, along with much of his U.S. Army Marksmanship Unit Action Shooting Team, had missed the entire 2010 shooting season to this point while deployed to Afghanistan. As such, there was a feeling out there that a lot of *different* competitors were winning 3GN Shoot-Offs, and that was great, but it would soon be over when Horner stepped back onto the line.

Horner made his return in August at the Rocky Mountain 3-Gun, an amazing natural terrain course of fire that challenges competitors with elevation, terrain, and lots of difficult rifle shooting—all elements tailor made for the skill set of one Daniel Horner. Still, with a layoff of several months while deployed, competitors didn't know quite what to expect of Horner's return. They didn't have long to find out. Any rust that might have existed was quickly dusted off, as Horner dominated the field to win Tactical Optics and qualify for his first 3GN Shoot-Off. But then, in the first round, an amazing thing happened.

Of all the people he could have drawn, Horner pulled former Army Marksmanship Unit teammate and friend Robby Johnson, now shooting for Remington. On any other weekend it would

have been a remarkable coincidence (though certainly not completely unexpected in a field limited to just eight competitors). But, this was no ordinary shooting weekend for Horner and Johnson. Beyond Horner's return from deployment, beyond his return to 3-gun, tragedy had struck the AMU family. It was this weekend where both had just learned of the death of one of their former AMU teammates, Army Ranger Master Sgt. Jared N. Van Aalst, who was killed in action only days before, in Afghanistan. It should go without saying that the emotions were running understandably high for each of the competitors that day. For Johnson, he took tragedy and turned it into a slice of triumph and claimed his first 3GN victory.

"I got a call first thing Thursday morning about my friend

Jared N. Van Aalst, who was killed in action," Johnson said. "It was very tough to think about the match, but I had a lot of friends and supporters call me. Jared was a competition shooter at heart and an AMU guy, and he taught me a lot about shooting. It was cool to give it my best effort and come out on top and dedicate the win to him."

In that opening round matchup, at the buzzer it was Horner who was first to the rifle position, yet he struggled to stay steady from a standing position against the barricade. Meanwhile, Johnson, a former Army Ranger sniper, went one-for-one through five of six rifle plates

Robby Johnson took home $5,000 from Safariland for his 3GN Shoot-Off win following the 2010 Rocky Mountain 3-Gun.

to establish a comfortable lead through the shotgun portion of the Shoot-Off. Although Horner accelerated through the shotgun poppers and pistol rack, the lead was too much to overcome, as Johnson stayed smooth to the stop plate.

"He does a lot for the Army and the AMU," Johnson said of Horner following the event. "He was almost Soldier of the Year. We kind of clicked the whole time we were in. We got super close and we still talk on the phone all the time. I try to shoot with him as much as I can to get as many pointers as I can. It's a friendship I'll have for life."

With Horner eliminated, and despite Johnson's win, the consensus favorite now seemed to be Shoot-Off specialist Jerry Miculek, who had cruised to comfortable wins in his first two match-ups, knocking off Burton Thompson and Craig Underdown. However, after out-shooting Horner, Johnson remained steady and defeated Eric Miller to set up a finals showdown versus Miculek.

"The whole time, I thought to myself that there was no shame in getting beat by Jerry, but the competitive spirit in me ... I just went out and gave it everything I had, I wasn't going to give it to him," Johnson said.

Nor would the elder statesman of 3-gun, who seemed extremely focused after a first-round exit to Taran Butler in his previous 3GN Shoot-Off. But, after shooting the second of the two semi-final match-ups, and with little break before the finals, Miculek was clearly winded, as the 6,500-plus feet above sea level seemed to take its toll on the Louisiana native. As such, Miculek struggled to

settle in at the rifle barricade, while Johnson easily pulled to the early lead. Similar to the Horner match-up, Miculek mowed through the shotgun poppers at an intense rate, but it wasn't enough. Johnson kept his composure and cleaned the pistol rack to the stop plate and the victory, along with $5,000 from Safariland.

"With Jerry, there was a lot of pressure, because it was the last match, the money was on the line, and I was going against the best Shoot-Off guy in the world," Johnson said. "I knew I had to go for it, because I wasn't going to win going slow."

For 3GN, the result was yet another exciting, high-drama finish featuring the top athletes in the sport. With the inaugural season winding down, there was some clear momentum, and high expectations, heading into the final weekend of the 3GN season—the USPSA Multi-Gun Nationals, followed the by $40,000 3-Gun Nation Championship!

USPSA Multi-Gun Nationals & 3-Gun Nation Title 2010

At USPSA Multi-Gun Nationals, 3GN threw its first curve ball to the sport since its debut at Superstition earlier in the season. It was a pitch that became a bit controversial with some competitors, but nevertheless created tremendous excitement.

The controversy surrounded 3GN's decision to offer 10 Wild Card slots for competitors at USPSA Multi-Gun Nationals. For those who had been chasing 3GN points all season, some eyebrows were raised. But, from our point of view at 3GN, there were several reasons for opening up the qualification a bit.

For starters, the 2010 3-Gun Nation Tour hadn't been announced until a few weeks after SHOT Show that year, which allowed very little time before the first match of the season, Superstition Mountain. By that time, most of the competitors had much, if not all, of their entire 3-gun season already planned. Match entries had been sent, time had been taken off work, and travel plans had been booked. So, the timing of everything left those of us at 3GN feeling as though not everyone had received a fair shot at attending enough qualifying matches that first season. Right or wrong, that was our perception that year.

Another reason we opened up those slot was because USPSA had agreed to host the first 3GN Championship, an event that would be held in conjunction with the Multi-Gun Nationals, in Las Vegas. Throughout the season, each match that partnered with 3-Gun Nation hosted a 3GN Shoot-Off, giving top shooters an additional and large cash incentive to shoot that particular match. While 3GN didn't have a plan for the USPSA Nationals, then USPSA President Mike Voigt pushed hard for us to find a way to more fully include their match into the mix, and we accepted the challenge.

Finally, there was the issue of Daniel Horner and the other members of the U.S. Army Marksmanship Unit. Deployed for much of the 2010 3-gun season, it was mathematically impossible for those shooters to qualify for the 2010 3GN Championship upon their return from Afghanistan. Some felt, and complained mightily in public forums, that we put the Wild

Card slots on the line just so Horner would have the opportunity to shoot his way into the 3GN Championship. That was partially true. In fact, we never shied away from admitting that wanting Horner in the championships played a part in the decision. But beyond that, we recognized that deployed active duty soldiers then, as they do now, get a pass on certain aspects of our qualification processes. Still, while Horner (and now even teammate Tyler Payne), is unquestionably at the top of the sport, some felt and still do feel our decisions amounted to preferential treatment. Well, maybe it is. But for those who serve, that seemed right to us.

Regardless how anyone felt about Wild Cards that first season, their presence had an obvious effect on the 3GN Cham-

pionship. Along with Horner, past 3GN Shoot-Off winner Rob Romero and USPSA Nationals Champion Ted Puente shot their way into the big show and then placed high enough in the four-stage 3GN Championship match to earn a slot in the Final 16.

As talented as the entire top-tier field was, all eyes were on Horner once he'd qualified into the Shoot-Off. Early on, he'd looked predictably unstoppable, with dominating wins over veterans Kerry Dematos and Tony Holmes, which set up a semi-finals match-up with Ironman 3GN Shoot-Off winner Dave Neth.

But, Neth was equally impressive in his first two runs, knocking out Ty Gentry and SureFire's Barry Dueck, seemingly recapturing the same rhythm and pace he'd set in Parma to win $5,000 in June.

As Horner and Net stepped to the line in the finals, one could feel a shift in the atmosphere. The crowd seemed to sense what was coming. Two confident, athletic shooters, who were both clearly in the "zone," were about to square off. Without a doubt, this was going to be the most exciting run of the 2010 3GN Tour.

At the horn, each man exploded out of the start box, reaching the rifle barricade in step and each dropping into a reverse-kneeling position. Horner's trigger broke first, instantly followed by Neth's, a distinct "pop-pop" cadence that continued throughout the rifle plate, with each firing SCARs to knock down the 100-yard targets in turn.

Few competitors were as dialed in as Dave Neth, during the 2010 3GN Championship Shoot-Off.

U.S. Army Marksmanship Unit's
Daniel Horner celebrates winning
the inaugural 3GN Championship, in
2010, along with a $25,000 payday
from Leupold Tactical Optics.

"I got into the rifle position
and shot the best I'd shot so far
and thought I was ahead. Then
I looked up, and he was already
finished and I thought I better
go faster," Horner said. "It's a
blast out here competing with
people. Guys like Dave, you can't
ask for better. This is a blast!"

Horner's half-count of a lead
evaporated at the shotgun
position, when both men simultaneously grabbed their SLP
shotguns and ripped through the
five poppers and two clays before
grounding the shotgun and
sprinting to the pistol rack.

Here again, as each com-
petitor hammered away with an
FNX 9, they went shot for shot
through the pistol rack. Finally,
the crowd rose to its feet, just as
Horner accelerated through the
cross-over stop plate, sending it

down an instant before Neth's
fell in turn. It was an amazing
run by both competitors.

"My run was good—even
perfect—I wouldn't take it back,"

Neth said. "But I can't feel bad
losing to Daniel Horner."

In a season of many firsts, the
Horner/Neth run provided the
most overwhelming "wow" mo-

(l. to r.) Bruce
Piatt, Daniel Horner
and Dave Neth took
home the big prizes
following the first
3GN Championship,
in 2010.

(above) Dave Neth became the first repeat winner in the 3GN Shoot-Off after his 3rd place finish in the 2010 3GN Championship Shoot-Off.

(right) Bruce Piatt's 2010 3GN Championship Shoot-Off run ended in a second place finish and a $10,000 payday from U.S. PALM.

ment thus far for 3-Gun Nation. More so than ever before, two competitors who were clearly firing on all cylinders, two outstanding, veteran competitors, stepped to the firing line with an immense sense of anticipation had hung over the crowd. The entire crowd just seemed to *know* something special was about to happen.

"We all knew what it took to make those shots," said Miller. "And that's why everybody was just in awe. Their run represents the pinnacle of what we all strive to do, and we saw it from both of them, at the same time, and on the same stage. And it was awesome. That's why everybody just went nuts, because everybody understood what they had just seen."

Over the course of two 3GN seasons, across 13 different Shoot-Off events, and with hundreds of individual bouts now in the books, the 2010 Horner/Neth run still ranks as my favorite. It had it all—two top flight shooters, expectations from a very enthused crowd, a tremendous amount at stake, and both shooters stepping to the line with uncommon focus and will. They both flat-out laid it down, and the result was nothing short of epic. The only thing that could have possibly made the run any better was if it had been for all the money and the title of 3GN Champion.

This is not to say the remaining semi-final match-up lacked drama or interest. Instead, it featured two 3-gun veterans and Shoot-Off specialists, Jerry Miculek and Bruce Piatt. Miculek had advanced to the semis with a first-round win over Kalani Laker, before go-

ing on to knock out the AMU's Tyler Payne. Meanwhile, Piatt had been forced to work his way through a figurative "murderer's row" of heavy hitters. After taking out veteran 3-gunner Kurt Miller in the first round, Piatt next faced Taran Butler, who was on everyone's short list to potentially win the title. But Piatt stayed measured during the rifle position, got his hits, and held on as Butler got fast on the trigger and tried to run him down during the shotgun and pistol positions.

"I knew I was leaving the rifle ahead of him, because I heard him still shooting," Piatt said. "I went faster than I wanted to on the shotgun, and I kept missing a plate on the pistol, which put me in panic mode. I had to settle back down, and once I did, was able to pull through."

After losing their semi-final match-ups, Miculek and Neth regrouped and toed the line to square off once more to determine the third-place winner, which included $5,000 on the line from Timney Triggers. Neth maintained much of the speed he'd showcased against Horner, cruising to the win and becoming the first repeat winner on the 3GN Tour.

"I got what I earned," Miculek said, congratulating Neth. "Dave shot a good one."

Piatt's run through the 3GN Championship Shoot-Off marked was one of consistency, as the veteran shoot-off competitor was deliberate on the rifle, fast on the shotgun, and smooth on the pistol. With consecutive wins over Miller, Butler, and Miculek, Piatt had proven to be a giant killer. But on this day, Horner, regarded as America's

best 3-gunner, was too much for anyone to overcome.

Horner cruised to a dominating win, becoming the first competitor to claim the title 3-Gun Nation Champion and taking home the largest payday in the history of 3-gun—$25,000 from Leupold Tactical Optics. For his second place finish, Piatt earned a $10,000 check from U.S. P.A.L.M.

But, the night belonged to Horner. Upon defeating Piatt, the often reserved and cool competitor thrust his fists skyward, followed by a smile that lit up the Nevada desert.

"Sixteen shooters for $25,000, if that doesn't get you fired up, I don't know what will," said Kevin Trepa, Vice President Tactical Sales & Marketing for Leupold Tactical, during the check presentation. "We are real proud to be a part of this and hope this becomes something that's an annual fixture."

"I'd like to thank all the sponsors and staff that made this event happen, and to the Army for letting me be here," said Horner, following his historic win.

Ozark 3-Gun Championship 2010

Only two weeks after Horner's amazing run through the USPSA Multi-Gun Nationals to secure a Wild Card slot, after finishing first in the 3GN Championship match to earn the top seed in the Shoot-Off, and after running the table there to become the inaugural 3GN Champion, it was time to start all over again. In what felt like a matter of minutes between events, the 3GN Tour was off again, this time heading to Osage, Missouri, at the Lake of the Ozarks for the Ozark 3-Gun Championship.

The Ozark presented yet another natural terrain course of fire over the Missouri foothills, challenging competitors with small, knock-over steel pistol targets, a massive round-count shotgun stage, and lots of movement over rolling terrain. Again Horner dominated the action, including an impressive win over Taran Butler to pick up a division win and advance into the 3GN Shoot-Off.

Horner looked as though he was having another day like the one in Las Vegas, one where nobody could possibly beat him. But, facing Rob Romero in the finals, Horner delivered what was likely his slowest 3GN Shoot-Off run since a first-round Shoot-Off loss to Robby Johnson at Rocky Mountain 3-gun. Still, Romero struggled equally on the rifle, while Horner fought to regain his composure and find his rhythm. Ultimately, Horner recovered first, leaving the rifle position before Romero and cruising for the Shoot-Off win and $5,000, courtesy of Adams Arms and Samson Manufacturing. The win ran Horner's career 3GN earnings to $30,000, not bad for two week's work.

Last Days at Fort Benning

The next event on the 2011 3GN Tour guaranteed Horner wouldn't win his third consecutive 3GN Shoot-Off, if only because he was working the match itself. That match, though no one knew it at the time, was the swan song for one of the more important 3-gun venues in the sport's history—the Fort Ben-

Daniel Horner took home $5,000 from Adams Arms and Samson Manufacturing for his 3GN Shoot-Off win following the 2010 Ozark 3-Gun Championship.

ning 3-Gun Challenge. If nothing else, this match had ushered in the major 3-gun experience east of the Mississippi.

The Fort Benning 3-Gun Challenge had held its own shoot-off during the previous year's match, but, in 2010, *3-Gun Nation* partnered with them in a co-branded event.

Maybe, one day, the Fort Benning match will return, but, if not, the 3GN Shoot-Off we shared put one hell of an exclamation point on the end of Benning's run, via the efforts of one James Darst.

Darst, a veteran 3-gunner and Open division specialist who also happens to be incredibly skilled with a rifle, likely was not the overwhelming favorite in the final Shoot-Off field of eight. This field had Rob Romero, a past 3GN Shoot-Off winner and one of the rising starts in 3-gun, as well as Taran Butler, one of the most dominant shooters in the game. Greg Jordan, another rising star, was making the first of what will likely be many more 3GN Shoot-Offs, and Clint Upchurch, one of two Open shooters in the mix, was there to begin what would be an absolute breakout year for the South Carolina native. Rounding out the field were Robby Johnson, who'd won the 3GN Shoot-Off at Rocky Mountain and was ranking high on everyone's list; Bryan Ray, the non-sponsored shooter from Kentucky, who'd shown ample potential to win it all; and 14-year-old Katie Harris, who was shooting for Kurt Miller and the only clear underdog in this field.

His staunch competition wasn't to say that Darst wouldn't have been considered a threat, just, that, by now, the 3GN Shoot-Off fields seemed to be getting deeper and featuring younger and more athletic competitors than just a year before. Something was clearly changing about the face of 3-gun. Then, James Darst went out and put on what could be the most memorable individual

performance in a 3GN Shoot-Off to date, coming from behind once and holding off furious charges from two others, to win a 3GN Shoot-Off and $5,000 from the National Shooting Sports Foundation (NSSF).

Darst's remarkable run began with a first-round match-up against Rob Romero, winner of the 3GN Shoot-Off at the FNH Midwest 3-Gun, in May. At the horn, Romero exploded out of the start box and was first to the gun table, cleaning the rifle rack and building an early lead he maintained through shotgun and into the final pistol plate rack. But Romero stumbled, just slightly, missing a pistol plate. That's when Darst came roaring on by. Darst went one-for-one on the pistol rack, then missed the stop plate once before knocking it down just a fraction of a second before Romero—an incredible finish.

In the second round, it was more of the same, with Darst facing 3GN newcomer Greg Jordan, who'd qualified out of Tactical Optics. This time it was Darst who raced to the early lead, with Jordan struggling on the rifle. In a reversal, Darst then dropped one shot on the shotgun, while Jordan pushed the pace and ran the shotgun portion cleanly. Darst dropped one plate on the pistol rack, allowing Jordan to squeeze the gap, but Darst had just enough of a lead and recovered to knock over his stop plate a mere half-second before Jordan. Leaving the firing line before a roaring crowd, Darst was visibly spent.

With two narrow escapes under his belt, Darst stepped to the line for the final run against Taran Butler and opened up an early lead by cleaning the rifle plates first. Then, Butler accelerated through an amaz-

ing shotgun run, narrowing the lead to an easy closing distance going into the final pistol rack. Butler, known as one of the fastest pistol shooters in the country and owning several USPSA and IDPA titles, was now in serious contention. But Darst, known more for his rifle skills than his pistol shooting, laid down a phenomenal pistol run of his own, missing only one plate. Darst then transitioned to the stop plate first, a half-second ahead of Butler, who ripped four successive shots at his own stop plate in an effort to pound it past Darst's already moving plate. In the end, it was Darst's plate that fell first, giving the Texan his first 3GN victory.

James Darst celebrates his remarkable 3GN Shoot-Off performance following the 2010 Fort Benning 3-Gun Challenge.

(top l. to r.) The author presents James Darst with a $5,000 check from NSSF, with DPMS, Leupold Tactical Optics, SureFire, and AMU representatives.

(above) James Darst was all smiles following his 3GN Shoot-Off win.

CHAPTER 15

BACK AGAIN
3GN's Milestone Second Season

For 3-Gun Nation, the conclusion of the 3GN Shoot-Off at Fort Benning provided the first break in the action since the Superstition match some 10 months before. Over that time, 3GN had partnered with or hosted (including the 3GN Championship) nine major 3-gun matches, awarding $75,000 spread across eight different top-shelf 3-gunners. In short, we felt like we had laid the first bricks to what would become the foundation of a true professional shooting sport.

After the successful debut of the Tour and television show in 2010, and with the addition of new sponsors Cheaper Than Dirt!, Stag Arms, Ruger, and the National Shooting Sports Foundation, 3GN came into the 2011 Superstition Mountain Mystery 3-Gun ready to shake things up.

Superstition Mountain Mystery 3-Gun 2011

Two changes were top on our list. First, the 3GN Shoot-Off stage and the guns used by the competitors would be changed continuously in Season Two. This was a very important component to the shooters involved. Second, the style of the television show would now feature a select group of competitors, showing the sport through *their* eyes. This is a perspective not very important to the match itself, but paramount to the viewer at home.

One of the first competitors we chose to feature at Superstition was Keith Garcia. Our initial 3GN Shoot-Off winner, now returning to the original venue of his win, Garcia would be the first 3-gunner to have the opportunity to defend his 3GN Shoot-Off title. The only problem, if you could call it that, was that the list of competitors at the 2011 Superstition match was absolutely stacked. Suddenly, there were more top competitors fighting at the same time, at the same venue, and with more money and prizes on the line. This, *this*, was the "3GN Effect."

To imagine Garcia would repeat in this extremely deep field actually seemed a bit of a stretch going in. To complete the entire match wearing a microphone for sound, with a huge production

crew in tow recording his every move, well, that would be simply tremendous—at least to everyone except Garcia himself, that is. From the jump, Garcia exhibited swagger and confidence, and then he looked to the camera and said he was going to win.

"In 2010, everything was new, and I didn't know what to expect," Garcia said. "I love to compete, so my mind-set was just to go for broke and try to beat whoever's in front of me. In 2011, though, I knew what to expect, and that gave me confidence I could win."

After being one of four Tactical Optics competitors—from a field of nearly 200—to qualify for the Shoot-Off, Garcia made quick work of Kelly Neal, one of the more well-rounded competitors in the game. The win set up a semi-final match-up with Daniel Horner. The tension ramped up considerably for the bout.

In that match-up, each competitor laid down tremendously fast shotgun runs to pull virtually even as they headed into the rifle arrays, where Garcia pulled a full plate lead going into pistol. However, Garcia struggled to disengage the external safety on his pistol, allowing Horner to blow past him and gallop through the pistol speed plates.

It seemed Garcia's fate was sealed, but, in a rare loss of precision, Horner missed his last plate and Garcia roared past to the stop plate. Ultimately, the match-up was a full-scale roller coaster of emotion for both competitors, leaving Horner stunned and Garcia intensely animated.

"As I entered the last box to shoot the handgun, I was ahead of Daniel and I could see the victory in my grasp," Garcia said. "Unfortunately, I struggled to

get the safety off the handgun, and Daniel started shooting before I did. I started hitting the targets as fast as I could, but I knew I would be hard pressed to catch up. As I got to the stop plate, I saw him hit his a fraction before mine, and they both went down. That's when I noticed one of his poppers still up, and I realized I had won. That was a great feeling, and I reacted to that."

In the Finals, Garcia faced Taran Butler, and after battling evenly through the shotgun arrays, it was Butler who jumped out to the first lead on the rifle plates. Butler built a two-plate advantage and seemed headed for his second 3GN win, before he got hung up on and went to war with a rifle plate. That was all the opening Garcia needed. He settled in, cleaned the rifle plate rack, and outlasted Butler through the pistol poppers to nail the stop plate and the victory.

"I felt the shotgun run was one of my best ever, so I knew we would be getting to the rifle at least even," Garcia said. "I heard him start hitting plates, so I knew I was behind, but I just settled in and started taking down the plates, not thinking about what Taran was doing. When I came off the rifle, I saw he was still shooting, so, at that point, I could feel another big check in my arms!"

The victory gave Garcia his second 3-Gun Nation Shoot-Off win, the first successful defense of a title, and a cash payout of $5,000 from Gun Vault. Meanwhile, the event marked the first time 3GN had established cash payouts for the entire Shoot-Off field, with AP Custom providing another $2,400 for second-through eighth-place finishers.

Preceding the main event, *3-Gun Nation* also debuted the inaugural 3-Gun Nation Team Event, presented by Brownells. Taking the top overall Lady and Junior competitors as Team captains, and then drawing at random to complete two, three-person squads, the first 3GN Team Event featured Team Kay Miculek (Lady) versus Team Katie Harris (Junior).

Harris, who also took top Lady honors in Tactical Optics, remarkably drew two other women, FNH USA's Dianna Liedorff and Tasha Hanish, to complete her squad. Meanwhile, Team Kay was filled out with Ernie Beckwith and Chris Temple.

In this event's debut, it was all Team Katie, as the captain sprinted out to the first position and laid down a smoking shotgun run to give her team the early lead. Hanish maintained a slight edge over Miculek through the rifle, before Liedorff cruised through the pistol arrays and earned her squad the win. For their performance, each member of Team Katie received a check for $500 from Brownells.

This first Team Event set the stage for what was to come later in the 2011 season at West Virginia, when the first 3GN Lady and 3GN Junior champions would be crowned via the 3GN Shoot-Off. Staged as the first real recognition of female and junior champions on such a large scale in 3-gun, the points race to qualify for these races proved a hot topic throughout the 2011 3-gun season.

MGM Ironman 2011

In June 2011, the 3GN Tour made its second return stop, with a trip back to the MGM Ironman. And, after qualifying for the 3GN Shoot-Off once again, it looked as though we might have another successful 3GN Shoot-Off defense, this time from the hands of Dave Neth.

But this was a different Ironman for sure. For starters, Neth had scaled way back on competitive shooting, due to work demands. Second, the field was much deeper the second time around, meaning it would be tough for anyone to win. And the format of Ironman itself provided an interesting twist. To permit more competitors entry into the match, the 2011 Ironman was split into back-to-back matches. The first was held for the smaller divisions, while the second contained the larger Tactical Optics field. The impact was that half the field had three days to prepare, at least mentally, for the Shoot-Off.

The first round featured a re-match of the previous final-round bout between Chuck Anderson and Dave Neth. It was a thrilling contest, with Anderson jumping all over Neth out of the gate. He shot a phenomenal pistol run, before cleaning his rifle and holding on as Neth picked up the SLP and nearly ran him down.

"Last year, I was *completely* surprised by getting into the Shoot-Off," Anderson said. "I didn't have the chance to really think about it before having to get up and perform. This year, I had several days to think about it and strategize. While this was my second Shoot-Off to compete in, I had gotten a front row seat to the Championship Shoot-Off and the Ozark match Shoot-Off.

"Last year I had two good runs and completely fell apart on the third," he continued. "Dave Neth beat me—badly. I'm pretty sure he could have shot it left-handed and still come out on top. This year I drew him in the first round, and that was probably the most stressed out I'd been in all the match-ups. Dave was also really close to beating me in that first round, and things could have ended very differently."

But Anderson moved on, as did Daniel Horner, with a first round win over Ironman veteran Matt Burkett. The two had a competitive run going, with Horner maintaining a lead heading into the final shotgun arrays. Unfortunately, shotguns had failed to be placed in the staging boxes, the first of several dramas to unfold in one of the wildest 3GN Shoot-Offs to date. After catching their breath, the two ran the course of fire again, and Horner expanded his lead over the first run for a comfortable win.

"By the time the first round was over, I was the only one who hadn't had to reload the handgun," Anderson said. "Most of the guys fired several shots after the load. I figured that if I could just stick to using that first magazine, I'd do okay."

In the second round, Anderson took on his second consecutive local favorite, MGM's Travis Gibson, who had won Limited. Like Neth, Gibson had many supporters in the stands, making for a loud scene, as Anderson once again jumped out to a big lead with the FNS 40 pistol and cruised to the rifle and shotgun. Gibson, however, was granted a re-shoot after a shotgun malfunction, and the two stepped to the line again. Despite the tension, Anderson regained his composure and laid down yet another blistering pistol run on his way to a semi-finals win.

Often considered the top 3-gunner in the country, AMU's Daniel Horner finished the 3GN Championship Match in first place, earning the top seed in the Shoot-Off.

In the other semi-final match-up, even more drama ensued. Daniel Horner, after seeming to win his bout against Barry Dueck, was forced to step to the line again, when a late re-shoot was issued by the controlling range officer. After much discussion, Dueck's shotgun was indeed found to have malfunctioned during his run and, per 3GN rules, he was granted the reshoot.

Like Anderson before him, Horner simply walked back to the line and made a spectacular run, winning and setting up the final showdown against Anderson.

"I was actually a lot more relaxed by the final round," Anderson said. "I figured I didn't have a lot to lose going into the final round. If I got beat, I got beat by Daniel Horner, and that's something we're all used to. I think there was more pressure on him to *not* get beat by the slow fat guy."

In that final run, Horner, as expected, was good. But Chuck Anderson was nearly perfect, going one for one on eight poppers and a six-plate rack, before ripping off seven for seven on the rifle and finishing with seven clay birds and the cross-over stop plate. The pistol-heavy course of fire set up perfectly for Anderson, and he took advantage by absolutely smoking the field with the FNS 40. In turn, Anderson recorded his first 3GN Shoot-Off victory and picked up a check for $5,000 from Warne Scope Mounts.

"It's really, really similar in feel to a Glock," Anderson said of his FNH pistol. "I've been shooting Production in USPSA for the last six years, mostly with the Glock pistol. I also just ran both matches with Glock handguns. Of the eight competitors, I was the only one who primarily shoots a striker-fired gun in competition. I've been a law enforcement officer for 17 years and a firearms instructor for most of that. I tell my students every time, as long as the sights are aligned with the target when the gun fires, the bullet's going to hit the target. The FNS is no different. Line the sights up, pull the trigger 'til it goes bang, find the next target, and repeat. The FNS shot exactly where I aimed it, and the trigger was really very good for a Production firearm. I already contacted FNH this morning and told them

I'd love to buy one when they're available in the U.S."

In retrospect, the Shoot-Off at Ironman was extremely pistol heavy at 14 targets—eight poppers and a six-plate rack. On that day, with that set-up and under those conditions, many spectators walked away from the range convinced no one could have defeated Anderson.

Rocky Mountain & Ozark 3-Gun Championships 2011

By the time the 3GN Tour headed back to Raton, New Mexico, for the 2011 Rocky Mountain 3-Gun, a lot of discussion was quietly taking place regarding Daniel Horner. In terms of stages and match overalls, Horner remained as strong as ever, routinely dominating the field in Tactical Optics. But,

Daniel Horner, center, won $5,000 from Safariland following his 3GN Shoot-Off win at the 2011 Rocky Mountain 3-Gun.

in terms of 3-Gun Nation Shoot-Offs, Horner had suffered two surprising back-to-back defeats to Keith Garcia and Chuck Anderson. There was talk that maybe the field was starting to close the gap on the young Army phenom—but that's right when Horner promptly showed his teeth again.

In a thrilling final run, Horner outlasted a furious late pistol charge by Rob Romero to win an unprecedented third 3-Gun Nation Shoot-Off and a check for $5,000 from Safariland. The win at Raton ran Horner's career 3GN earnings to $36,500 over the course of single calendar year.

In that last match-up, Horner

had opened up a comfortable lead by the second rifle position, firing an FNH SCAR for the final run. Then, during the pistol arrays, Romero accelerated with the FN FNS pistol, closing ground on Horner. Ultimately, though, Horner's lead was too great. He stayed steady, got his hits, and held on for the win.

That win put to rest any back-room talk as to who was the most dominant shooter in the game. Yet, it also was made clear, again, that the face of 3-gun was changing, with strong showings by the likes of Romero, Greg Jordan, and Horner's teammate Tyler Payne faring better and better with each match-up against veterans such as Mike Voigt,

Horner defended his 3GN Shoot-Off win at Ozark in 2011, taking home another $5,000 check from Adams Arms and Samson Manufacturing.

Kurt Miller, Adam Popplewell, and others.

The following month, Horner continued his reinvigorated 3GN dominance, when the 3GN Tour returned to Missouri for the Ozark 3-Gun Championship. Horner defeated Clint Upchurch, Greg Jordan, and Rustin Bernskoetter on his way to a fourth 3GN Shoot-Off win, picking up a check for $5,000 from Adams Arms and Samson Manufacturing and running his 3GN Career earnings to $41,500—$30,000 more than the closest competitor.

That event also served to introduce yet another up-and-coming 3-gunner to the national stage. Missourian Rustin Bernskoetter knocked off Kalani Laker and James Casanova, emerging 3-gun talents in their own right, to set up the showdown with Horner in the finals. Bernskoetter was remarkably cool and collected in his 3GN debut, leav-

ing most observers confident the best was still yet to come from the non-sponsored shooter.

Setting the Stage

Following Ozark, the 2011 3GN season had one remaining points match left—the new FNH USA Championship, held that September in Glengary, West Virginia. For many competitors, FN represented one last opportunity for a mad dash for 3GN series points in hopes of qualifying for the 3GN Championship that would follow.

The level of anticipation was justified, as the stakes had been significantly raised over that of 2010, both in terms of venue and prize. Although the 2011/2012 3GN Championship match would begin in West Virginia, with four stages of fire and the top 16 qualifying for the 3GN Shoot-Off, after just one elimination Shoot-Off round, the action would

stop there. In an unprecedented move, the 3GN Championship Finale would then be held in Las Vegas, at night and under the lights, during the middle of SHOT Show, in January 2012—all filmed for airing on the new NBC Sports Network. And, as if that weren't enough, the cash payout to the winner would be doubled, with $50,000 going to the 3GN Champion from Leupold Tactical Optics and NBC Sports Network.

(opposite) Andrew Daun dumps his pistol and transitions toward his staged shotgun during the final stage of the 2011 3GN Championship match, in West Virginia.

After an intense four-stage match designed by Larry Houck, 16 competitors at West Virginia advanced to the elimination round of the 3GN Championship. Daniel Horner, Tommy Thacker, Phil Strader (who qualified on the final weekend at FNH USA), James Casanova, Jeff Cramblit, Kalani Laker, Rustin Bernskoetter, Adam Popplewell, Kelly Neal, Mark Hanish, Greg Jordan, Tyler Payne, Jerry Miculek, Taran Butler, Mike Voigt, and Clint Upchurch comprised a remarkable talent pool of 3-gunners bent on making history.

In the first match-up, FN's

Tommy Thacker squared off against defending 3GN Champion Daniel Horner, who jumped out to a good lead during the rifle position and was first to the stop plate. Then, word got to the firing line that many felt Horner's run had contained a fault, which would prevent his advancing. The only problem—the range officer officiating the event hadn't seen or called the fault.

A review of the 3GN video was conducted, and it was discovered that Horner had indeed failed to knock down one of the self-resetting MGM ReCon targets. Upon seeing the footage, Horner conceded that he'd lost the bout, and Thacker advanced to Las Vegas.

"My deepest apologies go out to the competitors involved in this unfortunate situation," said 3GN President Pete Brown, in a

press release. "A fault occurred and it was not handled properly, which is a direct reflection upon 3-Gun Nation. Due to this, our shooters were put in an uncomfortable situation and were subject to speculation. Their only job is to compete and have fun, which is our ultimate goal for everyone in the sport. One of our jobs is to make the proper ruling for any scenario that comes our way, and in this instance we failed. Steps are now being put in place to ensure this type of situation never happens again."

This was an unfortunate twist for all involved. A call had been missed and the competitors were forced into a tough situ-

Tommy Thacker runs a Stag Arms 3G Competition rifle during his winning run in the 3GN Championship elimination round of late 2011.

ation through no fault of their own. Had the call been made at the time—during the run—would Horner have been able to go back and neutralize the target before Thacker finished his run? I've watched the video many times, and I don't think so. The speed at which these runs take place is quite fast, with a lone dropped shot often being the difference between defeat and victory. Still, Horner is an uncommon athlete in this game and, if anyone would have been able to pull off the feat, it conceivably would have been him. We'll never know. Per 3GN rules, the correct call was eventually made, and the defending 3GN Champion was eliminated. What remained to be seen is what

Thacker would be able to do with the opportunity.

In the second match-up, Phil Strader, who'd needed a third score at the preceding FNH USA 3-Gun Championship just to qualify for the 3GN Championship Match, defeated James Casanova and advanced to Las Vegas. Jeff Cramblit knocked off Stag Arms' Kalani Laker in the next bracket, setting up a Las Vegas showdown with Rustin Bernskoetter, who'd come from behind on the pistol to knock out Adam Popplewell.

In the lower brackets, FN's Mark Hanish laid down perhaps the most impressive single run of the event, going through the match at a blistering pace to

beat Kelly Neal. That win set up a Las Vegas dual with USAMU's Tyler Payne, who'd narrowly edged Greg Jordan.

Finally, in a 3GN Shoot-Off rematch of the Titans, Taran Butler made an extremely impres-

(below) AMU's Tyler Payne (foreground) and Greg Jordan start their entertaining run during the elimination round of the 2011 3GN Championship Shoot-Off.

(opposite top) Team FNH USA's Mark Hanish runs an FN SLP during the 3GN Shoot-Off elimination round in West Virginia.

(opposite bottom) Taran Butler mows down shotgun clays during the elimination round of the 2011 3GN Championship Shoot-Off.

sive run on his way to knocking out Jerry Miculek, positioning him for a Las Vegas match-up with Mike Voigt, who'd defeated Clint Upchurch.

Vegas, Baby!

The sport of 3-gun officially announced its presence to the entire firearms industry during the 2012 SHOT Show, in Las Vegas. One had to merely walk down the aisles of the convention floor to take in how big the sport had become, with company after company utilizing 3-gun shooters and products specific to 3-gun to promote their brands. Benelli, FNH USA, Stag Arms, Samson Manufacturing, and on and on it went—3-gun shooters were doing demos in the show display booths, high-speed match footage played on high-definition screens and tricked-out 3-gun rifles and shotguns were pawed over in the booths. And the one topic that tied all this 3-gun buzz together was the "Rumble on the Range," the 3GN Championship Finale.

The stage for this match was bigger than anything the sport had ever seen. Brownells, Stag Arms, and the NRA, along with a host of other companies, had thrown in support to sponsor the biggest night in 3-gun history. Busses were rented to transport the fans, free food and drink were provided, a select vendors' row highlighted event sponsors, and music and a live video feed was set up to entertain the fans.

Jerry Miculek, Patrick Flannigan, and other "Hot Shots" stars warmed up the crowd. Then

A competitor engages targets from a required shooting box during the 2011 3GN Championship.

3GN TV host and country music star Mark Wills performed an awesome rendition of the National Anthem, followed by thunderous applause. Game *on*.

The first match-up featured FNH USA's Tommy Thacker versus Remington's Phil Strader. In terms of sponsors, this was FN blue versus Remington green, as shooters representing two of the oldest names in gunmaking squared off.

Thacker stormed out of gate in the match-up, getting off the eight-target shotgun station first and widening the gap with a strong rifle run across six steel plates. Thacker struggled on the 12-plate pistol rack, paused for a moment, took a breath, and regained his composure to finish strong and advance to the semi-finals.

"I was pretty amped up for the first run," Thacker said. "I was listening to the music, trying to stay in the groove and relax. I was thinking *Don't let this stuff get to you. It's a mental game now. Your skill set is not going to change.* I played it over and over in my mind; I knew what I had to do."

In the second of the first-round match-ups, veteran 3-gunner Jeff Cramblit faced breakout star Rustin Bernskoetter, who had looked dominant in his elimination round win in West Virginia. But in Las Vegas, Bernskoetter struggled on the rifle, while Cramblit put together a solid run, advancing to the semi-finals.

FNH USA's Mark Hanish opened his 3GN finale with

Team FNH USA's Tommy Thacker runs the shotgun portion of the 3GN Shoot-Off Finale in Las Vegas.

an absolutely blistering shotgun run, while his opponent, USAMU's Tyler Payne ran his shotgun dry and was forced to reload to finish that array. That was all the lead Hanish would need, remaining steady through to the stop plate.

The final match-up of the first round featured two 3-gun powerhouses in Mike Voigt and Taran Butler. To many, the Championship would likely be decided in this opening round bout, a pick-'em match-up by Vegas standards. But it was Voigt who was dialed in and made the cut.

In the first semi-final match-up, Thacker came out strong on the rifle again, building an early lead over Cramblit. Thacker, though, was solid on the shotgun and then maintained his lead throughout the pistol rack to make it to the finals.

In the final semi-final bout, Hanish again jumped to a fast start with an incredible shotgun run, while Mike Voigt suffered a catastrophic mistake. Going equally fast, Voigt inadvertently left a shotgun popper standing, not noticing the standing steel target until he had abandoned an empty shotgun back at the staging box and was on the run halfway to the rifle position. Voigt scrambled back to the shotgun, then accelerated through the rifle and attacked the pistol rack at a furious pace, but it was too little too late. Hanish hit the stop plate first to advance.

Before the largest crowd ever to watch a 3-gun match, and with the largest cash prize in the history of the sport, Team FNH USA's Tommy Thacker and Mark Hanish stepped to the line to see who would become the 3-Gun Nation Champion.

In the best-of-three final rounds, Thacker again looked dominating in the first, staying even with Hanish on shotgun and surging ahead on rifle before finishing strong on MGM's Propeller plate rack, a wicked spinning target mechanism that tested accuracy and timing.

After a brief break in the action, Thacker and Hanish stepped to the starting box for round two, and the crowd noise began to build. The horn screamed, and each competitor hurled themselves toward the shotgun station. Hanish, as he had the entire night, leaned in and ripped off the rounds in the SLP in one continuous long bark. Thacker put on the show next, dropping down with an FN SCAR into a barricade-supported position to surgically fire Federal Tracer ammunition into the night, their fiery explosions bursting on disappearing rifle steel. For a moment, two Propeller plate racks spun in near slow motion, before Thacker's final plate stuck into the sand. He transitioned to the stop plate, squeezed the FNS trigger, and the bullet found its mark. The crowd erupted.

"Unbelievable," Thacker said, trying to put the enormity of the moment into words. "The only thing I can think is that I am so blessed, and everything happens for a reason. The only thing I can think is to thank God. Coming into this, I knew everything was right. I was in the zone more than I'd ever been, and, after the first run, I knew I was going to win this thing."

For the win, Thacker claimed the title of 3-Gun Nation 2011/2012 Champion, along with a cash payout of $50,000 from Leupold Tactical Optics

and NBC Sports Network. For finishing second, Mark Hanish received a Barrett MRAD rifle package and a check from Brownells for $2,500. In the consolation round, a gimpy Mike Voigt overcame a pulled muscle and limped to victory over Jeff Cramblit, winning $5,000 from Timney Triggers. Each 3GN Finale competitor received a check for $2,000, with

Stag Arms providing $2,000, Shooters Connection supplying $2,000 and DoubleStar ponying up $6,000 in prize money. In all, the Las Vegas payouts totaled $67,500, with an additional $15,000 in products distributed to the competitors. That money raised the total 3GN cash payout for 2011/2012 to more than $150,000 in cash prizes for the full 3GN Tour.

For FNH USA's Ken Pfau, the night surely put a very large exclamation point on what had been several years in the making—forming a 3-gun team, sponsoring major matches, and sponsoring the 3GN Tour and television show.

"On behalf of FNH USA, we would like to congratulate Tommy Thacker and Mark Hanish for their outstanding perfor-mance during the 3-Gun Nation Championship," said Pfau following the match. "Since joining Team FNH USA, both Tommy and Mark have demonstrated time and time again that they are superior marksmen. Their dedication to the sport of 3-gun contributed to their success in this final match and showcases FNH USA's commitment to the sport of 3-gun."

3GN Pro Series

The Rumble on the Range had a tremendous effect—the 3GN Effect—on the firearms industry that week during SHOT Show. Aside from the tremendous buzz that reso-nated throughout the convention center, the event itself was covered by most major firearm industry outlets, including television, web, and print. Amazingly, the 3GN Finale was featured in both web and print coverage by the *Las Vegas Review-Journal*, whose story highlighted a large photo of Mike Voigt in competition—now *that's* mainstream media coverage of a practical shooting event!

The success of the Rumble on the Range also propelled the next step in the evolution of 3GN—the 3-Gun Nation Pro Series. In 2012, the top 64 qualified 3-gun competitors, based on results from the entire 2011 3-gun season, will compete in an elite, professional tournament series. Pro shooter Rob Romero was brought in as 3GN's new Director of Competition to create a challenging course of fire for pro-level 3-gunners in a made-for-TV format.

"I'm really looking forward to shooting at some new venues with the Pro Series and adding some new flavors to the game," said 3GN Pro Series competitor James Casanova, who shoots for Carbon Arms. "The new targets and match structure sound interesting and entertaining.

Tommy Thacker accepts his historic check for $50,000 from Leupold Tactical Optics and NBC Sports Network for becoming the 2011-2012 3GN Champion.

The sport is an absolute blast to play, but watching it has been kind of hard. I think this setup will be a way to make it easier for spectators to see what's going on and keep it interesting for them, which will ultimately bring more people to the sport. It's also going to be a great opportunity to get together with a bunch of outstanding shooters and amazing people to have fun and learn with and from."

The 3GN Pro Series represents yet another new era in the sport of 3-gun, the dawn of real, professional shooting sports league. As we like to say at 3GN, "You ain't seen nothin' yet!"

3GN also launched Semi-Pro and Amateur Division races to complement the already successful Divisional, Lady, and Junior Points Series, giving competitors of all skill levels a tournament series in which they could compete on a national stage. A 3GN Club Series program was also launched, providing competitors with matches to shoot without ever traveling from their home range, while still giving them a way to compare their results with competitors across the country.

Ultimately, 3-Gun Nation is poised to provide a tourna-

Ken Pfau (center) celebrates with his two Team FNH USA teammates, Mark Hanish (left) and Tommy Thacker (right), following the all-FN final at the 2012 3GN Championship Finale.

ment structure applicable for every level of 3-gun competitor and foster competition all over the country. In short, 3-Gun Nation strives to build a nation of 3-gunners, forever legitimizing the sporting purpose of the firearms used in action shooting and further strengthening the 2nd Amendment that protects so much of what we all hold so dear.

SUPERSTITION MOUNTAIN MYSTERY 3-GUN, INTERNATIONAL MULTI-GUN ASSOCIATION (IMA) RULES

Revised October 20th, 2011

1 General Conduct & Dispute Resolution

1.1 Eye protection is mandatory for participants, spectators & officials at the event site.

1.2 Ear protection is mandatory for participants, spectators & officials while on or near a stage.

1.3 No participants or spectators shall consume or be under the influence of alcohol or non-prescription drugs at the event site. Any participant found to be impaired as a result of legitimate prescription drugs may be directed to stop shooting and requested to leave the range.

1.4 Participants and spectators are expected to conduct themselves in a courteous and sportsmanlike manner at all times. Any person who violates this rule may be ejected from the event site at the Match Director's discretion.

1.5 Clothing with any offensive or obscene logos, sayings, pictures or drawings will not be worn or displayed while at the event site.

1.6 Participants may be subject to event disqualification for safety or conduct violations. Disqualification will result in complete disqualification from the event, and the participant will not be allowed to continue nor be eligible for prizes.

1.7 A participant shall be disqualified for unsportsmanlike conduct. Examples of unsportsmanlike conduct include:

1.7.1 Cheating, such as:

1.7.1.1 Intentionally altering a target prior to the target being scored to gain advantage or avoid a penalty.

1.7.1.2 Altering or falsifying score sheets.

1.7.1.3 Altering the configuration of firearms or equipment without permission of the Match Director.

1.7.2 Threatening or assaulting other participants or Event Officials.

1.7.3 Disruptive behavior likely to disturb or distract other participants while they are shooting.

1.7.4 Willful disregard of Event Official instructions.

1.8 The final decision on all disqualifications and reshoots will be made by the Range Master or the Match Director.

1.9 Any rule not explicitly covered by this document will be resolved with a ruling by the Match Director or his designee. Rulings by the Match Director or his designee will be final, and will serve as a precedent for the duration of the event.

1.10 To have a matter arbitrated, a participant may obtain an Arbitration Request Form from the CRO of the stage in question. The completed Arbitration Request Form and the arbitration fee (US$100 cash) must be submitted to the Match Director within one hour of the time noted on the score sheet.

1.10.1 The Match Director will review the evidence, hear testimony, take counsel and issue a ruling before the end of the event.

1.10.2 If the arbitration is approved, the arbitration fee will be refunded. If the arbitration is disapproved, the arbitration fee is forfeit.

1.10.1 Safety violations are not subject to arbitration.

2 Safety

2.1 All International Multi-Gun Association (IMA) events will be run on cold ranges.

2.1.1 Participants firearms will remain unloaded at the event site except under the direction and immediate supervision of an Event Official.

2.2 Firearms may only be handled and/or displayed in a designated safety area.

2.2.1 Safety areas will be clearly marked with signs.

2.2.2 No firearm may be loaded in a safety area.

2.2.3 No ammunition (including dummy ammunition or snap caps) may be handled in a safety area.

2.3 Firearms may be transported to, from and between stages only in the following conditions:

2.3.1 Handguns must be cased or holstered, decocked and with the magazine removed.

2.3.2 Rifles and shotguns must be cased, secured muzzle up or muzzle down in a stable gun cart/caddy, or carried slung with the muzzle up.

Actions must be open and detachable magazines removed. The use of high-visibility open bolt indicator devices is recommended as a courtesy to other event participants.

2.4 A participant who causes an accidental discharge will be stopped by an Event Official as soon as possible, and shall be disqualified. Examples of accidental discharge include:

2.4.1 A shot, which travels over a backstop, a berm or in any other direction deemed by Event Officials to be unsafe. Note that a participant who legitimately fires a shot at a target, which then travels in an unsafe direction, will not be disqualified.

2.4.2 A shot which strikes the ground within 10 feet of the participant, except when shooting at a target closer than 10 feet to the participant.

2.4.2.1 Exception - a shot which strikes the ground within 10 feet of the participant due to a "squib".

2.4.2.2 In the case of a shot striking a prop where the projectile is deflected or does not continue to strike the ground, if an Event Official determines that the projectile would have struck the ground within 10 feet of the participant had it not been deflected or stopped by the prop, the provisions of 2.4.2 shall apply.

2.4.3 A shot which occurs while loading, reloading or unloading any firearm.

2.4.3.1 Exception - a detonation which occurs while unloading a firearm is not considered an accidental discharge. A "detonation" is defined as the ignition of the primer of a round, other than by action of a firing pin, where the projectile or shot does not pass through the barrel (e.g. when a slide is being manually retracted, when a round is dropped etc.).

2.4.4 A shot which occurs during remedial action in the case of a malfunction.

2.4.5 A shot which occurs while transferring a firearm between hands.

2.4.6 A shot which occurs during movement, except while actually engaging targets.

2.5 A participant who performs an act of unsafe gun handling will be stopped by an Event Official as soon as possible, and shall be disqualified. Examples of unsafe gun handling include:

2.5.1 Dropping a firearm, whether loaded or unloaded, at any time after the "Make Ready" command and before the "Range Is Clear" command.

2.5.1.1 Dropping an unloaded firearm before the "Make Ready" command or after the "Range Is Clear" command will not result in disqualification, provided the firearm is retrieved by an Event Official.

2.5.2 Use of any unsafe ammunition as defined in Section 3.

2.5.3 Abandoning a firearm during a stage in any location other than a safe abandonment location as stipulated in the stage briefing. Firearms may only be abandoned in one of the following conditions:

2.5.3.1 Loaded, safety catch fully engaged, muzzle pointed in the designated safe direction.

2.5.3.2 Completely unloaded (no ammunition in the firearm), detachable magazine removed, muzzle pointed in the designated safe direction.

2.5.4 Unloading any firearm in an unsafe manner, or discharging a firearm while not legitimately engaging a target.

2.5.5 Allowing the muzzle of a firearm to break the 180 degree safety plane.

2.5.5.1 In the case of a participant facing downrange, the muzzle of a loaded handgun may point slightly uprange while drawing or reholstering, so long as it does not point outside an imaginary circle of three (3) feet radius from the participant's feet.

2.5.6 Engaging a steel target in an unsafe manner, such as by:

2.5.6.1 Engaging steel targets with handgun ammunition at a range of less than 23 feet.

2.5.6.2 Engaging steel targets with shotgun birdshot ammunition at a range of less than 16 feet.

2.5.6.3 Engaging steel targets with shotgun buckshot ammunition at a range of less than 23 feet.

2.5.6.4 Engaging steel targets with shotgun slug ammunition at a range of less than 131 feet.

2.5.6.5 Engaging steel targets with rifle ammunition at a range of less than 164 feet.

2.5.7 Allowing the muzzle of a firearm to point at any part of the participant's body during a course of fire (i.e. sweeping).

2.5.7.1 Exception - sweeping of the lower extremities (below the belt) while drawing or re-holstering a handgun, provided that the participant's fingers are clearly outside of the trigger guard.

2.5.8 Using a tube-type shotgun speed-loading device without a primer relief cut.

2.5.9 Pointing a firearm, whether loaded or unloaded, in any direction deemed by Event Officials to be unsafe.

3 Ammunition

3.1 Handgun ammunition shall be 9mm Parabellum (9x19mmNATO) or larger, unless otherwise stipulated under equipment division rules.

3.2 Rifle ammunition shall be .223 Remington (5.56x45mmNATO) or larger, unless otherwise stipulated under equipment division rules.

3.3 Shotgun ammunition shall be 20 gauge or larger, unless otherwise stipulated under equipment division rules.

3.3.1 Birdshot must be no larger than #6 birdshot, and be made from lead or bismuth only. Iron/steel/tungsten birdshot is unsafe and prohibited.

3.4 Ammunition containing tracer, incendiary, armor piercing, steel jacketed or steel/tungsten/penetrator core projectiles is unsafe and prohibited.

3.5 A chronograph may be used by Event Officials to verify compliance with Heavy Metal division power factor requirements. Participants may be selected for testing on any basis approved by the Match Director. The chronograph procedure is as follows:

3.5.1 An Event Official will collect five (5) rifle rounds and five (5) handgun rounds from the participant.

3.5.2 One (1) of the rifle bullets and one (1) of the handgun bullets will be pulled and weighed to determine actual bullet weight.

3.5.3 Up to four (4) of the rifle rounds and up to four (4) of the handgun rounds will be fired by an Event Official over the official chronograph.

3.5.4 Power factor will be calculated according to the equation: PF = Bullet Weight (grains) x Velocity (fps) / 1000.

3.5.5 At least one (1) of the rifle rounds and at least one (1) of the handgun rounds must make the required power factor.

4 Firearms

4.1 All firearms used by participants must be serviceable and safe. Event Officials may inspect a participant's firearms at any time to check they are functioning safely. If any firearm is declared unserviceable or unsafe by an Event Official, it must be withdrawn from the event until it is repaired to the satisfaction of the Range Master.

4.2 Firearms capable of fully automatic- or burst-fire ("machine guns") may be used only in semi-auto mode (i.e. not more than one (1) round fired with each pull of the trigger). Violation of this rule will incur a 30 second time penalty per occurrence.

4.3 Participants must use the same firearms (handgun, rifle and shotgun) for the entire event.

4.3.1 If a participant's firearm becomes unserviceable, that participant may replace their firearm with another of a substantially similar model, caliber and sighting system only with the approval of the Match Director.

4.4 Participants generally may not reconfigure any firearm during the course of the event. Explicitly prohibited acts include changing caliber, barrel length, shotgun magazine tube length, sighting systems and/or stock style. Explicitly permitted acts include installing or removing support devices (e.g. bipods), slings and other minor accessories (e.g. scope covers).

4.4.1 If a participant's firearm becomes unserviceable, that participant may repair their firearm with directly equivalent replacement parts. If replacement parts result in a significant change to the firearm configuration, then the repair must be approved by the Match Director.

4.5 Unless otherwise stipulated in the stage briefing, required firearms will begin the stage in the following ready conditions:

4.5.1 Handgun: Loaded to division start capacity and holstered. In the case of single-action autos or double-action autos with manual override safeties, the safety catch must be in the "safe" position. In the case of double-action autos & revolvers, the hammer must be down/forward.

4.5.2 Rifle: Loaded to division start capacity and held in the low ready position. Safety catch must be in the "safe" position.

4.5.3 Shotgun: Loaded to division start capacity and held in the low ready position. Safety catch must be in the "safe" position.

4.5.4 Participants may not touch or hold any firearm loading device or ammunition after the "Standby" command and before the "Start Signal" (except for unavoidable touching with the lower arms).

5 Equipment Divisions

5.1 Participants will declare one equipment division at the beginning of the event.

5.1.1 Equipment divisions are: Open, Tactical Scope, Tactical Limited, Heavy Metal Scope and Heavy Metal Limited.

5.1.2 Failure to meet all of the equipment and ammunition requirements for the declared division shall result in the participant being placed into Open division. If the requirements of Open division are not met, the participant's scores will be excluded from the final event results.

5.2 Open division

5.2.1 Handgun

5.2.1.1 Handgun holsters must safely retain the handgun during vigorous movement, and must completely cover the trigger. The belt upon which the handgun holster is attached must be worn at waist level. Shoulder holsters and cross draw holsters are prohibited.

5.2.1.2 Magazine length may not exceed 170mm.

5.2.2 Rifle

5.2.2.1 Supporting devices (e.g. bipods) are permitted, and may begin any stage folded or deployed at the participant's discretion.

5.2.3 Shotgun

5.2.3.1 Speed loading devices and/or detachable box magazines are permitted.

5.2.3.2 Tubular speed loading devices must feature a primer relief cut.

5.3 Tactical Scope division

5.3.1 Firearms must be of a factory configuration. Prototype firearms are specifically prohibited. Internal modifications are permitted providing they do not alter the external appearance of the firearm.

5.3.2 Handgun

5.3.2.1 Handgun holsters must be a practical/tactical carry style and must safely retain the handgun during vigorous movement.

Semiautomatic pistol holsters must completely cover the trigger. Revolver holsters must completely cover the trigger and the cylinder. The belt upon which the handgun holster is attached must be worn at waist level. Shoulder holsters and cross draw holsters are prohibited.

5.3.2.2 Electronic sights, optical sights, extended sights, compensators, muzzle brakes or barrel porting are prohibited.

5.3.2.3 Magazines length may not exceed 170mm in the case of single column magazines, and may not exceed 140mm in the case of staggered column magazines.

5.3.3 Rifle

5.3.3.1 Not more than one (1) electronic or optical sight is permitted.

5.3.3.2 A supplemental magnifier may be used with the permitted optical sight provided the magnifier does not contain an aiming reticle,

cannot be used as an aiming device by itself, and remains mounted in the same location on the rifle for the duration of the event. A participant may use the magnifier in either the magnified or unmagnified mode without restriction.

5.3.3.3 Supporting devices (bipods, etc.) are prohibited.

5.3.3.4 Compensators and muzzle brakes may not exceed 1 inch in diameter and 3 inches in length (as measured from the barrel muzzle to the end of the compensator).

5.3.3.5 Drum magazines are prohibited.

5.3.4 Shotgun

5.3.4.1 Only tubular magazines are permitted.

5.3.4.2 Electronic sights and optical sights are prohibited.

5.3.4.3 Supporting devices (bipods, etc.) are prohibited.

5.3.4.4 Barrel devices designed/intended to reduce recoil or muzzle movement (e.g. compensators, barrel porting) are prohibited.

5.3.4.5 Speed loading devices and/or detachable box magazines are prohibited.

5.3.4.6 Not more than nine (9) rounds total may be loaded at the beginning of any stage, unless otherwise stipulated in the stage briefing.

5.4 Tactical Limited division

5.4.1 Firearms must be of a factory configuration. Prototype firearms are specifically prohibited. Internal modifications are permitted providing they do not alter the external appearance of the firearm.

5.4.2 Handgun

5.4.2.1 Handgun holsters must be a practical/tactical carry style and must safely retain the handgun during vigorous movement.

Semiautomatic pistol holsters must completely cover the trigger. Revolver holsters must completely cover the trigger and the cylinder. The belt upon which the handgun holster is attached must be worn at waist level. Shoulder holsters and cross draw holsters are prohibited.

5.4.2.2 Electronic sights, optical sights, extended sights, compensators, muzzle brakes or barrel porting are prohibited.

5.4.2.3 Magazines length may not exceed 170mm in the case of single column magazines, and may not exceed 140mm in the case of staggered column magazines.

5.4.3 Rifle

5.4.3.1 Not more than one (1) non-magnified electronic or optical sight is permitted. Electronic or optical sights originally designed to be capable of any magnification (whether used or not) are pro-

hibited.

5.4.3.2 Supporting devices (bipods, etc.) are prohibited.

5.4.3.3 Compensators and muzzle brakes may not exceed 1 inch in diameter and 3 inches in length (as measured from the barrel muzzle to the end of the compensator).

5.4.3.4 Drum magazines are prohibited.

5.4.4 Shotgun

5.4.4.1 Only tubular magazines are permitted.

5.4.4.2 Electronic sights and optical sights are prohibited.

5.4.4.3 Supporting devices (bipods, etc.) are prohibited.

5.4.4.4 Barrel devices designed/intended to reduce recoil or muzzle movement (e.g. compensators, barrel porting) are prohibited.

5.4.4.5 Speed loading devices and/or detachable box magazines are prohibited.

5.4.4.6 Not more than nine (9) rounds total may be loaded at the beginning of any stage, unless otherwise stipulated in the stage briefing.

5.5 Heavy Metal Scope division

5.5.1 Firearms must be of a factory configuration. Prototype firearms are specifically prohibited. Internal modifications are permitted providing they do not alter the external appearance of the firearm.

5.5.2 Handgun

5.5.2.1 Handgun holsters must be a practical/tactical carry style and must safely retain the handgun during vigorous movement.

Semiautomatic pistol holsters must completely cover the trigger. Revolver holsters must completely cover the trigger and the cylinder. The belt upon which the handgun holster is attached must be worn at waist level. Shoulder holsters and cross draw holsters are prohibited.

5.5.2.2 Electronic sights, optical sights, extended sights, compensators, muzzle brakes or barrel porting are prohibited.

5.5.2.3 Magazines length may not exceed 170mm in the case of single column magazines, and may not exceed 140mm in the case of staggered column magazines. Magazines may be loaded with not more than ten (10) rounds.

5.5.2.4 Minimum caliber is .44".

5.5.2.5 Minimum power factor (bullet weight x velocity/1000) is 165.

5.5.3 Rifle

5.5.3.1 Not more than one (1) optical sight is permitted.

5.5.3.2 A supplemental magnifier may be used with the permitted optical sight provided the magnifier does not contain an aiming reticle, cannot be used as an aiming device by itself, and remains mounted in the same location on the rifle for the duration of the event. A participant may use the magnifier in either the magnified or unmagnified mode without restriction.

5.5.3.3 Supporting devices (bipods, etc.) are prohibited.

5.5.3.4 Compensators and muzzle brakes may not exceed 1 inch in diameter and 3 inches in length (as measured from the barrel muzzle to the end of the compensator).

5.5.3.5 Magazines may be loaded with not more than twenty (20) rounds.

5.5.3.6 Minimum caliber is .30".

5.5.3.7 Minimum power factor (bullet weight x velocity/1000) is 320.

5.5.4 Shotgun

5.5.4.1 Only tubular magazines are permitted.

5.5.4.2 Electronic sights and optical sights are prohibited.

5.5.4.3 Supporting devices (bipods, etc.) are prohibited.

5.5.4.4 Barrel devices designed/intended to reduce recoil or muzzle movement (e.g. compensators, barrel porting) are prohibited.

5.5.4.5 Speed loading devices and/or detachable box magazines are prohibited.

5.5.4.6 Not more than nine (9) rounds total may be loaded at the beginning of any stage, unless otherwise stipulated in the stage briefing.

5.5.4.7 Minimum bore size is 12 gauge.

5.6 Heavy Metal Limited division

5.6.1 Firearms must be of a factory configuration.

Prototype firearms are specifically prohibited. Internal modifications are permitted providing they do not alter the external appearance of the firearm.

5.6.2 Handgun

5.6.2.1 Handgun holsters must be a practical/tactical carry style and must safely retain the handgun during vigorous movement.

Semiautomatic pistol holsters must completely cover the trigger. Revolver holsters must completely cover the trigger and the cylinder. The belt upon which the handgun holster is attached must be worn at waist level. Shoulder holsters and cross draw holsters are prohibited.

5.6.2.2 Electronic sights, optical sights, extended sights, compensators, muzzle brakes or barrel porting are prohibited.

5.6.2.3 Magazines length may not exceed 170mm in the case of single column magazines, and may not exceed 140mm in the case of staggered column magazines. Magazines may be loaded with not more than ten (10) rounds.

5.6.2.4 Minimum caliber is .44".

5.6.2.5 Minimum power factor (bullet weight x velocity/1000) is 165.

5.6.3 Rifle

5.6.3.1 Not more than one (1) non-magnified electronic or optical sight is permitted. Electronic or optical sights originally designed to be capable of any magnification (whether used or not) are prohibited.

5.6.3.2 Supporting devices (bipods, etc.) are prohibited.

5.6.3.3 Compensators and muzzle brakes may not exceed 1 inch in diameter and 3 inches in length (as measured from the barrel muzzle to the end of the compensator).

5.6.3.4 Magazines may be loaded with not more than twenty (20) rounds.

5.6.3.5 Minimum caliber is .30".

5.6.3.6 Minimum power factor (bullet weight x velocity/1000) is 320.

5.6.4 Shotgun

5.6.4.1 Only tubular magazines are permitted.

5.6.4.2 Electronic sights and optical sights are prohibited.

5.6.4.3 Supporting devices (bipods, etc.) are prohibited.

5.6.4.4 Barrel devices designed/intended to reduce recoil or muzzle movement (e.g. compensators, barrel porting) are prohibited.

5.6.4.5 Speed loading devices and/or detachable box magazines are prohibited.

5.6.4.6 Not more than nine (9) rounds total may be loaded at the beginning of any stage, unless otherwise stipulated in the stage briefing.

5.6.4.7 Minimum bore size is 12 gauge.

5.6.4.8 Manually operated shotguns (e.g. pump action) only are permitted.

6 Scoring & Penalties

6.1 Stage score will be based on straight time plus penalties.

6.1.1 Unless otherwise stipulated in the stage briefing, IPSC cardboard "shoot" targets must be neutralized by receiving either one (1) A-zone hit, one (1) B-zone hit or two (2) hits anywhere in the scoring area. Examples of neutralized targets include:

6.1.1.1 One (1) hit in the upper A–zone or B-zone.

6.1.1.2 One (1) hit in the lower A-zone.

6.1.1.3 Two (2) hits anywhere in the scoring area, in any combination of the C-zone and/or D-zone.

6.1.2 IPSC cardboard "shoot" targets that are not neutralized will incur time penalties as follows:

6.1.2.1 One (1) hit in the C-zone or D-zone only = 5 second penalty (Failure To Neutralize).

6.1.2.2 No hits on target, but target was engaged = 10 second penalty (Un-hit Target).

6.1.2.3 No hits on target, and target was not engaged = 15 second penalty (Target Not Engaged).

6.1.3 Only holes made by bullets/slugs/pellets will count for score/penalty. Evidence that the bullet made the hole must be present on the target (i.e. crown or grease ring/mark). Holes made by shrapnel, fragments, wads or flying debris will not count for score/penalty.

6.1.4 Knock-down targets (e.g. Pepper Poppers) must fall to score. Swinging/flashing targets must react in the manner prescribed in the stage briefing. An Event Official may call hits.

6.1.5 Knock-down/swinging/flashing targets that do not fall/react will incur time penalties as follows:

6.1.5.1 Target did not fall/react, but target was engaged = 10 second penalty (Un-hit Target).

6.1.5.2 Target did not fall/react, and target was not engaged = 15 second penalty (Target Not Engaged).

6.1.6 Knock-down targets will be calibrated before the event begins.

6.1.6.1 Handgun targets will be calibrated with a 9mm handgun using factory ammunition.

6.1.6.2 Shotgun targets will be calibrated with a 20 gauge shotgun, barrel length not to exceed 26", using a factory 2. dram, ounce load of #7. or #8 birdshot.

6.1.6.3 The Range Master will designate specific supplies of 9mm and 20 gauge ammunition, and one or more handguns and shotguns, to be

used as official calibration tools only by the Range Master or designated testing personnel. Designated calibration firearms and ammunition are not subject to challenge.

6.1.7 Frangible targets (e.g. clay pigeons) must break by gunfire to score. A target with a significant piece visibly detached is considered "broken".

6.1.8 Frangible targets that do not break will incur time penalties as follows:

6.1.8.1 Target did not break, but target was engaged = 10 second penalty (Un-hit Target).

6.1.8.2 Target did not break, and target was not engaged = 15 second penalty (Target Not Engaged).

6.1.9 Scoring hits on designated "No Shoot" targets will incur a 5 second penalty per hit, up to a maximum of 2 hits per no-shoot. Steel "No Shoot" targets must fall to score. Frangible "No Shoot" targets must break to score.

6.1.10 Failure to follow procedures prescribed in the stage briefing will result in a 5 second penalty.

6.1.10.1 If a competitive advantage is deemed to have been gained, procedural penalties may be applied on a "per shot" basis.

6.1.10.2 Enhanced procedural penalties may be applied at the Match Director's discretion if a participant willfully and egregiously violates stage procedures.

6.1.10.3 The rendering of any assistance or advice to a participant who is actively engaged in a stage ("coaching") by any person other than an Event Official is prohibited. Event Officials may penalize the "coach" and/or the participant with a procedural penalty for each occurrence. Persistent coaching may be subject to the provisions of rules 1.4 and/or 1.7.

6.1.11 Additional penalties may be applied as stipulated in the stage briefing.

6.1.12 Stage Not Fired (SNF) penalty is 500 seconds per stage not fired.

6.1.13 The Match Director may specify a time limit for completing any stage by stating it clearly in the stage briefing. If a participant exceeds the time limit, they will be stopped by an Event Official and the stage will be scored as shot with all applicable miss and TNE penalties.

6.2 Stage Points

6.2.1 Stage points will be calculated separately for each equipment division.

6.2.2 Stage points will be awarded to participants according to their stage time relative to the fastest time on that stage, using the equation $STAGE\_POINTS = (FASTEST\_TIME / PARTICIPANT\_TIME) \times 100$.

6.2.3 Total points accumulated for all stages will determine the event placement by division.

6.2.4 Highest score wins.

7 Awards

7.1 One or more of the following individual participant categories may be recognized at the discretion of the Match Director:

7.1.1 Lady: Participants who were of the female gender at birth.

7.1.2 Junior: Participants who were under the age of 18 years on the first day of the event.

7.1.3 Senior: Participants who were over the age of 55 years on the first day of the event.

7.1.4 Super Senior: Participants who were over the age of 65 years on the first day of the event. Super Seniors may enter Senior category only if

Super Senior is not being recognized.

7.1.5 Military: Current or honorably retired military personnel.

7.1.6 Law: Current or retired full-time law enforcement officers with arrest powers.

3-GUN NATION PRO SERIES
RULES 2012

SECTION 1 – RULES

1. SAFETY RULES

1.1 Participants are subject to event disqualification for violation of any rule or regulation in sections 1 or 2. Exception: Section 2: Stage Disqualifications (rule 2.8.1 & 2.8.2) Safety violations will not be subject to arbitration.

1.2 All 3GN Produced Events will be run on COLD RANGES.

1.2.1 COLD RANGE (definition): Participants' firearms will remain unloaded at the event site except under the direction of an event official.

1.3 Designated Safety Areas

1.3.1 The Safety Areas will be clearly marked with signs.

1.3.2 Unloaded firearms may be handled and/or displayed only in the Safety Areas.

1.3.3 No ammunition may be handled in any Safety Area.

1.4 Rifles, Shotguns and Pistols (carry from vehicle or between stages)

1.4.1 Rifles & shotguns must be cased or if hand carried slung with the muzzle up. Carts whereby muzzle is pointed downward is approved.

1.4.2 Rifles & shotguns must be carried with actions open and detachable magazines removed. Actions can be closed only if a empty chamber flag is in place.

1.4.3 Shotgun ammunition shall be 20 gauge or larger - #7.5 LEAD SHOT or smaller where required by the stage description. Steel shot specifically not allowed. Use of steel shot is a safety violation and will result in a participant's (EDQ) Event Disqualification.

1.4.4 On stages, the Ready Condition for Rifles and Shotguns must be "Loaded and on Safe", magazine loaded, round in chamber and Safety Engaged.

1.5 Handguns (carry between stages)

1.5.1 Handguns must be cased or remain in holster, magazine removed except under the direction of Range Officers on a stage.

1.5.2 Handguns must be carried with the "Hammer/Striker Down."

1.5.3 On stages, the Ready Condition of handguns must be "Unloaded", magazine loaded and inserted, hammer/striker down with an empty chamber.

1.6 No competitors shall consume or be under the influence of alcohol or non-prescription drugs at the event site. Any participant found to be impaired and deemed unsafe as a result of legitimate prescription drugs may be directed to stop shooting and requested to leave the range.

1.7 Eye protection is mandatory for participants, spectators & range personnel at the event site.

1.8 Ear protection is mandatory for participants, spectators & range personnel while on or near a course of fire.

1.9 Grounding Firearms

1.9.1 During the course requirements of a 3GN stage, a participant may be required to ground a firearm in order to transition to another. The location and position of the grounded firearm will be specified in the Written Stage Briefing. A participant shall transition firearms by safely grounding a firearm using either of the following acceptable and safe methods: Safety Condition 1 or 2:

1. Loaded, safety engaged. Note: Passive Safeties in Operational condition will satisfy the safety engaged requirements. "2011" style grip safeties, "Safe Action" striker safeties or passive trigger safeties fall under this rule. Note: For purposes of 3GN Rules, "Passive Safety" means: Any safety that engages automatically and disables the firearm from discharging while the firearm is not being handled. Note: For purposes of 3GN Rules, "Operational" means: The safety operates correctly as intended. To not be disabled or altered in which the safety features no longer prevents the firearm from discharging while the firearm is not being handled. Example: "Pinning the grip safety"

2. Unloaded. Note: For purposes of 3GN Rules, "unloaded" means: A. Empty chamber and empty source (tube or magazine); or B. Empty chamber and magazine completely removed.

2. EVENT DISQUALIFICATIONS

2.1 An Event Disqualification (EDQ) will result in complete disqualification from the event and the participant will not be allowed to continue. Competitor will not be eligible for prizes. All disqualifications will be issued by the DOC and all reshoots will be issued by the CRO or DOC. Safety violations will not be subject to arbitration. Reshoots: In the case of a stage that has not been completely reset prior to the start signal or a target that falls on it's own after the start signal, the CRO will stop the competitor as soon as possible and grant a reshoot to the competitor. Note: The Stage in question will be reset and competitor will be given a choice to reshoot immediately or have their position moved to the bottom of the order and will be the last competitor to complete the Course of Fire (COF) for that squad.

2.2 Disqualification for Negligent Discharge

A participant who causes a negligent discharge must be stopped by a Range Officer as soon as possible. A negligent discharge is defined as follows:

2.2.1 A shot, which travels over a backstop, a berm or in any other direction deemed by the event organizers as being unsafe. Note that a participant who legitimately fires a shot at a target, which hits and then travels in an unsafe direction, will not be disqualified.

2.2.2 A shot which strikes the ground within 10 feet of the participant, except when shooting at a target closer than 10 feet to the participant.

a. Exception - a bullet, slug, or shot which strikes the ground within 10 feet of the participant due to a "squib".

b. In the case of a shot striking a prop where the bullet, slug, or shot is deflected or does not continue to strike the ground, if the Range Official determines that the bullet, slug, or shot would have struck the ground within 10 feet of the participant had it not been deflected or stopped by the prop, the provisions of 2.2.2 shall apply.

2.2.3 A shot which occurs while loading, reloading or unloading any firearm after the "Make Ready" command and/or before the "Range is Clear" command.

a. Exception - a detonation, which occurs while unloading a firearm, is not considered a shot or Discharge subject to an event disqualification, however. Rule 5.1 may apply.

Detonation (definition): Ignition of the primer of a round, other than by action of a firing pin, where the bullet, slug or shot does not pass through the barrel (e.g. when a slide is being manually retracted, when a round is dropped).

2.2.4 A shot which occurs during remedial action in the case of a malfunction.

2.2.5 A shot which occurs while transferring a firearm between hands.

2.2.6 A shot which occurs during movement, except while actually shooting at targets.

2.3 Grounding a firearm in any condition not outlined in rule 1.9 will result in disqualification.

2.4 A participant shall be disqualified for:

2.4.1 Dropping a firearm, or

2.4.2 Dropping a firearm while loading/unloading, or

2.4.3 Dropping a firearm, whether loaded or unloaded, at anytime after the "Make Ready" command and before the "Range is Clear" command. This includes any firearm, loaded or unloaded, that falls after being grounded during the course of fire.

2.4.3.1 Dropping an unloaded firearm before the "Make Ready" command or after the "Range is Clear" command will not result in disqualification, provided the firearm is retrieved by an Event Official.

2.4.4 Steel shot specifically not allowed. Use of steel shot is a Safety Violation and will result in a participant's (EDQ) Event Disqualification.

2.5 A participant shall be disqualified for allowing the muzzle of his/her firearm to break the 180 degree Safety Plane (except while holstered, drawing or re-holstering.)

2.6 A participant shall be disqualified for unsportsmanlike conduct.

2.6.1 Cheating:

a. Intentionally altering targets prior to the target being scored to gain advantage or avoid a penalty.

b. Altering or falsifying score sheets.

c. Altering the configuration of firearms or equipment to gain advantage (see rule 5.3 & 5.4)

2.6.2 An Event Disqualification (EDQ) will be issued for Shotgun start total violation Rule (6.3.8).

2.6.3 An Event Disqualification (EDQ) will be issued for Pistol Magazine OAL violation Rule (6.2.4). Rule (6.1.5) will apply.

d. A course of fire must never require or allow a participant to touch or hold a firearm loading device or ammunition after the "Standby" command and before the "Start Signal" (except for unavoidable touching with the lower arms)

2.6.4 Threatening or assaulting other participants or staff personnel.

2.6.5 Disruptive behavior in an attempt to disturb other participants while they are shooting.

2.7 ALL disqualifications and re-shoots will be issued by the DOC.

Stage Disqualifications:

2.8 Stage Disqualification (SDQ) will result in the lowest ranking stage time posted overall multiplied by three (3) for the competitor on the stage in violation, but competitor will be allowed to continue and finish the match.

Competitor will still be eligible for prizes. Final decision will be with the DOC. Safety violations will not be subject to arbitration.

2.8.1 A Stage Disqualification (SDQ) will be issued for a grounded firearm in an "Unsafe" condition. A competitor whose firearm is observed to be in violation of Rule 1.9.1 (Condition 1 or 2) will not be touched, handled or moved before competitor is brought back to firearm in question for the firearm clearing portion of the stage. The competitor will show the RO that the firearm is "Unloaded" or the "Safety" is in fact engaged. After the inspection the RO will determine the next course of action.

a. The competitor in violation will be issued a (SDQ) for a violation of Rule (1.9.1). Final decision will be with the DOC.

b. The competitor continues in the match to the next Course of Fire (COF)

3. SPORTSMANSHIP AND CONDUCT

3.1 Participants and spectators are expected to conduct themselves in a courteous, sportsman-like manner at all times.

3.2 Clothing with any offensive or obscene logos, sayings, pictures or drawings will not be worn or displayed while at the event site/range.

4. AMMUNITION

4.1 No tracer, incendiary, armor piercing, steel jacketed or steel/Tungsten core ammunition is allowed.

A $100 fee shall be assessed for any competitor found in violation of rule (4.1) per each steel target engaged and or damaged. Fines will be made payable the day of the offense.

4.2 Pistol/revolver ammunition shall be 9x19 or larger.

4.3 Rifle ammunition shall be .223 Remington (5.56 NATO) or larger.

4.4 Shotgun ammunition shall be 20 gauge or larger - #7.5 LEAD SHOT or smaller.

Steel shot specifically not allowed. Use of steel shot is a Safety Violation and will result in a participant's (EDQ) Event Disqualification.

5. FIREARMS

5.1 All firearms used by participants must be serviceable and safe. Range Officers may demand examination of a participant's firearm or related equipment, at any time, to check they are functioning safely. If any such item is declared unserviceable or unsafe by a Range Officer, it must be withdrawn from the event until the item is repaired to the satisfaction of the Range Master.

5.2 If a participant's firearm becomes unserviceable during competition, that participant may replace his/her firearm with another of the same model, caliber and sighting system approved by the DOC or his designee.

5.3 For purposes of this ruling, a "firearm" consists of a specific caliber, receiver, barrel, stock and sighting system combination.

5.4 The same firearm system, for each gun, per Rule 5.3, shall be used during the entire event.

5.5 Participants will not reconfigure any firearm during the course of the entire event, (i.e. change caliber, barrel length, shotgun magazine tube length, sighting systems or stock style.) This will be considered Unsportsmanlike Conduct. Note: Shotgun Choke changes are allowed.

6. FIREARM DIVISION – Tactical

6.1 Handgun – Tactical

6.1.1 Firearms must be of a factory configuration.

6.1.2 Internal modifications are allowed providing they do not alter the original factory configuration of the handgun.

6.1.3 Firearms with custom or factory installed electronic sights, optical sights, extended sights, compensators or barrel porting are NOT allowed in this division.

6.1.4 Magazines used shall not exceed 170 mm OAL (overall length) for single stacks, and shall not exceed 140 mm OAL for staggered magazines.

6.1.5 Competitor magazines are subject to inspection at any time for OAL violations. A 3GN Official Magazine gauge will be made available for competitors at the beginning of all stages of fire.

6.2 Rifle - Tactical

6.2.1 Firearms must be of a factory configuration (see Rules 5.3, 5.4 & 5.5)

6.2.2 Internal modifications are allowed providing the modifications do not alter the original factory configuration of the rifle.

6.2.3 Scoped rifles may be equipped with no more than one (1) optical sight.

6.2.3.1 A magnifier may be used with an optical sight in this division without violating the "one optic" rule, provided:

a. The magnifier does not contain an aiming reticule.

b. The magnifier cannot be used as an aiming device by itself.

c. The magnifier is mounted in the same location on the rifle for the entire event.

If these provisions are satisfied:

d. The magnifier will not be considered a second/separate optic.

e. The competitor may start and use the magnifier in either the magnified or unmagnified mode without further restriction.

6.2.4 Rifle supporting devices (i.e. bipods, etc.) are not allowed in this division.

6.2.5 Compensators are allowed in this division provided the compensator is not larger than 1 inch in diameter and 3 inches long, measured from the barrel muzzle to the end of the compensator.

6.3 Shotgun – Tactical

6.3.1 Shotguns must be of a factory configuration (see Rule 5.3)

6.3.1.Conventional tubular magazine fed shotguns, only, allowed in this division.

6.3.2 Barrel length may not be changed for the duration of the event.

6.3.3 Internal modifications are allowed providing the modifications do not alter the original factory configuration of the shotgun.

6.3.4 No electronic or optical sights are allowed on shotguns in this division.

6.3.5 No shotgun supporting devices (i.e. bipods, etc.) are allowed in this division.

6.3.6 No compensators or porting on barrels allowed in this division.

6.3.7 No shotgun speed loaders are allowed in this division.

6.3.8 No shotgun in tactical division may START with more than 9 rounds total in the shotgun.

7. HOLSTERS AND EQUIPMENT

7.1 Handgun holsters and equipment - Tactical

7.1.1 Holsters must be a practical/tactical carry style and must be able to safely retain the handgun during vigorous movement

7.1.2 The holster material must completely cover the trigger on all semiautomatic pistols. Revolver holsters must completely cover the trigger and the cylinder.

7.1.3 The belt upon which the holster and magazine/speed loader pouches are attached must be worn at waist level.

7.1.4 Due to safety concerns shoulder holsters and cross draw holsters are disallowed.

8. DIVISION

8.1 Tactical

8.1.1 Participant will compete with a Tactical Handgun (Rule 6.1), Tactical Scoped Rifle (Rule 6.2) and a Tactical Shotgun (Rule 6.3)

9. SCORING

9.1 Scoring per stage will be straight time plus penalties

9.1.1 Any 3GN reactive paper target designated as a "shoot" target must have either one (1) "Center" hit in the 8" Red circle OR have (2) hits anywhere inside the 17.25" Black scoring circle to avoid penalty.

Examples of scoring targets include:

a. One (1) hit in the "Center" (8" Red Circle)

b. Two (2) hits anywhere in 17.25" Black scoring circle to avoid penalty

9.1.2 Example of scoring and penalties on 3GN reactive paper targets:

a. One (1) "Center" hit in the 8" Red circle = no penalty

b. Two (2) hits in any combination inside the 17.25" Black scoring circle or the 8" Red center circle = no penalty

c. One (1) hit in the 17.25" Black scoring circle and NO scoring hit in the 8" Red center circle = 2.5 second penalty (Miss on Target MOT)

e. Target Not Engaged (TNE)= 2.5 second penalty for not making the minimum two hits anywhere on the target plus 2.5 seconds, per target, for the TNE PROCEDURAL for a total penalty of 5 seconds per target added to time.

f. Only holes made by bullets will count for score/penalty. Evidence of the actual bullet must be present on the target, i.e. crown or grease ring (mark) on the hole. Holes made by shrapnel, fragments or flying debris will not count for score/penalty.

9.1.3 Knock down (KD) style plates must fall to score.

Note: If KD style plate is struck by a Rifle OR Pistol bullet and edges, turns or spins the target but does not fall the competitor will get score/credit for KD plate in question.

Note: Any KD plate engaged with SHOT must FALL to score!

9.1.4.1 Failure to knock down a KD plate will result

in a 2.5 second penalty.

9.1.4.2 Failure to engage a knock down (KD) plate will result in a Target Not Engaged (TNE)= 2.5 second penalty for not knocking down the KD plate plus 2.5 seconds, per target, for the TNE PROCEDURAL for a total penalty of 5 seconds per target.

9.1.5.1 Frangible targets (Clay bird) must break (one BB hole is a break) to score.

9.1.5.2 Failure to engage a frangible (Clay bird) plate will result in a Target Not Engaged (TNE)= 2.5 second penalty for not breaking frangible target plus 2.5 seconds, per target, for the TNE PROCEDURAL for a total penalty of 5 seconds per target.

9.1.6 Procedural penalties, 5 seconds per shot, may be assessed for failing to follow the stage directions as written in the stage description. Shooting outside the defined shooting area.

9.1.7 Procedural penalties, 5 seconds, may be assessed for failing to follow stage procedures.

9.1.8 Maximum time for any stage (including target penalties) is 250 seconds.

9.1.9 The course of fire starts with the "Make Ready" command and ends after the "Range is Clear" command.

9.2 Rifle Targets:10" & 4" round KD plates and 3GN reactive paper targets.

9.2.1 Pistol Targets:10" & 4" round KD plates, 3GN reactive paper targets and 4"x10" square KD plates.

9.2.2 Shotgun Targets:4"x10" square KD plates and frangible/clay targets.

9.2.3 Total time accumulated for all stages will determine the event placement.

9.2.4 Lowest time wins.

10. APPEALS

10.1 Decisions are made initially by the stage's Chief Range Officer.

10.2 If the complainant disagrees with the CRO's decision, the Director of Competition (DOC) will be called to make a ruling in the matter. The decision of the DOC will be final. Safety violations will not be subject to arbitration

BRM3G RULES

1. Safety Rules

1.1 Participants are subject to match disqualification for violation of any rule or regulation in sections 1 or 2.

1.2 The BRM3G Championship match will be run on a COLD RANGE.

1.2.1 COLD RANGE (definition): Participants firearms will remain unloaded at the match site except under the direction of a match official.

1.3 Designated Safety Areas

1.3.1 Safety Areas will be clearly marked with signs.

1.3.2 Unloaded firearms may be handled and/or displayed only in the Safety Areas.

1.3.3 No ammunition may be handled in any Safety Area.

1.4 Rifles & Shotguns (carry from vehicle or between stages)

1.4.1 Rifles & shotguns should be cased or carried/slung with the muzzle up or down.

1.4.2 Rifles & shotguns should be carried with actions open and detachable magazines removed.

1.5 Handguns (carry between stages)

1.5.1 Handguns must be cased or remain in holster, magazine removed except in designated Safety Areas, or under the direction of Range Officer(s) on a stage.

1.5.2 On stages, the Ready Condition of handguns must be "Hammer Down" for DA autos & revolvers, and "Cocked & Locked" for SA autos or DA autos with manual override safeties.

1.6 No participants or spectators shall consume or be under the influence of alcohol or non-prescription drugs at the match site before or during shooting. Any participant found to be impaired and deemed unsafe as a result of legitimate prescription drugs may be directed to stop shooting and requested to leave the range.

1.7 Eye protection is mandatory for participants, spectators & range personnel at the match site.

1.8 Ear protection is mandatory for participants, spectators & range personnel while on or near a stage of fire.

2. Disqualifications

2.1 Match disqualification will result in complete disqualification from the match. Shooter will not be allowed to continue with the match and will not be eligible for prizes nor a free entry into next year's match. Final decision is with the Match Director.

2.2 Match disqualification for negligent discharge.

2.2.1 "Negligent Discharge" is defined as the discharge of a firearm in an unsafe manner or unintentionally in which a projectile (bullet) strikes the ground within 3 feet of the competitor or range officer, or outside the confines of the backstop.

2.3 A participant shall be disqualified from the Match for dropping a loaded firearm, or dropping a firearm while in the loading or unloading process.

2.4 A participant shall be disqualified for allowing the muzzle of his/her loaded firearm to break the safety plane (except while holstered, or reholstering.)

2.5 A participant shall be disqualified for unsportsmanlike conduct.

2.5.1 Cheating

2.5.1.1 Intentionally altering targets prior to them being scored to gain an advantage or to avoid a penalty

2.5.1.2 Altering or falsifying score sheets.

2.5.1.3 Altering the configuration of firearms or equipment to gain advantage (See rule 5.3, 5.4, 5.5, 7.1.4).

2.5.2 Consuming or be under the influence of alcohol or non-prescription drugs at the match site while shooting is taking place.

2.5.3 Shooting prohibited ammo (see 4).

2.5.4 Failing to help reset and/or tape targets. (One warning will be issued by the RO on the stage.)

2.5.5 This is not an all inclusive list of unsportsmanlike conduct.

2.6 A participant shall be disqualified for unsafe gun handling. This includes, but is not limited to: handling a gun while people are down range, handling a gun on a stage without permission of the range officer, abandoning a gun in an unsafe manner or direction.

2.7 Stage Disqualifications may be issued for various infractions at the discretion of the Range Master or Match Director.

2.8 All disqualifications will be issued by the Range Master or Match Director.

3. Sportsmanship & Conduct

3.1 Participants and spectators are expected to conduct themselves in a courteous, sportsmanlike manner at all times. Disputes will be handled promptly and fairly by the Range Master.

3.2 Clothing with any offensive or obscene logos, sayings, pictures or drawings will not be worn or displayed while at the match site/range.

3.3 Any competitor with a proven handicap may request, or be required, to shoot the courses of fire other than intended, but may incur a penalty in time/points per string or per stage. The Match Director will rule on any such request on a case-by-case basis.

3.4 Range Officers may assess additional "unsportsmanlike conduct" penalties to competitors that intentionally fail to make a good faith effort to engage and hit targets on order to gain advantage. The Range Master and Match Director shall be the final arbiters of any such penalties.

3.5 Reshoots may only be authorized by the Range Master or Match Director.

4. Ammunition

4.1 No tracer, incendiary, armor piercing, steel jacketed, or steel core ammunition is allowed.

4.2 Pistol/revolver ammunition shall be 9x19 or larger.

4.3 Rifle ammunition shall be .223 Remington (5.56 NATO) or larger.

4.4 Shotgun ammunition shall be 20 gauge or larger, LEAD SHOT & SLUGS ONLY.

4.4.1 No steel shot ammunition allowed.

4.4.2 Slugs may be prohibited on some targets.

4.5 Use of prohibited types of ammunition may result in a stage or match disqualification.

5. Firearms

5.1 All firearms used by competitors shall be serviceable and safe.

5.2 If a competitor's firearm becomes unserviceable during competition, that competitor may replace his/her firearm with another of the same, or similar, model, caliber and sighting system approved by the Match Director or the Range Master.

5.3 For purposes of this ruling, a "firearm" consists of a specific caliber, receiver, barrel, stock, and sighting system combination.

5.4 The same firearm system, for each gun, per Rule 5.3, shall be used during the entire match.

5.5 Competitors may not reconfigure any firearm during the course of a match. (i.e. change caliber, barrel length, shotgun magazine tube length, sighting systems or stock style; changing shotgun choke tubes is not considered a reconfiguration).

5.6 Certain firearm supporting devices may be prohibited by the Match Director.

5.6.1 Supporting devices that risk excess damage to props or pose a risk to shooters are prohibited. (i.e. the Hedgehog and like products are not allowed)

6. Firearms Classifications (Open Class, Tactical Class Iron or Scoped, Heavy Metal)

6.1 Handgun

6.1.1 Open Class

6.1.1.1 No limitations on accessories (see rule 5.3, 5.4, 5.5)

6.1.1.2 Magazine length may not exceed 170 millimeters.

6.1.2 Tactical Class

6.1.2.1 Handguns must be of a factory configuration.

6.1.2.2 Internal modifications are allowed providing they do not alter the original factory configuration of the handgun.

6.1.2.3 Handguns with custom or factory installed electronic sights, optical sights, extended sights, compensators or barrel porting are NOT allowed in this class.

6.1.2.4 Magazines used shall notexceed 170 mm OAL (overall length) for single stacks, and shall not exceed 140 mm OAL for staggered magazines.

6.1.3 Heavy Metal Class

6.1.3.1 Handguns must comply with Tactical Handgun rules with the following exceptions.

6.1.3.2 Handguns must be .45 caliber.

6.1.3.3 Magazines may not be loaded with more than 10 rounds at any time.

6.2 Rifle

6.2.1 Open Class

6.2.1.1 No limitations on accessories (see Rule 5.3, 5.4, 5.5).

6.2.2 Tactical Class

6.2.2.1 Rifles must be of a factory configuration (see Rule 5.3,5.4, 5.5).

6.2.2.2 Internal modifications are allowed providing the modifications do not alter the original factory configuration of the rifle.

6.2.2.3 Tactical Optics Class rifles may be equipped with no more than one (1) optical sight.

6.2.2.4 Tactical Iron Class rifles may be equipped with one non-magnifying optic which is in the same plane as standard iron sights and the bore-line (if in addition, the sights must co-witness) in addition to or in place of Iron sights.

6.2.2.5 Rifle supporting devices (i.e. bipods, etc.) are not allowed in this class.

6.2.2.6 Rifle may have a compensator that is no more than 1" in diameter and 3" in length.

6.2.3 Heavy Metal Class

6. 2.3.1.1 Rifles must comply with Tactical Class rifle rules.

6. 2.3.1.2 Rifles will be .308 Winchester (7.62 x 51 NATO) or larger caliber.

6. 2.3.1.3 Heavy Metal Class rifles may be equipped with one non-magnifying power optic which is in the same plane as standard iron sights and the bore-line (if in addition, the sights must co-witness) in addition to or in place of Iron sights.

6. 2.3.1.4 No magazine shall have more than 20 rounds loaded at any time.

6.3 Shotgun

6.3.1 Open Class

6.5.1 No limitations on accessories (see Rule 5.3, 5.4, 5.5).

6.5.2 Shotgun detachable magazines and speed loaders are allowed in Open Class.

6.5.2.1 Shotgun speed loaders must have a primer relief cut.

6.5.3 Magazine tube length may not be changed for the duration of the match.

6.3.2 Tactical Class

6. 3.2.1 Shotguns must be of a factory configuration (see Rule 5.3, 5.4, 5.5).

6. 3.2.2 Internal modifications are allowed providing the modifications do not alter the original factory configuration of the shotgun.

6.3.2.3 No electronic or optical sights are allowed on shotguns in this class.

6.3.2.4 No shotgun supporting devices (i.e. bipods, etc.) are allowed in this class.

6.3.2.5 No compensators or porting on barrels allowed in this class.

6.3.2.6 No shotgun in Tactical class may be loaded

with more than 9 rounds at any time, or hold over 8 rounds in the magazine tube.

6.3.2.7 No shotgun speed loaders or shotguns with detachable magazines are allowed in this class.

6.3.2.8 Magazine tube length may not be changed for the duration of the match.

6.3.3 Heavy Metal Class

6.3.3.1 Shotguns must comply with Tactical Shotgun rules.

6.3.3.2 Only 12 gauge shotguns are allowed in this class.

6.3.3.3 Only pump actions are allowed in this class.

7. Holsters and other Equipment –All classes

7.1 The handgun holster must be capable of retaining the handgun during the vigorous movement that may be required or otherwise encountered during the courses of fire.

7.2 The handgun holster must allow the competitor to safely draw and reholster the handgun without causing the muzzle to point in an unsafe direction.

7.3 The holster material must completely cover and protect the handgun's trigger.

7.4 The competitor shall use the same handgun holster for the duration of the match.

7.5 Spare ammunition, magazines, speed loaders, and other equipment must be secured in pouches, pockets and/or carriers on the competitor's person or firearm.

7.6 The competitor may not abandon any equipment during a course of fire except detachable magazines, speed loaders, or ammunition clips, unless so directed by the Range Officer and/or stage description.

8. Classes

8.1 Open Class

8.1.1 Any Open Class gun OR Open Class equipment puts the competitor in Open Class for the entire match.

8.1.2 Competitor will shoot firearms which comply with the Firearms Classification rules for Open Class.

8.2 Tactical Class-Iron Sighted Rifle

8.2.1 Competitor will shoot firearms which comply with the Firearms Classification rules for Tactical Class, but must use a rifle with iron sights.

8.3 Tactical Class-Scoped Rifle

8.3.1 Competitor will shoot firearms which comply with the Firearms Classification rules for Tactical Class, but must use a rifle with an (one) optical sight.

8.4 Heavy Metal Class

8.4.1 Competitor will shoot firearms which comply with the Firearms Classification rules for Heavy Metal Class.

9. Scoring

9.1 Scoring per stage will be straight time plus penalties. A maximum time allowed to shoot any stage may be set prior to the start of the match.

9.1.1 Any paper target designated as a "shoot" target requires two (2) hits inside the scoring perforations on the target. (Slug targets MAY be exempted from this rule and only require one (1) hit inside a designated scoring ring.) A Vickers scoring system will be used with 0.5 seconds added to the competitor's raw time on the stage for each point down (or each point not earned) on the paper targets on a stage.

9.1.1.1 The best two hits on paper will be scored.

9.1.1.2 Paper targets which have less than the required number of hits will receive a 5 second penalty for each hit less than that required number. (The penalty is 10 seconds per hit required if the target is > 100 yards from the shooting position.)

9.1.1.3 Example of scoring and penalties on paper targets:

a. "A," "B," or "0" zone hits = no penalty

b. "C" or "-1" hit = 0.5 second penalty

c. "D" or "-3" hit = 1.5 second penalty

d. A paper target engaged by firing at least one round at it, but with no hits, is a Failure To Neutralize. Such a target will receive a minimum of a 10 second penalty for the miss/misses.

e. A paper target which is not engaged by firing at least one round at it will receive a minimum of a 10 second penalty for not making the required hit(s) on the target plus 5 seconds, per target, for a Target Not Engaged (TNE) procedural for a total minimum penalty of 15 seconds per target added to time.

9.1.1.4 Paper targets used in the match may be IPSC (old style), the new IPSC "Classic", TSA, IDPA targets, or any other similar target approved by the Match Director.

9.1.2 Designated "No Shoot" targets will incur a 5 second penalty for each hit.

9.1.3 Non-Paper Targets

9.1.3.1Knock down style targets (i.e. poppers or other steel) must fall to score.

9.1.3.2 Frangible targets must break to score. (One BB hole is a break.)

9.1.3.3 Swinging style rifle targets must be struck solid enough to cause the hidden "flash card" to be visible to the Range Officer. The Range Officer may call hits.

9.1.3.4 Engaging a frangible, knock-down or swinging style target by firing at least one round at it but not breaking it, knocking it down or causing the target to react will result in a 10 second miss penalty per target. If the target is located > 100 yards from the shooting position, the penalty for the miss is 15 seconds.

9.1.3.5 A frangible, knock down or swinging style target which is not engaged by firing at least one round at it will receive an additional 5 second penalty for a Target Not Engaged (TNE) procedural per target added to time.

9.1.4 Procedural penalties, 5 seconds per target, may be assessed for failing to follow the stage directions as stated in the stage briefing.

9.1.5 Procedural penalties, 5 seconds, may be assessed for failing to follow stage procedures.

9.1.6 Stage Not Fired (SNF/DNF) penalty: A competitor shall receive zero (0) match points for each such stage.

9.1.7 A Maximum Time shall be established for each stage (180 seconds unless otherwise noted). Upon failure to complete the stage within the maximum time, a shooter will be stopped by the Range Officer and assessed a stage time equal to the Maximum Time plus all applicable penalties.

9.1.8 Higher penalties may be imposed for desig-

nated high value targets.

9.2 Stage Points

9.2.1 Stages will be assigned a point value based on the number of guns required to be used in the stage.

9.2.1.1 100 stage points to stages using one (1) gun.

9.2.1.2 125 stage points to stages using two (2) guns.

9.2.1.3 150 stage points to stages using three (3) or more guns.

9.2.2 FirstPlace (lowest time) for each stage, in each class, will receive 100% of the points available for that stage. Second place and below will receive points on a percentage basis from the first place time multiplied by the number of stage points.

9.2.3 All classes will be scored separately.

9.2.4 Total points accumulated for all stages will determine match placement by class.

9.2.5 Ties will be broken by an undisclosed Tie Breaker Stage designated by the Match Director.

9.2.6 Highest score in each class wins.

10. Arbitration Rules & General Principles

10.1 Administration –Occasional disputes are inevitable in any competitive activity governed by rules. It is recognized that at the more significant levels of competition, emotions run high and the outcome ismuch more important to the individual competitor. Remaining calm and rational while arbitrating disputes will make this unpleasant job easier.

10.2 Access –Protests may be submitted for arbitration except the actual scoring of targets. However, protests arising from a disqualification for a safety infraction will only be accepted to determine whether or not an infraction as described by the range official was in fact unsafe. The commission of the infraction may not be protested.

10.3 Appeals –Decisions are made initially by the Range Officer for the stage or area. If the complainant disagrees with a decision, the Range Master should be summoned and asked to rule. If a disagreement still exists, the Match Director must be summoned and asked to rule. His decision is final.

Yamil R. Sued photo

USPSA MULTI-GUN ADDENDUM 2012 EDITION

A) Introduction:

In the interest of responding to the interests of USPSA members, while seeking to preserve the unique attributes of USPSA competition, this provisional addendum has been prepared to provide a USPSA-authorized framework for matches involving more than one firearm type ("multi-gun matches").

The intent of this addendum is to enable USPSA clubs to run multi-gun matches within the context of the USPSA rules. Since this type of match represents a new type of USPSA competition, this addendum is provided on an experimental or provisional basis. The terms of this amendment have the weight and authority of the USPSA rules, and multi-gun matches may be run as USPSA events under the terms of this addendum, but with the understanding that this addendum may be amended, modified or withdrawn at any time.

This addendum and the authority of any guidelines relating to USPSA multigun matches will expire on Dec. 31st, 2012, unless formally extended or adopted for inclusion in the official USPSA rules by action of the USPSA Board of Directors.

Please note that throughout the provisional period, clubs are encouraged to provide feedback about this addendum and these provisional rules for multigun matches. Your input will help USPSA improve the clarity, quality and effectiveness of the rules relating to multi-gun competition.

B) Authority:

This addendum draws its authority from the current edition of USPSA rule books (e.g., Handgun rules, Rifle rules, Shotgun rules and Tournament rules), and should be considered a provisional amendment to those rule books.

The purpose of this addendum is to identify and address specific areas where the rules for multi-gun matches will conflict with or deviate from the rules for a single firearm-specific match or a tournament composed of two or more firearm-specific matches. Except as and unless noted otherwise in this amendment and within the context of a multi-gun match, the current editions of the USPSA rule book are to be considered the definitive sources of rules authority for USPSA competition.

C) Terms:

Except as and unless noted otherwise in this amendment, the terms "handgun", "shotgun" or "rifle" within the separate rule books are to be construed to mean "firearm" within the context of a multi-gun match, and are to be interpreted to apply to all firearm types.

D) General Regulations:

(i) Definition:

A "multi-gun match" is defined as a match (see 6.1.4) in which at least one stage involves the use of two or more different firearm types. A multi-gun match may involve any combination of handgun, rifle and shotgun usage, including stages which involve one, two or all three firearm types. Other than the use of multiple firearm types, all other provisions of 6.1.4 apply.

(ii) Notice:

Multi-gun matches must be clearly denoted as such in match notices, materials and publications, including match announcements, match entry forms, match calendar listings, and match confirmation letters. This is to ensure that competitors are fully informed as to multi-gun equipment requirements and the rules that will be in effect during the competition, and to distinguish multi-gun competitions from traditional match formats (single firearm-specific matches and tournaments composed of multiple firearm-specific matches).

(iii) Competition Divisions:

Divisions recognized in a multi-gun match will be those divisions defined in **Appendix A1-A5**. Each competitor must declare one division for the match (see 6.2.3), and all firearms used during the match must conform to the equipment requirements for the declared division. In the event that the division is not recognized, a competitor fails to declare a division or, at any time during the match, the competitor's equipment fails to comply with division equipment requirements, the provisions of 6.2.5 (including sub clauses) will apply.

(iii)a For scoring purposes, there will be no recognition of Revolver, Production or Limited-10 as separate handgun divisions within the context of a USPSA multi-gun match. All handguns will be scored as Limited, Tactical or Open, in accordance with currently-defined tournament aggregate divisions.

(iii)b "Heavy Metal Tactical" division within the context of a USPSA multigun match at this time will follow the guidelines of the newly formed Heavy Metal division in the USPSA Tournament and **Appendix A5** of the Multigun rules.

(iii)c If any firearm fails to meet the minimum power factor floor for the relevant Division, the competitor may continue shooting the match, but not for score or match recognition. Heavy Metal competitors failing to make major pf with any firearm (but does make minor) will be moved to an appropriate division instead of shooting for no score.

(iv) Competition Awards:

The award and/or prize protocol for a multi-gun match must be clearly published in relevant match materials, including entry forms and match books, if any. However, because of the complexities involved in combining the use of dissimilar firearm types within a single competition, the distribution of awards and/or prizes by firearm type (i.e., handgun-specific awards, rifle-specific awards, etc) is prohibited. Instead, awards and/or prizes will only be distributed according to placement in the combined multi-gun division standings.

(v) Stage Scoring Guidelines:

Multi-gun stages must be scored according to the methods listed in Section 9.2 of the USPSA rule book, including appropriate use of Power Factor for each firearm used. Time Plus scoring is listed in the supplement as an alternative scoring system for trial purposes.

Match Scoring Guidelines:

Multi-gun matches must be scored using EzWinScore version 4.03 or later. Competitors will be registered in the multi-gun match in a manner which reflects their declared Power Factor for each firearm type, and the single division which will apply for the entire match.

Stage Balance Guidelines:

While round counts may vary, a multi-gun match should provide a balanced test of firearms skills. Consistent with Tournament rule 2.3, total points available in any firearm discipline should not vary by more than 25% of the total points available in any other firearm discipline. A match which is heavily biased towards a specific firearm type does not represent a true test of skills across the disciplines and should be avoided.

For example, a multi-gun match in which the ratio of available points between handgun, rifle and shotgun is 30% / 30% / 40% would be considered balanced. A multi-gun match in which the ratio of available points is 20% / 30% / 50% is not considered balanced, because there is more than a 25% variance in available points between two disciplines.

Specific Rule Variances:

MG 1.1.5:

Competitors must be permitted to solve the challenge presented in a freestyle manner, and to shoot targets on an "as and when visible" basis; however, in a multi-gun course of fire the course description must define which targets are to be shot with which type of firearm. (Rule 4.3.1.10 is waived from 1.1.5 when the same self-indicating targets are engaged from multiple positions, courses of fire using these, may stipulate from which positions the targets may be re-engaged from).

MG 1.1.5.1:

Course designers may present challenges which provide the shooter options with regard to firearm use within the context of a multi-gun stage. Any such options must comply with sections MG-2.1.3, and MG-3.2, and must be consistent with all other sections in this document.

For example, a course designer may design a handgun-designated course with three target arrays: target array "A" must be engaged with handgun, the shooter may then engage either array "B" or array "C" with handgun, and finish by engaging the remaining array with shotgun. This would be considered a valid course of fire if minimum distances to any steel targets are valid no matter which option the shooter chooses, consistent with MG-2.1.3; and the course description appropriately designates targets by firearm type for each option, consistent with MG-3.2.

MG 1.2:

Multigun stages do not have a round count limitation.

MG 2.1.3:

Minimum distances for any metal target in a multi-gun match are the minimum distances defined for the firearm used to engage that target, as documented in the discipline-specific rule book for that firearm type. In the present (2008/2009) version of the rules, minimum distances for metal targets are defined as:

— Handgun: 23 Feet

— Shotgun (birdshot): 16 Feet

— Shotgun (slugs): 131 Feet

— Rifle: 164 Feet

All other provisions of 2.1.3 (including sub clauses) apply.

MG 3.2:

Written stage briefings for multi-gun stages must also include:

— Identification of specific targets to be shot with specific firearms

(i.e., T1-T4 are to be engaged with Handgun, T5-T8 with Rifle).

— Location and ready condition for all firearms used on the stage.

— Designation of locations and conditions where firearms may be abandoned

(Type-1, Type-2 or Type-3 as specified in MG 10.5.3)

All other provisions of 3.2 (including sub clauses) apply.

MG 4.2.1:

Any paper target approved for use in USPSA matches may be used in Multigun. Targets may be mixed on a stage to clearly define which targets are to be engaged with which firearm.

MG 4.3 USPSA Approved Multi-Gun Targets-Metal

MG 4.3.1

Approved metal targets for use in USPSA Multigun matches include any metal target that provides an adequate method of determining hits or misses other than by falling (self-indicating hits). Scoring metal targets by listening for hits is not permitted. Self-indicating targets when used in a Rifle COF may be engaged from multiple shooting locations as new targets. All types of metal targets may be used as scoring targets or no-shoots. They must be scored in accordance with the relevant Appendices.

MG 4.3.1.5

Scoring of metal targets will be per the Optional Enhanced Target Values Supplement

MG 4.3.1.5.1

Metal scoring plates will be scored as a hit, if the plate falls from a hit on the plate, base or supporting stand when the plate is shot at.

MG 4.3.1.7

Metal scoring targets need not be painted after each competitor.

MG 4.3.1.10

Self-indicating targets when used in a Multi-Gun COF, may be engaged from multiple shooting locations as new targets. All types of metal targets may be used as scoring targets or no-shoots.

MG 5.1.2:

Minimum cartridge for each firearm type in a multi-gun match is the minimum cartridge defined for the firearm, as documented.

MG 5.1.7:

Competitors must use the same firearms throughout the match. For purposes of this rule, a firearm is considered to be the combination of a specific caliber, barrel, stock or grip, sighting system, and fixed magazine or magazine tube if applicable. Competitors must not reconfigure any firearm (i.e., change caliber, barrel, stock or grip style, sighting system, and fixed magazine or magazine tube) during the course of a match.

All other provisions of 5.1.7 (including sub clauses) apply. Additionally, the provisions of Shotgun 5.2.5 apply.

MG 5.1.8:

Competitors may be required to use a prop gun supplied by the Match Director on a stage to start the course of fire; it may not be required to engage more than three (3) targets before abandoning it. The prop gun and all related ammunition and equipment will be provided by the host match officials and be the same for all competitor's. Should the equipment provided malfunction or fail; the competitor will be stopped immediately and given a reshoot once the malfunction has been repaired.

MG 5.1.9:

Competitors may be required to carry more than one firearm at a time, but must never be required or allowed to engage targets with more than one firearm at a time.

MG 5.2.1:

Except when within the boundaries of a safety area, or when under the supervision and direct command of a Range Officer, competitors must carry their firearms according to the discipline-specific rules. Refer to 5.2.1 (and subsections) in the current Handgun, Rifle or Shotgun rules for details regarding specific carry conditions and requirements.

All other provisions of 5.2.1 (including subsections) apply.

MG 5.2.5.3:

Due to the varied equipment requirements in a multi-gun match, belts, holsters, belt-mounted magazine holders and speed-loading devices and any other equipment worn or carried by the shooter may be changed, repositioned or reconfigured between stages, provided that such reconfiguration is compliant with MG-5.1.7, and all equipment is in a rules-compliant configuration prior to the start of the shooter's attempt on the Course of Fire.

MG 5.2.7:

Tie down holsters and holsters with the heel of the butt below the top of the belt are allowed. All other provisions of 5.2.7 (including sub clauses) apply.

MG 5.6:

Any Rifle and/or Handgun and associated ammunition may be tested at any time. In the event that the ammunition fails to make declared power factor, the actual (measured) power factor will be used for scoring. Shotguns and ammunition must be 20 gauge or larger (must be 12 gauge in Heavy Metal divisions). Shotguns will be scored major. All other provisions of 5.6 (including subsections) apply.

MG 5.7.7:

In the event that a Range Officer terminates a course of fire due to a suspicion that a competitor has an unsafe firearm or unsafe ammunition (e.g. a "squib" load), the Range Officer will take whatever steps he deems necessary to return both the competitor and the range to a safe condition. The Range Officer will then inspect the firearm or ammunition and proceed as follows:

5.7.7.1

If the Range Officer finds evidence that confirms the suspected problem, the competitor will not be entitled to a reshoot, but will be ordered to rectify the problem. On the competitor's score sheet, the time will be recorded up to the last shot fired, and the course of fire will be scored "as shot", including all applicable misses and penalties (see Rule 9.5.6).

5.7.7.2

If the Range Officer discovers that the suspected safety problem does not exist, the competitor will be required to reshoot the stage.

MG 6.1.4:

The provisions of 6.1.4 are waived to allow the use of more than one type of firearm within the context of a multi-gun match. All other provisions of 6.1.4 apply.

MG 6.2.6:

Disqualification during a multi-gun match is disqualification for the entire competition. Tournament rule 2.8 is not applicable in a multi-gun match. Disqualified competitors will not be allowed to continue in the match, and are not eligible for match prizes or awards.

MG 8.1:

Ready conditions for each firearm type are the ready conditions as documented in the discipline-specific rule book for that firearm type. Note that a course of fire may require that a firearm be "staged" (prepared and placed prior to the start signal in a specific position and condition for use later during the course of fire). In such cases the written course description must define the position, condition and location of the staged firearm(s). Stage designs must be configured in so that firearms, when staged, are compliant with the requirements in 10.5.2, and positioned in such a way that no person is ever allowed or required to pass in front of the muzzle of a staged firearm. All other applicable provisions of 8.1 (including sub clauses) apply.

MG 8.3.1:

Where more than one firearm will be used during a course of fire, the Range Officer will direct and supervise the competitor through the process of preparing all firearms. The Range Officer will give the "Make Ready" command, signifying the start of the Course of Fire, and will then direct and supervise the competitor through the process of preparing and positioning any "staged" firearms. The Range Officer will then accompany the competitor to the start position and direct the competitor to prepare the firearm to be initially used on the stage, prior to assuming the ready position. The initial "Make Ready" command defines the start of the "Course of Fire" regardless of how many firearms are subsequently prepared, loaded and/or staged following that command. All other applicable provisions of 8.3.1 (including sub clauses) apply.

A "pre-loading" area may be used on any stage, subject to the Range Master's discretion. The "pre-loading" area must be in a safe position and orientation,outside the active stage boundaries but still well within the confines of the berm, and must be clearly and obviously marked to distinguish it from a Safety Area or other use. Competitors may "pre-load" in this area only under the active direction and supervision of a Range Officer.

"Pre-loading" activity begins with a "Make Ready" command, and is to be considered part of the Course of Fire. As such, "pre-loading" activity, including transporting loaded guns to staging or start position(s), is subject to the provisions of relevant safety regulations, including (but not limited to) 10.4.3 (shot while loading), 10.5.1 (handling firearm without RO supervision), 10.5.2 (unsafe muzzle direction), 10.5.3 (dropped gun), 10.5.9 (finger inside trigger guard during loading), etc.

MG 8.3.6:

Where more than one firearm is used during a course of fire, the Range Officer will give the command "If You Are Finished, Unload And Show Clear" and will supervise the shooter through the appropriate procedure for clearing the most recently used firearm (see 8.3.6, 8.3.7). When that procedure is complete, the Range Officer will accompany the shooter to any firearms abandoned during the course of fire (see MG-10.5.3), and repeat the procedure to supervise the clearing of each firearm in turn. Only when ALL firearms have been cleared will the Range Officer declare "Range Is Clear" (8.3.8). In order to reduce stage clearance time, a Range Officer may be assigned to clear "abandoned" firearms at the Range Master's discretion. After ensuring that the range is clear and no person is downrange of the abandoned firearm, the RO shall verify that the abandoned firearm is in a legal abandoned state (eg, properly positioned, and safety-on or empty as appropriate per MG 10.5.3). Upon verifying the condition, the RO may clear the firearm and transport the cleared firearm to a rack or other location behind the line. The

Range Officer is responsible for the safe handling of the firearm during this process, including (but not limited to) muzzle direction. All other applicable provisions of 8.3.6, 8.3.7 and 8.3.8 (including sub clauses) apply.

MG 9.3:

A competitor's score is calculated by identifying the highest value stipulated number of hits on each target which are of the appropriate caliber, as determined by the firearm specified for use on that target in the course instructions.

Any hit(s) upon the scoring surface of a scoring paper target which is/are determined to have been fired from the incorrect firearm for that target shall not be scored and, unless there are scoring hit(s) from the correct firearm, any resulting Miss penalties shall apply. In the case of steel or frangible targets, any hits by the non-specified firearm which result in that target being unavailable for further engagement shall be scored with Failure To Shoot At and Miss penalties.

Any hits on a paper or metal penalty target will be scored in accordance with

the appropriate provisions of 9.4.2 and 9.4.3. All other provisions of 9.2 and 9.4 apply. Also note that violation of firearm-specific minimum distances (see 2.1.3 and 10.5.17, 10.5.15, 10.5.12) may result when a metal target is engaged with the incorrect firearm.

MG 10.3.1:

A competitor who commits a safety infraction or any other prohibited activity during a USPSA multi-gun match will be disqualified from the entire match, and will be prohibited from attempting any remaining courses of fire in that match regardless of the schedule or physical layout of the match.

MG 10.5.3:

Within the context of a multi-gun stage, a competitor may be required to "abandon" a firearm in order to use another firearm. In this context, an "abandoned firearm" is a firearm which the competitor has used, placed on the ground or other stable object in accordance with course requirements, and subsequently moved more than one (1) yard away from. In a multi-gun stage, the provisions of 10.5.3.2 are waived to allow specific ways in which a firearm may be "abandoned" during a course of fire. There are three ways in which a firearm may be legally "abandoned" during a course of fire:

Type 1) A stage may provide a device which retains the firearm in a safe and stable position and orientation. Examples of suitable devices include boxes (with or without lids) which have sides high enough to prevent the firearm from being dislodged; tubes or barrels arranged to hold the firearm in place, etc. Any such devices must be securely fixed in a safe position and orientation, so that a firearm placed within is pointed towards a berm or other safe direction, cannot easily or inadvertently be dislodged, and so that no person may pass in front of the muzzle of a firearm placed in the device. Stage designers and setup crews when using grounding boxes, should be built with consideration of the various firearms with optics and detachable magazines (shotgun, handgun and rifle). Padding should also be provided to avoid damage to a firearm. If a firearm is placed in such a device, the firearm may be abandoned in any "ready condition" defined in Section 8.1 When a loaded firearm is safely placed within such a device, the shooter may move downrange of the abandoned firearm (subject to course instructions and constraints).

— Abandoning a loaded firearm in the device in an improper condition (eg, loaded and safety off) will result in a Match DQ.

— Abandoning a loaded firearm outside of such a device and subsequently moving downrange of it will result in a Match DQ.

Type 2) A stage may provide a location for the firearm which does not provide positive retention. Examples of this type of placement would include a marked location on a table, a flat surface, a referenced location on the ground, etc., where there are no raised sides or other devices designed to keep the firearm from being inadvertently moved after placement. If a firearm is placed in such a location, the firearm may be abandoned in any "ready condition" defined in Section 8.1 When a firearm is abandoned in a non-retention location, the shooter may NOT move downrange of the abandoned firearm (subject to course instructions and constraints) UNLESS the firearm is UNLOADED (see Option 3, below).

— Abandoning a loaded firearm in the location in an improper condition (e.g., loaded and safety off) will result in a Match DQ.

— Abandoning a loaded firearm in a non-retention location and subsequently moving downrange of it will result in a Match DQ.

Type 3) Whether or not the stage provides a specific device or location for an abandoned firearm, a firearm may be abandoned if it is in an UNLOADED ready condition (as defined in 10.5.13 for each firearm type). If an UNLOADED firearm is abandoned, the shooter may move downrange of the abandoned firearm (subject to course instructions and constraints).

— Abandoning a loaded firearm in a non-retention location and subsequently moving downrange of it will result in a Match DQ.

Note: UNLOADING a firearm in an unsafe manner, including but not limited to 10.4.1 (shot in unsafe direction), 10.4.2 (shot hits ground within 3 yards), and 10.4.6 (shot while moving and not engaging targets) will result in a Match DQ.

Note: If the shooter remains within 1 yard of the firearm as specified in **MG 10.5.3.2, the firearm is not considered abandoned. The options, simplified:**

— **1: Loaded and on safe (or empty) and in a retention device = free to move downrange.**

— **2: Loaded and on safe (or empty) but NOT positively retained = lateral movement only.**

— **3: UNLOADED = free to move downrange.**

All abandoned firearms, whether loaded or unloaded, must always be oriented with the muzzle pointing in a safe direction as defined in 10.5.2, and safemuzzle direction for any abandoned firearms must be specified in the course description. Abandoning a firearm in an unsafe location, position or orientation (e.g., pointing in an unsafe direction) will result in a Match DQ. Props, markings or other devices may be used to indicate the safe muzzle direction of an abandoned firearm.

Stage designs must be configured in such a way that no person is ever allowed or required to pass in front of the muzzle of an abandoned firearm, whether loaded or unloaded. An abandoned firearm found to be pointed in an unsafe direction or which results in any person passing in front of the muzzle will be considered a violation of 10.5.2 or 10.5.5, as appropriate. When a firearm is abandoned, all other relevant provisions of 10.5.3 apply.

10.5.3.3 Handling a second firearm during abandonment

A competitor may, during abandonment of one firearm, handle his second firearm to be used without penalty, providing all safety aspects are followed. (ex. Abandoning a shotgun, and a handgun is to be used for the next array of targets, the competitor may draw the handgun while in the act of abandoning the shotgun). Neither firearm may be fired while competitor has both in hand.

APPENDIX A1 DIVISIONS MULTIGUN

Multigun Appendix A1 is a brief overview of the rules, not a substitute for the complete rules in the handgun, shotgun and rifle rule books. It also explains the additional restrictions and allowances compared to the HG, R and SG rules.

USPSA MultiGun Open Division

Division Rule brief Multigun allowances Multigun restrictions

Rifle Open Rifle No No

Minimum caliber N0

Power Factor 320 major/150 minor

Compensator Yes, any size

Optics Yes, multiple allowed

Bipods Yes

Max. number of rounds in magazine No

Division Rule

Brief Multigun Allowances Multigun restrictions

Shotgun Open shotgun No No

Minimum gauge 20 ga

Action type Any

Compensator/Porting Yes

Optics Yes

Max. number of rounds in magazine 10 rounds +1 for loaded start

Division Rule brief Multigun allowances Multigun restrictions

Handgun Open handgun Yes No

Caliber .355 Minimum

Power Factor 165 major/125 minor

Compensator/Porting Yes

Optics Any

Magazine Length 171.25 mm maximum

Max. number of rounds in magazine No

Holster Lower/Tie down OK

APPENDIX A2 DIVISIONS MULTIGUN

USPSA MultiGun Limited Division

Division Rule brief Multigun allowances Multigun restrictions

Rifle Limited Rifle Yes Yes

Minimum Caliber No

Power Factor 320 major/150 minor

Compensator 1.00" X 3.00" Max.

Optics One non magnified No variable powered

Bipods No

Max. number of rounds in magazine No

Division Rule brief Multigun allowances Multigun restrictions

Shotgun Limited Shotgun No No

Minimum Gauge 20 ga.

Action Type Any

Compensator/Porting No

Optics No

Max. number of rounds in magazine 8 Rounds +1 for loaded start

Division Rule brief Multigun allowances Multigun restrictions

Handgun Limited Handgun Yes No

Minimum Caliber .355 minor/.400 major

Power Factor 165 major/125 minor

Compensator/Porting No

Optics No

Magazine Length 141.25 mm Max. length, 171.25 mm in Single Stack guns.

Max. number of rounds in magazine No

Holster Lower/Tie downOK

APPENDIX A3 DIVISIONS MULTIGUN

USPSA MultiGun Tactical Division

Division Rule brief Multigun allowances Multigun restrictions

Rifle Tactical Rifle No No

Minimum Caliber No

Power Factor 320 major/150 minor

Compensator 1.00"X 3.00" Max.

Optics Maximum one

Bipods No

Max. number of rounds in magazine No

Division Rule brief Multigun allowances Multigun restrictions

Shotgun Limited/Tactical No No

Minimum Gauge 20 ga.

Action Type Any

Compensator/Porting No

Optics No

Max. number of rounds in magazine 8 Rounds +1 for loaded start

Division Rule brief Multigun allowances Multigun restrictions

Handgun Limited Handgun Yes No

Minimum Caliber .355 minor/.400 major

Power Factor 165 major/125 minor

Compensator/Porting No

Optics No

Magazine Length 141.25 mm Max.171.25 for Single Stack Guns

Max. number of rounds in magazine No

Holster Lower/Tie down OK

APPENDIX A4 DIVISIONS MULTIGUN

USPSA Multigun Heavy Metal Limited Division

Division Rule brief Multigun allowances Multigun restrictions

Rifle Limited Rifle No Yes

Minimum Cartridge No .308 Win/7.62x51

Power Factor 320 pf minimum

Compensator 1.00"X 3.00" Max.

Optics No

Bipods No

Max. number of rounds in Magazine 20 Rounds

Division Rule brief Multigun allowances Multigun restrictions

Shotgun Heavy Metal No No

Minimum Gauge 12ga.

Action Type Pump Only

Compensator/Porting No

Optics No

Max. number of rounds in Magazine 8 Rounds

Division Rule brief Multigun allowances Multigun restrictions

Handgun Limited 10 Handgun Yes Yes

Caliber Must be.45 ACP

Power Factor Minimum 165 pf

Compensator/Porting No

Optics No

Max. number of rounds in magazine 10 +1 for loaded start

Holster Lower/Tie down OK

APPENDIX A5 DIVISIONS MULTIGUN

USPSA Multigun Heavy Metal Tactical Division

Division Rule brief Multigun allowances Multigun restrictions

Rifle Tactical Rifle No Yes

Minimum Cartridge .308 Win/7.62x51

Power Factor 320 Minimum pf

Compensator 1.00"X 3.00" Max.

Optics Maximum one

Bipods No

Max. number of rounds in magazine 20 Rounds +1 for loaded start

Division Rule brief Multigun allowances Multigun restrictions

Shotgun Limited/Tactical No Yes

Minimum Gauge Must be 12 ga

Action Type Any

Compensator/Porting No

Optics No

Max. number of rounds in magazine 8 Rounds +1 for loaded start

Division Rule brief Multigun allowances Multigun restrictions

Handgun Limited 10 Handgun Yes Yes

Caliber .400 minimum

Power Factor Minimum 165 pf

Compensator/Porting No

Optics No

Max. number of rounds in Magazine 10 Rounds +1 for loaded start

Holster Lower/Tie down OK

APPENDIX C1

Calibration of Poppers

Initial Calibration

1. The Range Master must designate a specific supply of ammunition and one or more handguns to be used as official calibration tools by officials authorized by him to serve as calibration officers.

2. Prior to commencement of a match, the calibration ammunition must be chronographed using the procedure specified in Appendix C2. The calibration ammunition, when tested through each designated handgun, must achieve a power factor between 119-124 sub-minor to qualify.

3. Once the supply of ammunition and the designated handguns have been tested and approved by the Range Master, they are not subject to challenge by competitors.

4. The Range Master must arrange for each popper to be calibrated prior to the commencement of a match, and whenever required during a match.

5. For initial calibration, each metal scoring target must be set to fall when hit within the calibration zone with a single shot fired from a designated handgun using the calibration ammunition. The shot must be fired from a minimum of 10 yards.

6. Calibration Challenges. If, during a course of fire, a popper does not fall when hit, a competitor has three alternatives:

   a. The popper is shot again until it falls. In this case, no further action is required and the course of fire is scored "as shot".

   b. The popper is left standing but the competitor does not challenge the calibration. In this case, no further action is required and the course of fire is scored "as shot", with the subject popper scored as a miss.

   c. The popper is left standing and the competitor challenges the calibration. In this case, the popper and the surrounding area on which it stands must not be touched or interfered with by any person. If a Match Official violates this rule, the competitor must reshoot the course of fire. If the competitor or any other person violates this rule, the popper will be scored as a miss and the rest of the course of fire will be scored "as shot". If the popper falls for any non-interference reason (e.g. wind action), before it can be calibrated.

Section 4.6 will apply, and a reshoot must be ordered.

7. In the absence of any interference, or problem with a target mechanism, a calibration officer must conduct a calibration test of the subject popper (when required under 6(c) above), from a minimum of 10 yards of the target with the match calibration ammo. The following will apply:

1. If the first shot by the calibration officer hits on or below the calibration zone and the popper falls, the popper is deemed to be properly calibrated, and it will be scored as a miss.

2. If the first shot fired by the calibration officer hits the popper anywhere on its frontal surface and the popper does not fall, the calibration test is deemed to have failed and the competitor must be ordered to reshoot the course of fire, once the popper has been recalibrated.

3. If the first shot fired by the calibration officer hits above the calibration zone, the calibration test is deemed to have failed and the competitor must be ordered to reshoot the course of fire once the Popper has been recalibrated.

4. If the first shot fired by the calibration officer misses the popper altogether, another shot must be fired until one of 7(a), 7(b) or 7(c) occurs.

8. Note that authorized metal plates are not subject to calibration or challenge (See Rule 4.3.1.6).

MG Appendix C2 (Target Values):

In general, target values for Multi-Gun matches are as defined in Appendix B of the relevant rule book(s). It may be desirable, however, to use enhanced target values to ensure practical and competitive target engagement. Please refer to the separate supplement, "Enhanced Target Values", for information and guidelines. Frangible flying birds will be scored at 10 point value with an option of 20 point value should the MD choose, and to have been considered disappeared once they land.

Disclaimer:

These rules and guidelines are expressly provided on a provisional basis for a period of time, during which they are subject to change. It is recommended that competitors NOT make equipment purchase decisions based on provisional materials, as future changes and refinements may affect the applicability of that equipment for competition purposes.

Call To Action:

These provisional rules are provided so that clubs may try them out, see what works, and provide feedback to USPSA. The USPSA Board wants to ensure that USPSA competitions are relevant and interesting to USPSA members. During this provisional period, we will be paying a great deal of attention to feedback that we receive from members and clubs, about the experiences gained at Multi-Gun Matches. You can help

USPSA by reporting back to us what works, and what doesn't, so that we can make the final rules as clear and complete as possible. Please help us, by trying these rules out, letting us know how they work, and how they can be improved.

SUPPLEMENT

Additional scoring methods to Comstock.

"Time Plus"

Time Plus will be scored as follows:

MG 9.1: Scoring per stage will be straight time with bonus' for accuracy.

9.1.1

Any IPSC cardboard target, designated as a "shoot" target must have either one (1) "A" hit OR two (2) hits anywhere inside the scoring perforations on the target (i.e. minimum 2 "D" hits) to avoid a penalty. Examples of neutralized targets include:

a. One hit in upper A/B zone

b. One "A" hit on lower A zone

c. Two hits anywhere in scoring area (i.e. – minimum of two "D" hits) to avoid penalty.

9.1.2

Example of scoring and penalties on paper targets:

a. One "A" zone hit or one hit in the upper A/B zone = no penalty

b. Two hits in any combination "C or D" = no penalty

c. One C or D hit only = 5 second penalty (Failure to neutralize)

d. No hits on target but target was engaged = 10 second penalty

e. Target Not Engaged (TNE)= 10 second penalty

for not making the minimum two hits anywhere on the target plus 5 seconds, per target, for the TNE PROCEDURAL for a total penalty of 15 seconds per target added to time.

9.1.3

Designated "No Shoot" targets that are hit will incur a 5 second penalty for each hit.

9.1.4

Knock down style targets (i.e. poppers) must fall to score. Poppers will be calibrated using the proper calibration gun and ammo for the discipline being used on such targets

9.1.5

Failure to engage a knock down or swinging style target will result in a 15-second penalty. (10 seconds for not making the hit and 5 seconds TNE.)

9.1.6

Engaging a frangible, knock-down or swinging style target but not breaking it (one BB hole is a break), knocking it down or causing the target to react will result in a 10 second penalty per target. R.O. may call hits.

9.1.7

Procedural penalties, 5 seconds per shot, may be assessed for failing to follow the stage directions as written in the stage description.

9.1.8

Procedural penalties, 5 seconds, may be assessed for failing to follow stage procedures.

9.1.9

Stage Not Fired (SNF) penalty, 500 seconds per stage not fired.

9.1.10

Maximum penalty time for any stage (including target penalties) is 500 seconds.

9.1.11

Disappearing targets and flying birds. The course description must stipulate that these will be scored as a bonus target when hit and a non-penalty miss when not. Bonus' are scored as time off the shooters stage time and the amount should reflect the difficulty of the target itself.

MG 9.2: Stage Points

9.2.1

First Place (lowest time) for each stage, in each division, will receive 100 points; Second Place and below will figure points on a percentage basis of the 100 from 1st Place.

9.2.2

Total points accumulated for all stages will determine the match placementby division.

9.2.3

Highest score wins.

Score-Card Design:

Three Typical approaches are:

Range Scoring:

After a shooter's attempt at the Course of Fire, the Range Officer will score targets as normal, with one additional step: the firearm type must be recorded on the scorecard for each hit. In the case of the "additional column" type of scorecard, this is simply a matter of calling out the firearm type as each hit is scored. For example:

"Alpha Bravo, Pistol" (scorer would enter 1-A and 1-B, and a "P" in the firearm column)

"Alpha Charlie, Rifle" (scorer would enter 1-A and 1-C, and an "R" in the firearm column)

"Delta Mike, Rifle" (scorer would enter 1-D and 1-M, and an "R" in the firearm column) In the case of the "separate section" type of scorecard, this is even easier: simply ensure that the hits are recorded on the correct section of the scorecard. For example:

"Alpha Bravo, Pistol" (scorer would enter 1-A and 1-B in the Pistol section of the scorecard)

"Alpha Charlie, Rifle" (scorer would enter 1-A and 1-C in the Rifle section of the scorecard)

"Delta Mike, Rifle" (scorer would enter 1-D and 1-M in the Rifle section of the scorecard)

Note that there is no change in either approach to the procedure for recording No-Penalty Misses, No-Shoot hits or Procedurals, as the scoring values for those hits do not change for different Power Factors.

SUPPLEMENT – Optional Enhanced Target Values:

In a multi-gun stage, certain targets may prove to be "not worth shooting" when the standard target values are used (5 points for handgun steel, 5 points for clays, 5 or 10 points for rifle and shotgun steel). Using an extreme example, a plate at 500 yards may be "not worth shooting", given that the 5 or 10 points gained for a hit would likely cost the average shooter an inordinate amount of time. This supplement provides a provisional solution to the problem, by allowing matches to enhance the scoring values for targets within certain guidelines and constraints:

— Steel handgun target values may be doubled (10 points) at distances beyond 50 yards. Use of steel handgun targets beyond 100 yards is discouraged.

— Steel shotgun *shot* target values may be increased 10 points (to 15 points or 20 points) at distances beyond 20 yards. Use of steel shotgun targets beyond 35 yards is discouraged.

— Steel shotgun *slug* target values may be increased 10 points (to 15 points or 20 points) at distances beyond 50 yards. Use of steel shotgun targets beyond 100 yards is discouraged.

— Thrown frangible shotgun targets (i.e., A clay launched by a falling popper) will score 10 or 20 points per Multigun Appendix C2 and shotgun 4.4.1.2.

— Steel rifle target values may be increased 10 points for each 100 yards of distance. i.e.,

0-99 yards value is 5 or 10 points

100-199 yards value may be increased up to 15 or 20 points

200-299 yards value may be increased up to 25 or 30 points

300-399 yards value may be increased up to 35 or 40 points

Etc.

Enhanced target values for steel should comply with the following constraints:

— Enhanced target values are defined at the discretion of the course designer or match director, before the match begins. There is no requirement that steel target values be enhanced; this supplement only provides an option that the course designer may use to make targets "worth shooting".

— Enhanced target values should be used only to ensure competitive equity and to remove any competitive "benefit" which might arise by choosing to ignore a distant target. Enhanced target values should not be used abusively or punitively (eg, assigning high target values to difficult shots, resulting in a large number of "zero-scores" on a stage).

— Enhanced target values should be used sparingly, in order to preserve "balance" in the stage designs. It is recommended that no more than 50% of the points in any stage be derived from "enhanced target values".

— Enhanced target values apply to steel or thrown/launched frangible targets only. Providing enhanced scoring values for paper targets is not supported.

— Stage descriptions must clearly identify enhanced-value targets.

— Per 9.4.4, Comstock Misses will be worth twice the value of a scoring hit (eg, a miss on a 30-point target will be penalized 60 points).

— Per 9.2.3.2, steel targets are not applicable in Virginia Count stages.

— Per 9.2.4.5, Miss penalties do not accrue in Fixed Time stages.

— Per 10.1.2, Procedural Penalties will always incur twice the maximum scoring value of a hit on a paper target (10 points).

— It is NOT required that all steel on a stage have the same value. Steel target values may be mixed on a single stage.

— Where feasible, colors should be used to indicate target values (eg, yellow ribbons near 10-point rifle targets, orange ribbons near 20-point rifle targets, red ribbons near 30-point rifle targets, etc.).

Stats Procedures:

Enhanced target values will require some pre-planning on the part of stats, in three areas: score-card design, match setup, and stats entry.

Scorecard design:

It is important to distinguish steel targets by value in the design of the scorecard. It is recommended that there be different scorecard "lines" for each target value. A sample scorecard is shown on previous pages: Note that there are separate "lines" for 5-point, 10-point and 25-point rifle steel. There are many ways to accomplish this, but it is important to have the scorecard provide places to record how many hits there were at each level of value.

Match Setup:

In EZWinScore 4.03, the recommended approach is to set up all stages with 5-point steel targets. During EZWS setup for each stage, however, the number of targets should be manipulated to represent the appropriate number of points possible on steel targets.

In the sample scorecard shown on previous pages, there are:

4 5-point handgun steel targets

2 5-point rifle steel targets

2 10-point rifle steel targets (count as 2 hits each)

2 25-point rifle steel targets (count as 5 hits each)

Adding them together, those targets comprise a total of 100 possible points on steel, so the stage should be set up with 20 5-point steel targets, even though there are only 10 actual targets available to the shooter.

About the Author

Author Chad Adams

Chad Adams was raised on healthy doses of football, basketball, shooting, and fishing in the southeastern Kentucky town of Corbin. When not playing traditional sports, Adams spent countless summer days plinking with friends or chasing bass on Laurel Lake.

In 1998, after attending the University of Kentucky, Adams joined the United States Marine Corps. He served four years with the Corps, which included assignments to the 3rd Marine Division, FAP to Marine Corps Base Camp Butler, Okinawa, Japan, along with two years at the ceremonial and oldest post of the Marine Corps—Marine Barracks Washington, D.C., otherwise known as "8th & I."

Following his career in the Marine Corps, Adams was hired by NRA Publications, where he worked his way from Assistant and Associate Editor with *Shooting Illustrated* to Associate and then Managing Editor for the *American Rifleman*. It was with *American Rifleman* that Adams first began to work in outdoors television, first as a reporter and producer for *American Rifleman Television*, then creating and hosting *American Guardian Television*.

In 2010, Adams and business partner Pete Brown created a new company, the National 3-Gun Association (N3GA). The N3GA operates the 3-Gun Nation Pro Series Tour, the premiere competition platform for the top 3-gunners in America. The N3GA also runs several point series for varying skill levels, as well as women and junior shooters in partnership with major 3-gun matches across the country. The N3GA also recently launched the 3-Gun Nation Club Series, the first national club-level competition format of its kind.

The driving force behind the N3GA is its coverage of 3-gun, most notably the 3-Gun Nation Pro Series Tour on the television show *3-Gun Nation*, airing on the NBC Sports Network. The company's website, www.3GunNation.com, has become the leading news source for the entire sport of 3-gun.

Adams is the Vice President of N3GA, Co-Executive Producer for *3GN* TV, and Editor in Chief of 3GunNation.com. He resides in his home state of Kentucky, with his wife, Amy, and three children, Peyton, Hunter, and Brody.

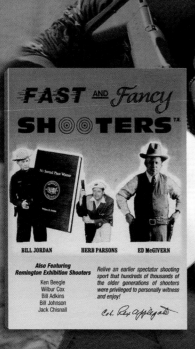
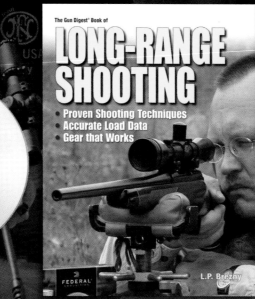
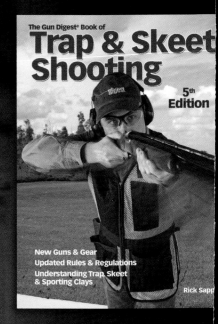